COMPARING PUBLIC POLICIES: NEW CONCEPTS AND METHODS

SAGE YEARBOOKS IN POLITICS AND PUBLIC POLICY

Sponsored by the

Policy Studies Organization

Books in this series:

1. What Government Does (1975)
   MATTHEW HOLDEN, Jr. and DENNIS L. DRESANG, *Editors*
2. Public Policy Evaluation (1975)
   KENNETH M. DOLBEARE, *Editor*
3. Public Policy Making in a Federal System (1976)
   CHARLES O. JONES and ROBERT D. THOMAS, *Editors*
4. Comparing Public Policies: New Concepts and Methods (1978)
   DOUGLAS E. ASHFORD, *Editor*

VOLUME IV. SAGE YEARBOOKS IN POLITICS AND PUBLIC POLICY

COMPARING PUBLIC POLICIES
New Concepts and Methods

DOUGLAS E. ASHFORD

Editor

SAGE Publications Beverly Hills / London

For information address:

SAGE PUBLICATIONS, INC.
275 South Beverly Drive
Beverly Hills, California 90212

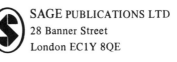

SAGE PUBLICATIONS LTD
28 Banner Street
London EC1Y 8QE

Printed in the United States of America

International Standard Book Number 0-8039-0904-7 (cloth)
International Standard Book Number 0-8039-0905-5 (paper)

Library of Congress Catalog Card No. 77-79492

FIRST PRINTING

CONTENTS

SERIES EDITOR'S INTRODUCTION

This is the fourth volume in the series of *Yearbooks in Politics and Public Policy* published by Sage Publications in cooperation with the Policy Studies Organization. Each volume has dealt with a different general approach to analyzing the causes and effects of alternative public policies. The first volume on *What Government Does,* edited by Matthew Holden, Jr., and Dennis L. Dresang, provides an overview of various substantive policy problems from a political science perspective, including problems relating to economic regulation, environmental protection, health, welfare, education, art, legislative reform, and urban government. The second volume on *Public Policy Evaluation,* edited by Kenneth M. Dolbeare, provides an analysis of the problems involved in seeking to evaluate alternative public policies, including problems of conceptualization, measurement, ideology, research objectives, experimental research design, cross-sectional analysis, and operations research in both a general policy context and with specific applications to crime control. The third volume on *Public Policy Making in a Federal System,* edited by Charles O. Jones and Robert D. Thomas, also deals with a variety of policy problems, but in the context of using federalism as a key variable in explaining the causes and effects of alternative public policies.

This fourth volume on *Comparing Public Policies: New Concepts and Methods,* like the first three, deals with a general approach to public policy analysis rather than one or a few specific substantive policy problems. Also like the previous volumes, this symposium is mainly based on a conference that involved bringing together prominent experts in the field to inventory what has been done and especially to indicate new concepts and methods for further developing the field. The relevant conference was held in autumn, 1976, at Cornell University under the auspices of the Western Societies Program of the Cornell Center for International Studies and under the coordination of Douglas E. Ashford who is the director of the Western Societies Program. The book covers the logic of comparative policy analysis, the institutions, the economic theory, and policy as the determinant of politics.

Having a cross-national perspective on policy problems as this book has can be justified in terms of developing broader theories of the causes and effects of alternative public policies than can be developed by merely working with states or cities within the United States or another single country at one point or even many points in time. Having such a perspective also has practical significance in terms of providing insights into what policies ought to be adopted in light of given goals, constraints, and environmental circumstances. For example, an analysis of the effects of abortion policies in the United States made during the 1960s might lead one to conclude that making abortions easier to obtain has virtually no effect on decreasing deaths from illegal abortions, unwanted births, or other social indicators. In reality, however, the slope or marginal rate of return of relevant social indicators to the leniency of abortion policy might be quite substantial if the units of analysis had been countries where there is a wider range of scores on the leniency variable than among American states. Like many policies, abortion policy may have an S-shaped relation to its goals such that the slope is relatively flat at low levels and high levels on the policy, but relatively steep in the middle. Determining the role of possibly fundamental policy causes like industrialization, capitalism-socialism, and democracy-dictatorship also cannot be meaningfully done within the limited variation of American states rather than U.N. members.

The main problem in cross-national policy comparisons is the difficulty of holding constant other variables that may affect the goal indicators besides the policy variable. The traditional approach has been to use a cross-sectional analysis of many countries at one point in time and divide the countries into similar sub-samples, or use a form of predictive regression analysis that attempts to statistically control for differences among the countries. Those approaches, however, are limited by the number of countries available and by the difficulty of determining what variables to control for. As an improvement on that methodology, this book advocates and illustrates an increased concern for time series analysis. By comparing a set of 10 or N countries before and after they adopt a policy, one generally controls for extraneous variables better than comparing 10 countries that have adopted the policy with 10 countries that have not. For example, it would probably be more meaningful to do an interrupted time series on a set of countries to determine the effects on sex crimes of legalizing pornography, than to compare countries that legally allow pornography with those that prohibit it, although with either approach one would want to consider other causal variables. Both approaches can be combined by trying to compare countries over time that have adopted a policy with related countries over the same time periods that have not adopted the policy. Likewise, over time analysis may be especially helpful in determining the effects of policy causes like population change, the business cycle, or per capita income.

Related to the control problem and the use of time series analysis is the problem of determining the degree of reciprocal causation between policies and other variables. For example, does crime occurrence increase anti-crime efforts on a cross-national basis, or do anti-crime efforts decrease crime, or both, or neither? If one uses countries at one point in time to determine the relationship, the slope tends to be positive regardless which variable is used as a dependent variable and regardless what other variables are held constant. If, however, one uses countries at two points in time and relates crime occurrence as an effect at time t back to anti-crime expenditures as a cause at time t-1, holding constant crime occurrence at time t-1, then the relation tends to be negative and substantial. Likewise, if one relates anti-crime expenditures as an effect at time t back to crime occurrence as a cause at time t-1, holding constant anti-crime expenditures at time t-1, then that relation tends to be positive and substantial. Thus, with two points in time data, we are able to show there is a negative relation in one direction and a positive relation in the other, and in which direction the relation is stronger. This also illustrates the relevance of the concepts and methods of cross-national comparisons to cross-state and cross-city comparisons.

The above conceptual and methodological problems emphasize the use of empirical data which may be more difficult to obtain at the cross-national level than the subnational level. As a result, there may be even more need in cross-national theory building and practice for the use of deductive modeling to analyze the causes and effects of alternative public policies. The most useful models for deducing the effects of policy changes on society or social changes on policy may be models that assume political decision makers and people in general try to maximize their perceived expected benefits minus costs. Models like that are not only helpful in the absence of hard evaluation data, but may be especially helpful for determining the effects of changes before the changes occur even if data might be available afterwards. For example, one can predict many effects of the adoption of a pollution tax on business or managerial polluters from such a model without having to adopt the tax. Likewise, one can probably better explain why some countries have adopted national health insurance and others have not by using such a model to understand the choices made by legislators in the adopting countries and the opposite choices made by legislators in the other countries. Related models are advocated in this book especially in the section on Economic Theory and Comparison.

Future volumes in this series may be published at the rate of two per year in view of the increasing popularity of the policy studies field in general and the series in particular. The fifth volume is tentatively entitled *Public Policy Strategies in America: Past, Present, and Future* under the editorship of Theodore J. Lowi and Alan Stone. It provides a set of surveys of important policy problems with an emphasis on the legislative, judicial, and administrative action in each problem area. Like the other volumes in the series, it also emphasizes the causes and effects of alternative policies. The sixth volume is tentatively entitled *Politics and Public Policy,* and is under the editorship of Aaron Wildavsky and Judith May. Like most of the previous volumes, it will be mainly based on the best papers presented at the preceding annual meeting of the American Political Science Association. That volume will be followed by *Policy Studies and Public Choice* under the editorship of Douglas Rae and Stephanie Cameron. Its general policy analysis approach will emphasize the use of rational choice deductive models in explaining public policy decisions, and in analyzing what decisions ought to be made to maximize given goals within realistic constraints. That will make seven volumes in this series which may be both an effect of the dynamic new policy analysis orientation within political and social science, and hopefully a cause of the continued expansion of that important orientation.

Stuart S. Nagel
Urbana, Illinois

VOLUME EDITOR'S INTRODUCTION

Why add another book to the growing number of comparative volumes dealing with policy studies? The answer can only be that it is a fascinating subject which has attracted increasing interest among political scientists. It deserves closer examination. For several decades political science has neglected the complexity of policy formation, implementation and its results. The more conceptual answer might be that comparing policies across states is different from comparing a single policy across states or several policies within a state. It is this question that generated the conference of comparative policy at Cornell in October, 1976. Does cross-national comparison of policies have a different objective than studying policies in isolation, either within or across states?

Although we are beginning to see more comparative policy studies, particularly of the same policy across states, there is still relatively little discussion of the analytical and conceptual problems of comparison itself. For many, this may seem an unproductive endeavor in the face of a challenging and provocative new area of inquiry. But the question remains as to how this research will ultimately blend, possibly illuminate, the nature of political inquiry itself. This question came up repeatedly in a seminar on comparative public policy taught by Professors Pempel and Katzenstein and myself at Cornell. Our discussion provided substantial encouragement to pursue the comparative issue further. The group of scholars brought together at Cornell had done cross national policy studies. They were asked to pump their minds about their experience and to focus attention on the analytical questions themselves. As one might expect, each had his own way of approaching the overall question, but we did focus on the justification and promise of comparative public policy studies.

Perhaps the best way of introducing the issues surrounding the comparative analysis of policy is to acknowledge the fundamental questions of any comparative inquiry. There are, I think, three basic ways of comparing. Each has advantages and disadvantages which are to be found in the essays in this volume. There are, first, simple descriptive efforts using typologies, which has been a classic form of analysis. Typologies are a simple and effective device to deal with complexity. Because comparative politics has always worked with numerous systems, the second approach has been to study variation within systems. An interest in the performance of political systems and the results of public policies has added enormously to the possibilities for intrasystemic comparison. The third and long-standing concern is with variation among systems which address basic normative questions. Using aggregate data important progress has already been made in comparing policies in the works of Pryor and Wilensky.

Typologies are, I think, a way of clarifying and hopefully establishing the importance of certain key dimensions used in the definition of types. They are a step toward the formation of more general theories and seek to penetrate situations of complexity. Classification has real shortcomings. A great deal of energy can be wasted on sorting out events and data around definitions that do not lead to theory, as the early biologists discovered. The dimensions tend to be stated in dichotomous form and, therefore, may establish unjustified polarities in our thinking. The dynamics of a typology are often unclear, that is, how a situation moves from one type to another within the typology.

But typologies also have very immediate and practical advantages, especially for comparison. Surely one of our first concerns in studying policies across nations is to describe how countries have approached similar problems such as health, pollution, and civil rights. If we can agree on the essential characteristics of policies found in every country, then typologies serve an important organizing function. They may even, as Lowi would argue, denote characteristic forms of politics. Typologies provide the beginnings of a theory and enable us to accumulate rudimentary and scattered evidence, such as case studies, in a way that may lead to more general theory. But they also tend to give less attention to the historical and institutional differences that shape policy within nations. The definitions of the types must be drawn from characteristics of policies themselves, and in doing so we may indeed miss some of the most interesting possibilities for new discoveries using comparative policy analysis.

One of the interesting results of our discussion at Cornell was how little the contributors felt typologies held the key to future work on comparative policy. Though the Lowi typology is the root of his essay, he moves beyond his early formulation by posing testable hypotheses. Anderson would argue that typologies have limited usefulness because they are essentially academic devices depending on our own special definition of what goes on in government. As such, they are not likely to consider decision making in the context of policymakers nor are they likely to provide us with ways of organizing policy data that will penetrate the world of real choices. Section II, in particular, deals with alternatives to description. All the authors are trying to develop ways of formulating policy analysis around the crucial aggregations or groups that make policy. Though we still talk of types of policy and even use the simple sectoral distinctions among kinds of policy, our discussion in this section moves over into a concern with intrasystemic differences of the policy process.

Within system variations seem to be a step toward encompassing the historical and institutional complexity that classification may ignore. This kind of policy analysis is now well established for specific countries, particularly in the elaborate comparisons of state and regional differences that are done for the United States. Such research began with the more manageable, quantifiable differences within countries, but is now being extended to center-local relations, voter influence in electoral systems, and budgetary processes. A focus on internal variation may, of course, take several forms in comparing policies: how policies arrive on the political agenda, how policies are implemented, or how policies seem to respond to certain basic choices such as equality versus growth. Thus, it is not the case that internal variations themselves solve the dilemmas of looking for a more systematic theory, as the papers of Teune and Marmor show. There must still be some arbitrary definitional quality in deciding what are the internal variations of greatest potential import in building new theory.

In my view, the great attraction of this form of comparison is that it may indeed lead to important discoveries about the power structure of the modern state, as I try to show in my essay. Perhaps the most interesting thing about policy formation, implementation and evaluation, however one wishes to divide the policy process, is that there are important structural similarities across all or most policies for any one state. As such differences are understood for a number of states, we may approach something like a comparative policy explanation of the state that rivals the one provided by behavioral and economic models of policy. More than this, it is conceivable that with the growth of the state itself, a policy based formulation of state power may be a more accurate representation of how the modern state functions than those built on formulations of electoral, legislative, or party politics.

Several of the essays raise questions about the undone work at the intrasystemic level of comparison. Rich is particularly clear in his criticism of science policy studies. The utilization of science is a very different problem from that of how it may effect key relationships in the state. In this highly developed field of comparative policy studies, there remains much to learn about how science and technology actually affect the agenda, procedures, and expectations of government. Similar questions are raised by Marmor, Bridges, and Hoffman. My own essay suggests that the analysis of structural relationships within states will lead us toward better ways of specifying the politically significant differences of the policy process. As this is done we may learn of important gaps in typological approaches and we may also be able to deal more empirically with normative assumptions common to systemic level comparison of politics. Inescapably these concerns slip over into systemic differences.

Systemic comparison also has its arbitrary quality because the essential characteristics of systems as a whole must somehow be specified before policy comparison can begin. There are essentially two forms of this, corresponding roughly to the liberal and Marxist view of society. The Friedland-Alford-Piven essay corresponds to the latter view, seeing class struggle and inequality as the dynamic for policy change and also as the basic description of policy. The liberal view is derived from rational self-interest of individuals, and leads to the deductive theories of policy suggested by Peretz and Kelley. Policy analysis of this kind is by far the best established in policy studies as a whole. It preoccupies the entire field of micro-economics and associated inquiry in cost-benefit analysis, social indicators, and decision theory. Whether the deductive theorists, after several decades of intensive effort, will be able to work from the individual to actual choice in society remains to be seen, just as it remains unclear whether the neo-Marxists will be able to disaggregate their systemic assumptions in a form that permits them to address policy choice.

Systemic comparison has, of course, a long history in the study of industrialization, social class, and participation. One immediately thinks of the work of Armstrong, Moore, and Bendix as well as of the major political philosophers themselves. In a curious way, policy was always at the forefront of much political philosophy. Bentham,

Mill, Marx, and Weber were not only intensely interested in some very practical problems of their day, but they were movers of men and often active in government itself. Comparative policy studies, particularly work aimed at the systemic level, constantly returns to these writers, and may have the constructive effect of reviving interest in the close association of values and politics.

The economic theories of politics which Kelley and Peretz examine have, of course, already had immense impact on policy insofar as economics can make concrete suggestions of considerably more reliability than politics. But their essays, I think, go deeper into the relation of liberal economic theories as they relate to how men are in fact motivated and organized. Though Peters and Heisler were not at the Cornell meeting, their essay, too, begins from the fundamental question of how ideology relates to policy. Their view that policy may itself lead to mobilization and stimulate political activity is neatly opposed to the Friedland, Piven, and Alford contribution, which sees legitimation as an increasingly difficult problem in the liberal state. The latter essay is also crucial to the balance of work in the volume for it conveys how many of the neo-Marxist writers are moving toward theories that enable them to disaggregate simple class theories into a form that can evaluate policy.

The essay notable for its omission in the above outline of our volume is the one by Anderson. Though it appears first in the volume, I place it last in my introduction because it raises very fundamental epistemological questions that none of the above authors confront. There remains in policy studies, as in every field of discourse, the primordial question of whether our language is adequate to the problem under consideration. Social science has its quota and more of jargon. Linguistic differentiation produces jargon as we try to express shades of meaning, intensity, and so forth. Anderson tries to convey the very difficult problems political scientists have "entering" the world of policymakers, and in doing so he may be raising a most important issue for the future of comparative policy studies.

In our discussion and our papers all the authors share a fascination which we hope will contribute to future comparative studies of policy. We considered whether policy may eventually become an independent variable in future political explanations, or in Lowi's terms, whether policy may determine politics. Anderson would be the first to remind us that we must be precise about the meaning of "determine." Thus, the typologies may provide insight into the kind of political exchange one might expect from different kinds of policies, but they say little about the significance of these exchanges across political systems. American politics studied through policy may turn out to be log-rolling politics. Are we, then, any wiser?

Policies determine politics in a very different sense in their application to the internal variation problem. Sectoral or structural similarities and differences found within any one country or in several countries may lead us to understand the political process, the capability of the state to resolve policy conflicts, and how policies arrive on the political agenda. But this is in many respects only specifying the parameters of policy rather better than we have been able to do using other comparative methods. Though I would argue that we must pay more attention to the historical and institutional constraints on policy before we try to compare in more specific (typological) or more general (systemic) terms, one might spend many hours over this kind of comparison and have little serious contribution to any specific policy issue.

The methodological problems, however, are the greatest when starting with very sweeping assumptions about the nature of man or society. Description ignores the problems of aggregation to real institutions and choices. Grand theory has the reverse limitation as one tries to disaggregate in order to state which policy should be changed or how institutions might be improved. These views also trigger intense feelings and appeal to very basic human needs. One could not imagine the systemic level concerns being discarded if only because the philosophical foundations on which each is built are well known and each in its own way needs reconsideration and explication.

As editor I must thank my coauthors for their patience as the essays were revised, cut, and reassembled. We can only hope that the enthusiasm we found among ourselves for this endeavor is somehow transmitted to the reader.

Douglas E. Ashford
Ithaca, New York

April 1977

PART I

LOGIC OF COMPARISON

1

THE LOGIC OF PUBLIC PROBLEMS: EVALUATION IN COMPARATIVE POLICY RESEARCH

CHARLES W. ANDERSON

University of Wisconsin

To identify and define a public problem, some standard of judgment must be invoked. Not everything that happens in a society is a political problem. Policymakers have to make a distinction between "problems" and "the way things are." Poverty is not a problem for a society which believes that the "poor are always with us"—or that they get precisely what they deserve. Poverty becomes a problem in the light of a principle: the poor have been treated unjustly, or society should aim at greater equality. Similarly, inflation is not ipso facto a policy problem. Inflation simply means that prices are rising; that is a condition rather than a problem. In some contexts, inflation may be regarded as a remedy rather than a difficulty—as an unconventional means of taxation, for example, or a roundabout way of reducing the burden of the public debt. For inflation to be regarded as problematic, some further criteria of public performance must be stipulated. Price instability is bad because of its impact on investor confidence, or because it represents a confiscation of some forms of private property, or because it redistributes wealth in socially undesirable ways. A policy problem, in short, is a political condition that does not meet some standard.

AUTHOR'S NOTE: *I am indebted to Douglas Ashford and Thomas Bossert for their helpful comments on earlier drafts of this paper.*

Problems can be appraised in the light of many different political principles. We talk frequently about the "common" problems of all industrialized societies, but these so-called shared problems—inflation, environmental deterioration, inequality, social conflict, participation, and the like—may have a wholly different kind of significance from one nation to the next, not only because of economic and social differences but because of the way such problems are evaluated and analyzed.

Policymakers and publics can set all kinds of puzzles and quandaries for themselves. Public problems are not just "out there" waiting to be dealt with. Policymaking is not simply problem-solving. It is also a matter of setting up and defining problems in the first place. Whether a nation perceives poverty, inflation, unemployment, or bourgeoise morality as a problem or merely a condition depends on the standards of judgment and the ideals of right order that are employed in making political evaluations.

There is, then, a normative element at the very heart of any effort to develop a systematic, comparative study of public policy. A policy is more than a state action or activity. It is a conscious contrivance, reflecting human purposiveness, and it is in some sense a moral act. A distinction is made somewhere between things that are good for the public and things that are bad. If policy analysis represents, as many think it does, a rather fundamental reconceptualization of political science, then the logic of evaluation (the normative element which underlies policy) is a matter of very great interest both in theory construction and in empirical research.

Seen in this light, a policy cannot be satisfactorily "explained" simply as a product of certain socioeconomic conditions, or a given configuration of political pressures, or as the outcome of a particular political process, all of which are dominant motifs in contemporary policy study. It is also necessary to know what people *thought* of prevailing socioeconomic conditions, what claims and grievances interested parties brought forward, and how they debated and assessed these problems.

There is another reason for the importance of the normative element in policy analysis. Many students of public policy see their work as "pure" political science, their object being to explain the product of government or better to comprehend the nature and dynamics of government through an examination of its product; others see their task as building a more positive, recommendatory political science with greater relevance to the problems of public choice or social criticism. Here policy analysis becomes frankly normative. The analyst's object is not merely to understand how policy evaluations are made, but to make a policy evaluation.

The line between pure and positive policy study is often hard to draw. The papers in this series are illustrative. Ashford and Lowi share the view that it is important to focus on policy so as to understand better the nature of the state. Both ostensibly address themselves to pure science questions. Yet the problems Ashford discusses–inertia, scale, and substitutability–all concern the performance of the state. At least a diagnostic question is raised, if not an evaluative one. Lowi explicitly argues that political science has a specialized concern in policy study, which is "the impact of policies on the political system itself." Friedland, Alford, and Piven reflect the subtle normative-empirical blend of concerns in any neo-Marxist study. The concept of "fiscal crisis" which James O'Connor introduces into this strand of contemporary social science theory is not merely an interesting policy dilemma for study. It also represents a *contradiction* in capitalist society, a construct full of evaluative significance in this mode of analysis.

Other papers are more explicitly evaluative. Henry Teune asks that empirical political science be given a fair test in comparative policy research, but does so on the ground that it will assist the process of public choice by making us more aware of alternatives and better able to anticipate consequences. Hoffman and Marmor explicitly use comparative policy analysis to answer such questions as: who benefits from health care services? what conceptions of justice are implicit in health policies? Their purpose is to derive lessons from comparative experience for policy planners. Paul Peretz argues for a specific *standard* for policy appraisal, the Maslovian hierarchy of needs, while Shefer presents notions of comprehensiveness, direction, interdependence, and reversibility as criteria for appraising policy-making systems. Kelley ultimately suggests the centrality of asking the question "who benefits?" in comparative policy study.

Most who do research in the field of public policy are generally willing to acknowledge, either reluctantly or brazenly, that normative analysis is part of it. Less likely to be recognized is that normative analysis has an analytic rigor of its own. In the division of labor of contemporary political science, normative argument–the critical examination of evaluative constructs and propositions–is the domain of political philosophy. Most policy analysts come from the empirical side of the discipline. Their concern is with data, modeling and the like. They seldom look on normative analysis as a body of technique with its own canons of procedure and standards of inquiry. Consequently, the normative element comes into policy analysis in ways that are often crude and unexamined. A value (say, equity or efficiency) is proposed, empirical indicators are fashioned, and an experiment is performed. Little effort is made to analyze the normative construct itself, to embed it in a logic of appraisal, much less to justify it as a plausible basis for political assessment. In the folklore of empirical political science, evaluative statements cannot be demonstrated. Consequently, the analyst is free to do as he pleases. The only rule of scholarship, it is held, is that the evaluative position be made explicit. Postulated values need neither be defended nor are they, in themselves, appropriately the subject of scholarly criticism. From the standpoint of the normative political theorist, this is both awkward and unfortunate.

On the whole, scholarly activity in normative political theory and policy analysis goes on in relative isolation. (There are exceptions, of course, in such journals as *Philosophy and Public Affairs,* in the interest in John Rawls among some policy-oriented economists, and in some neo-Marxist research.) The consequence is that writing on such basic conceptual problems as equality, justice, and representation proceeds at a highly abstract level, while policy analysis develops no effective rationale for its evaluative undertakings. It is as though students of political philosophy could scrutinize the policy problem of representation as it appeared in 17th-century England, but could not deal with questions of participation in 20th-century economic planning. Meanwhile, policy analysts become incapable of recognizing that their concern with cost-benefit analysis is only an episode in a long Western tradition of defining principles appropriate to judge the legitimacy and propriety of political activity.

Herein, I want to deal with some of the implications of taking seriously the evaluative element in policymaking, particularly in comparative policy research. First I will consider this in relation to the problem of empirical policy study. As I noted, different polities define the appropriate objects of public action in different ways. To compare policies at all, at some point we have to ask: "What problem are they trying to solve?" To do this, I suggest, we have to comprehend the logic of appraisal that we bring to bear in defining a "situation" as a "problem." Second, I will discuss the utility of this approach to the policy analyst as evaluator of the comparative performance of nations and regimes. Finally, I will take up some of the implications and assumptions of research into political evaluation in general.

THE "LOGIC OF EVALUATION" AS A UNIT OF ANALYSIS

The deliberation of public policy takes place within a realm of discourse. Policy evaluations may be made on ideological grounds; they may reflect the criteria of technicians or experts or they may be based on calculations of political advantage or group interest by partisan forces. There may be dispute and conflict within a society over which standards are appropriate to make authoritative commitments on public purposes. Nonetheless, policies are made within some system of ideas and standards which is comprehensible and plausible to the actors involved.

Political evaluation takes place within and between structured systems of discourse. To understand how public problems are appraised and policies analyzed, one has to know how these "logics" of political evaluation operate. These "models," "frameworks," or "logics" (terms I will use interchangeably), rather than simple beliefs, values, opinions, attitudes, and cognitions, become the basic unit of analysis for the normative dimensions of policymaking.

I will not try to define a logic of policy evaluation precisely. Concepts of even the most straightforward political phenomena—such as parties and interest groups—become fuzzy and controversial at the margins. However, what I have in mind is a logically interconnected system of ideas and norms that operates as a professional code of procedure in making public policy; it entails standards of how to judge and criticize policymaking performance. (Thus, only in some political systems is it significant to criticize a policymaker for not consulting "important interest groups." It only makes sense in some partisan contexts to note that a policy failed because it did not take into account "both the objective and the subjective conditions of revolution.")

This conception of a logic of political evaluation certainly includes formal ideologies, such as liberalism, Marxism, or Catholic corporatism. It also embraces such analytic modes of policy evaluation as incrementalism, profit maximization, organizational survival and so on, which may identify coherent systems of policy appraisal in some contexts. In this paper, however, I will concentrate almost exclusively on another form of policy evaluation logic which is of particular importance in contemporary policymaking: the language and logic of "expertise."

The process of policy reasoning is different in law, macroeconomics, diplomacy, military strategy, and urban planning. In each of these, there are different rules for identification of the problematic, different norms of evaluation, and different criteria for what would count as a solution and what would not. For example, a highway can be appraised by a military planner in terms of its strategic location, by a traffic engineer for carrying capacity and cost effectiveness, and by an environmentalist for its energy use and pollution implications in comparison with other modes of transport. The traffic engineer is "correct" in his solution to the policy problem if he designs the road to accommodate a projected increase in traffic over the long run. The environmentalist may find that the "best" solution is to underbuild the road so as to discourage reliance on the automobile. The same public work appears problematic in different ways for each of these specialists, whose appraisal is part of a larger framework of criteria of good performance.

We tend to identify the role of experts in modern government with technique. However, the actual role of professionals and experts in policymaking is probably more prescriptive than operational. The setting of standards of good practice is a large part of what professionalism means. Most policy sciences are such precisely because they provide standards for the appraisal of public programs. The conventional wisdom–that policymakers set objectives and technical specialists deal only with means–probably has the matter precisely backwards. In such distinct fields as law, forestry, consumer safety, nutrition, and welfare, the expert's essential purpose is to define standards, to use them to criticize existing policy, and to employ them as criteria for the identification of alternate, preferred programs.

The criteria of policy evaluation, and consequently of problem identification and resolution, are different in the various logics of policy reasoning. In fact, these frameworks of policy evaluation may be identified by the normative criteria they contain and by the standards of evaluation that set puzzles and quandaries for those who operate within them. The basic liberal principles of political evaluation–justice, freedom, equality, efficiency, the public interest, due process of law, and the like–all take on specific technical meaning in each of the logics of policy analysis. Furthermore, none of these frameworks for policy reasoning contains all of the norms of political evaluation in the ordinary language of political discourse in liberal society. Each emphasizes certain norms as crucial in defining public problems and identifying remedies.

Thus, in law, the central normative construct is rights. In economics, it is efficiency. In law, the essential public problem is to establish what counts as an injury, to define harms in relation to rights and remedies. In economics, the public problem is to assign costs appropriately so that an optimum allocation of resources can be achieved. *Thus, whether we regard an issue as a legal or an economic problem makes a great deal of difference.* Rights and efficiency are very different normative constructs. When we declare something to be a matter of right we do not count the costs. The establishment of a legal entitlement creates a prescriptive claim on resources. (We do not assess "opportunity costs" to school districts in weighing the merits of school busing to achieve educational equality.) Conversely, considerations of efficiency do not lead to legal entitlement. There is no way in the logic of liberal economics that one can construe a notion of *right* to profit or a specific claim on resources (Okun, 1975).

In any given polity or issue area, the language of political discourse may be conflictual or consensual in varying degrees. A high value may accrue to a dominant logic of decision making (civil rights are defined by legal argument); there may be struggle over which language of evaluation shall prevail (Marxists versus liberals, energy economists versus environmentalists). Policy languages may change and hybridize. (The Supreme Court accepts sociological reasoning and evidence as a basis for decision, management science borrows the norms of systems analysis from cybernetics.)

An understanding of the varying forms that political argument and policy evaluation may take is essential to the comparative study of public policy. The normative constructs of a specific logic of policy analysis may become virtual imperatives. In most advanced industrial societies, the Keynesian macroeconomic aggregates have become tantamount to an operational definition of the public interest. The test of a government's legitimacy is not that it rests on consent but rather that it achieves an optimum balance between the goals of economic growth, full employment, price stability, and trade equilibrium. The relationship of the modern economist to the policymaker is not unlike that of the Medieval monarch to his confessor. The scholastic theologian and the modern economist were each master of a complex canonical system against which the decisions of rulers were to be evaluated and according to which they could be justified.

By the same token, different nations may locate similar problems in distinct frameworks of policy reasoning. The issue of distributive justice acquires new dimensions if treated as a matter of full employment policies generated through macroeconomic management, transfer payments rendered through public services linked to progressive taxation, or socialization of the means of production.

Different nations may produce distinctive responses to seemingly similar problems because they locate the problem in different realms of policy discourse. Gary Freeman recently compared the way the status of racial minorities was appraised in Britain and France, against the background of the American experience (Freeman, 1975). In the United States, race relations were primarily evaluated—at least initially—as a legal problem concerning equal rights and equal protection. In Britain, however, at least until the late 1960s, as a policy issue race was seen in the perspective of immigration policy and Commonwealth relations. What was at issue was not equality before the law so much as the ethnic composition of the nation and the commitments and entitlements that had been created as a result of policies of decolonization and independence. In France, however, the status of ethnic minorities was seen in relationship to manpower policy and economic planning. The place of foreign workers in the economic system, their contribution to growth and their competition in the labor market with native Frenchmen were at issue. It is, of course, true that the differing responses of these nations had much to do with their distinctive historic experiences and ethnic characteristics; but their approaches to public policy and their conceptions of the race issue in public affairs cannot be understood without considering the various assumptions they made about evaluating the issue and the nature of the problem itself.

Students of comparative public policy should explore the structure of public debate and the logic of policy evaluation. Many intriguing questions come to mind. For example, one might ask whether there is a tendency toward differentiation or convergence in the normative systems used in assessing public problems. On the one hand, we proclaim the "end of ideology" and assert that "now we are all Keynesians." On the other hand, in the last generation or so, there has been an overwhelming proliferation of new forms of policy expertise, social criticism, and perspectives on the problematic. Has the public debate become more open and heterodox or has it become increasingly consensual and conventional? What are the patterns between nations and between policy areas? Where do the languages of expertise prevail, where partisan ideology, and where more open, "ordinary language" systems of policy evaluation?

THE COMPARATIVE EVALUATION OF POLICY

One of the tasks that policy analysis originally set for itself was the comparative appraisal of the policy performance of different kinds of political systems. The achievements of nations and regimes were assessed by the use of rates of economic growth, capital-output ratios, social indicators, and measures of income inequality. These are important questions for comparative policy research. We all have more than a passing interest in how centrally planned and modern capitalist economies perform in relation to one another; whether modern socialist and modern conservative governments differ much in their policy products; whether such highly regarded systems as the Swedish, Israeli, and Swiss are as good as their reputations; and if the Spanish, Italian, or South African governments are as bad or ineffectual as the conventional wisdom would have us believe.

The normal approach is to take some index of policy achievement that is available in relatively comparable form for a large number of politics and relate it to various economic, social, and political variables. One may be able to derive some inferences about the policy achievements of different kinds of political system or regime. This is all very well at one level of analysis. The difficulty is that such research, more or less by definition, excludes the intentions of policymakers, their models of political evaluation, as a significant variable. The result is that this kind of research contains a peculiar fallacy, which is that the analyst *may be trying to assess the performance of a government in relation to a problem it was not trying to resolve.* Of this problem, I wrote in an earlier paper: "A decent respect for the relativity of cultures and circumstances would seem to imply that an assessment of a government's intention is logically prior to an evaluation of its performance. The alternative is to risk normative ethnocentricity and ideological bias, if not sheer normative simple-mindedness" (Anderson, 1975:227).

Currently there is a great interest in the study of comparative inequalities; in much of this research it is implicitly or explicitly assumed that the reduction of inequality is an appropriate norm for evaluating the policy performance of nations and regimes (Jackman, 1975). However, the fact of the matter is that only very rarely in the evolution of the modern welfare state has income redistribution been a manifest objective of public policy. The characteristic institutions and programs that we identify with the welfare state evolved from logics of policy evaluation that varied greatly from nation to nation (Heclo, 1974).

For example, Bismarck was attracted to social insurance as a primary policy instrument at least partly because of its compatibility with the principles of corporatist political order. The risk-sharing character of insurance and the organizational autonomy of the insurance associations reflected the ideals of guild mutualism, while the tripartite contribution scheme was consistent with the regime of organic solidarities that was crucial to the corporatist conception of statecraft (Rimlinger, 1971).

English liberals and American progressives "received" social insurance as the central instrument of social policy on an entirely different basis. Compulsory social insurance intrigued turn-of-the-century reformers partly because it offered a resolution to a problem that was particularly vexing in any liberal model of policy evaluation—how to prevent individuals from rationally preferring public dependency to private self-support.

Very different conceptions of the problematic lay behind historic debates on welfare policy, but sheer equality was seldom evoked as the critical principle. In fact, the characteristic problem of welfare policy throughout most of the 19th and 20th centuries is probably better described as defining legitimate states of dependency. The basic riddle has been: When is an individual properly exonerated from the responsibility for self-maintenance? The scope of welfare policy has been largely determined by the answers that different governments have given to that question. Old age, illness, industrial accident seemed particularly compelling sources of individual vulnerability and grounds for exoneration from the duty of self-support in Imperial Germany. Unemployment, on the other hand, was first recognized as a legitimate condition of dependency in Britain, probably as a result of the work of reformers like Charles Booth, who tried to demonstrate that the individual frequently could not be held responsible for his failure to find work (Winch, 1969:52-53). Only in recent years, and particularly in the United States, has income itself been taken as a legitimate condition of dependency. In any event, it seems clear to me that the distinctive institutions of the modern welfare state cannot be traced to a preoccupation with the problem of inequality in the strict sense of the term.

It is, of course, plausible to do a normative assessment of comparative inequalities which might very well help those who endorse this as a significant index of the quality of public life in a society. But when are we justified in imputing a reduction in inequality to the consequences of public action? It might be that a nation achieved a reduction of inequality as an accidental byproduct of policies designed for entirely different purposes—as seems to have been the case in the recent British experience with inflation. Once again, studies of international inequality cannot serve as an index of policy performance unless we first demonstrate that such was the goal of public action. And if we are interested in *explaining* comparative inequalities, an analysis of the way the problematic in social policy is structured and defined would probably account for far more than such political "variables" as party competitiveness, electoral participation, and other fashionable political indicators.

The same question can be raised about many topics in comparative policy research. It is an issue in the appraisal not only of policy outputs but institutions as well. For example, the "success" or "failure" of French economic planning has been a prime topic for comparative policy study in recent years. Often, the French claim to have reconciled central planning with democratic practice and free enterprise is criticized on the ground that the institutions of planning were, at best, imperfectly democratic. French planning is normally appraised as a process characterized by close relationships between technocrats, the major government ministries and dominant industries. The consultative institutions fail by two criteria of democratic practice. They are not representative, either in the sense of engaging widespread participation or reflecting some postulated set of legitimate interests (labor and consumer interests are underrepresented and the commissions hardly reflect the ideological or partisan configuration of the nation). They were not authoritative, in the sense that they had no real decision-making autonomy, and could hardly overrule the intentions of the planners.

To be sure, the French economic planners left themselves open to this criticism because of their rhetorical insistence that they were engaged in "democratic" planning. However, at another level, the criticism is not germane at all. The planners did not fail to create representative institutions of consultation; rather, they had no intention of creating them at all. The object of participation was not to create democratic process but to further the economic objectives of the plan, which were to increase productivity, remove bottlenecks, and generally maximize economic growth. The selection of participants in the commissions of the plan was guided by no theory of popular, constituency, or interest representation. Instead, the criteria for selecting and excluding specific groups and interests were the participants' contribution to the information-gathering, "penetration," and coordination functions of the planning enterprise (Miller, 1976; Cohen, 1969; Anderson, 1977).

Of course, any form of social criticism gets its power from proposing standards of evaluation other than those ordinarily invoked. My plea is not that students of comparative policy eschew social criticism, but that we clearly distinguish this question from assessment of the performance of a polity or government. It is one thing to render a judgment on a regime on the grounds that it failed to do what it set out to do, and quite another to rate it against some universal norm of political achievement. The first strikes me as closer to the aim of an empirically based, comparative study of public policy. The second seems to derive from the activity of normative political theory. Both, I am arguing, are appropriate to the agenda of comparative policy studies so long as we are clear about their implications.

COMPARATIVE PERSPECTIVE AND NORMATIVE ANALYSIS

We can also use comparative analysis to help clarify fundamental evaluation dilemmas in policy analysis. It is at this level (rather than at "what works and what doesn't," which begs too many questions of international comparability) that comparative policy study may be useful to policymakers. As noted, we can identify and define public problems in various ways, depending on the standard of judgment we invoke. Any "technical" standard of policy evaluation contains normative implications. To use the classic formula of cost-benefit analysis (choose the alternative in which aggregate benefits are greater than aggregate costs) is to adopt efficiency as the criterion of choice. To use the "revised" conception of cost-benefit analysis and ask "Who pays, and who benefits?" implies choosing distributive equity as the appropriate standard of policy evaluation. Policymakers and policy analysts are frequently blind to the normative implications of their evaluational techniques. They seldom think that things could be otherwise. Comparative analysis can create apparent alternatives in conceptualizing public problems by analyzing the standards that different nations or jurisdictions apply in policy analysis.

A good example comes from the field of incomes policies. In a period of sustained inflation, every nation has to confront the possibility of direct governmental involvement in setting wages and prices, possibly through the mechanism of controls. Americans have far less experience in this area than most European nations and, in our public debate on the subject, we seem to be aware of only some of the issues such policies raise. There is a central normative riddle in any kind of incomes policy, which Europeans are well aware of, but which American commentators have hardly touched on at all. In any period of sustained wage controls, the issue of relative interprofessional wage levels will eventually have to be faced. This poses a fundamental question of distributive justice: what is one worker *entitled* to receive in relation to another?

In British postwar experience policymakers have used a variety of criteria to decide this issue. Productivity was the earliest standard they applied. Wage increases are *justifiable* if they result from increased productivity. The normative standard is derived from the logic of macroeconomic management. Wage increases in excess of productivity are inflationary. The effect is that workers in more productive industries, particularly those using advanced technologies, earn more than those in declining ones. According to the logic of political economy, this is as it should be. The principle of equity is that people should be paid in relation to their contribution to total social product. Furthermore, such a standard is consistent with a market distribution of factors of production. Labor mobility toward the more dynamic sectors *should* be encouraged.

However, the standard of productivity in deciding interprofessional wages, if applied universally, does raise serious questions of equity. These have long been discussed and debated in Britain. Some economic sectors are inherently more susceptible to rapid increases in productivity. Do workers in such sectors deserve higher wages than those in service occupations, for example, where productivity is more difficult to improve? Is productivity the most pertinent index of social value? To what extent do productivity increases represent a contribution by the worker and how much do they result from the introduction of laborsaving equipment, better management, and so forth? Does the worker *deserve* to benefit from such improvements unless they derive from his own greater exercise of skill, responsibility or effort? (Jones, 1973:69-73).

A second norm for evaluating interprofessional wages is the maintenance of traditional differentials. In British practice, this seems to come closest to representing the ordinary sense of "fairness" as the worker understands it. As Runciman and others have pointed out, for most people the sense of distributive justice is related not to the total distribution of income in society but to comparisons made with certain neighboring groups and occupations. Such appraisals seem rooted in certain long-term assumptions about relevant differences in skill, effort, and responsibility which should be maintained unless good reasons can be given to revise them. Yet as a norm of interprofessional wage adjustment in an incomes policy, the maintenance of traditional differentials can have devastating consequences, since a recognized demand at any point in the system brings collateral demands for similar adjustments throughout (Crouch, 1975: 215-242).

Since 1975, the British have experimented with an idea of justice that is virtually Rawlsian in character—that adjustments in interprofessional wages should be to the benefit of the "least well off." This was the implicit normative criterion of the Wilsonian "new social contract," which put indicated wage increases in pound and pence rather than percentage terms.

In Sweden, an alternative conception of distributive justice has been employed that has evolved into a highly sophisticated model of macroeconomic management. The basic norm endorsed by the Swedish trade unions is one of "equal pay for equal work." This implies, of course, that less productive industries will bear a larger wage burden than more productive ones. The Swedes accept the implication. The LO insists that workers in less prosperous sectors receive some of the benefits that have been won elsewhere in the economy. Such a principle is seen as a motor of productivity for the economy as a whole. Investment should move toward the more productive sectors, away from declining industries. Competitive market pressures and an active manpower and investment policy to assure factor mobility make the criterion of justice compatible (hypothetically) with the standards of macroeconomic management (Shonfield, 1965:199-210).

To survey the way in which different nations have appraised and debated the issue of equity that arises in connection with an incomes policy cannot answer the question of what standard should be applied. None of the criteria come close to representing a perfect reconciliation of the claims of distributive justice and the imperatives of macroeconomic management. (The Swedes, like the British, continue to experiment, trying to define an operationally persuasive base to judge the relative skill, responsibility, effort, "nastiness," and so forth in different occupations. I wish them well, but I fear they have opened a Pandora's box.) However, comparative analysis can, by explicating the logic of policy evaluation in other countries, do more to clarify the normative issues than pure, deductive conceptual analysis at the philosophical level or normal policy analysis as that craft is currently practiced. In order to understand how to *make* a normative assessment of a public problem, it is useful to know how such assessments are in fact *made*.

THE IMPLICATIONS AND ASSUMPTIONS OF POLITICAL EVALUATION RESEARCH

To undertake the study of political evaluation entails significant assumptions and implications, some of which are suspect, from the point of view of normal empirical social science research. The premises of such an enterprise should be made fully explicit.

THE REASONS OF STATESMANSHIP

To study the logic of public policymaking one must look at the language of political discourse—the way public actions are argued, explained, and justified. Doing this entails the significant assumption that what policymakers think and say makes a difference. Much of comparative policy analysis seems to proceed on the premise that the manifest rationale for public action is either suspect or irrelevant.

Those who study politics tend to be skeptical of those who practice it. They are not inclined to take the ostensible reasons for public policy at face value. The explicit rationale for public action is taken as "rhetoric," "window-dressing," or "rationalization." The *real* causes and motives for public action lie at a deeper level. To some extent, this attitude is simply a matter of healthy skepticism, but it is also an artifice of social science theory and procedure. For most social scientists, the reasons given for a public action do not count as an explanation for it. The purpose of the political scientist should be to give an account of a political phenomenon that is "nonobvious." From this point of view, the job of political science is to reconstruct political reality through a logic that is different from the manifest logic of politics itself.

In much comparative policy research, the rationale of policy is almost totally ignored. Public policymaking is not conceived as a realm of human intellectuation, judgment, ingenuity, and contrivance. Rather, policy is studied either as phenomenon or process. One might identify four basic approaches to the study of comparative public policy that have been fashionable of late. All of them ignore the factor of intent in policymaking. First, policy may be regarded simply as the product of the state–its "output." The task of the analyst is to infer the dynamics of the political order from an examination of its policy product. This project may be suggested by the cybernetic metaphor of the political system suggested in the models of Easton, Deutsch, and Almond. "Output" is to be related to "input" through the "conversion processes" of the political system. Politics is reduced to pure mechanism. The *reasons* of public policy have nothing whatever to do with the *explanation* of it.

The second familiar form of comparative policy research, the correlational analysis of the type Dye, Sharkansky, Hofferbert, and others practice is similar. Policy is the dependent variable. It can be explained through relationships with certain institutional and environmental characteristics for which statistics can be provided. Significant correlations become the "determinants" of public policy. The intentions of policymakers are simply irrelevant.

A third possibility is Marxist or functional sociology. Public policy is explained as a product of social structure or class conflict. Again, the manifest rationale for policy, the justifications adduced by policymakers, do not explain anything. They are merely symptoms of a deeper structure.

The fourth alternative seems to be to view policymaking as process. The analyst tries to illuminate the characteristic ways in which policymakers respond to problems. This is the method of Allison, March, Lindblom, Wildavsky, Heclo, Dror, and others. Here, to be sure, the policymakers themselves enter the picture. However, the reasons of policy are not yet a significant datum. It is the process rather than the content of policy that is at issue. Again, the objective is to provide a logic *for* policy that is different from the logic *of* policy itself.

If we are to investigate the logic of political evaluation we have to begin to attend closely to the nature of political argument and the language of political discourse in which the consideration and resolution of public issues is embedded. These are the raw materials of inquiry. We are interested not in what the system does, or what the process does, but what policymakers do, what the *activity* of policymaking is all about. This implies that we take the reasons of public policy seriously.

In our time, the latent functions of political activity have all but driven the manifest functions of politics from the eyes of social scientists. The manifest functions of politics include making authoritative decisions on behalf of a community, creating rights and concomitant duties, establishing standards of equity to govern the distribution of resources, and the allocation of public services. This is the work of policymaking. This is what policymakers do.

The latent functions of politics are the capture and maintenance of power, the protection and advancement of self-interest, the preservation and expansion of institutions and offices. The modern social scientist frequently does not feel that he has produced an explanation of public policy until he has reduced the manifest justification to the latent function. In the eyes of most political scientists and sociologists, this is what policymakers *really* do.

If one asks "What problem are these policymakers trying to solve?" a straightforward response might be that they are trying to stabilize prices without increasing unemployment. However, for most political scientists, what they are really doing is trying to get reelected, collecting IOUs for future logrolling, or contriving an expedient way out of "the fiscal crisis of the state."

If one were, by the same token, to ask a young scientist what problem he (or she) was trying to solve, he might reply that he was interested in cracking a further puzzle in the structure of the genetic code. He would review the logic of discovery in biochemistry to date, show why his problem was a significant one and how he designed his experiment to answer the question one way or the other. However, his activity might be explained in another way. It might be said that what he was *really* trying to do was to get tenure. One of these answers is facetious. But which one is it?

Politics takes place at a number of levels. To take the language of political discourse seriously, we do not have to abandon hard-headed realism. We can simply assume that interest underlies political argument. We can ask directly "What are they getting out of it?" when examining the rationale for a policy decision. But once we do this, the interesting problem is to examine the logic of the rationale itself. Because someone wants something or has an interest in it does not mean that he is entitled to it or that it would be good public policy to give it to him. On the other hand, a political actor may have an interest in something as well as a right to it.

AN ANALOGY TO SCIENTIFIC INQUIRY

The study of the logic of political evaluation seems to require an approach that has more in common with the philosophy of science than with normal social science empiricism. The object of such writers as Thomas Kuhn (1962), Stephen Toulmin (1961), and Karl Popper (1968) has been to try to comprehend the nature of scientific discovery. They look to what scientists do and why they do it, in terms of the aims of science and the logic of scientific procedure. By the same token, we might look at policymaking as a creative, intellectual, problem-solving activity, wherein goals, puzzles, and problems are defined by certain frameworks of reasoning. To examine the activity of public policymaking, we ask, among other things, what is meant by "solving" a public problem, just as philosophers of science ask what is entailed in "solving" a scientific problem. This implies that we can approach policymaking from the inside, from the standpoint of the policymaker, as well as from the outside, from the position of the detached observer. We have, first of all, to understand what policymakers think they are doing on their own terms; what reasons they give for what they do.

To understand the activity of a scientist, we look first to the intellectual structure of a scientific discipline. What takes shape as an interesting problem—what is significant and what is not, what counts as a mistake in reasoning and analysis—can only be understood if we first comprehend the "rules of the game," the structure of scientific reasoning.

The same sorts of questions can be asked about the activity of policymaking: What counts as a problem? What counts as a solution? What counts as a mistake? In science, as in policymaking, to answer these questions we have to look to the normative standards of the framework of reasoning, to the *grounds* that practitioners appropriately adduce, either in construction or criticism.

Scientific inquiry and political discourse are both basically forms of reasoned argument. The attorney or interest advocate makes a case. The policymaker justifies a decision. Similarly, the scientist gives reasons—argument and a certain structure of evidence—to support his contentions. Argument in either field must follow certain rules of "right reasoning."

Argument, in science or politics, is guided by two fundamental types of evaluative construct. The first is the paradigm case—what Toulmin calls the "ideals of natural order." In Newtonian mechanics, the abstract ideal of a body moving at uniform speed in a Euclidean straight line provides a criterion for identifying the "problematic." It tells us what aspect of a body's motion requires explanation. (No body does so move, of course; otherwise ships would run off the edge of the earth into outer space. But it is precisely the hypothesis that "an object in motion tends to remain in motion" that sets up the puzzle leading to the theoretical enterprise of modern physics [Toulmin, 1961:44-59].) Similarly, the model of the market in perfect competition tells us what aspects of economic organization are problematic in liberal political economy. Deviations from the paradigm case require explanation, and what is more important, they require *justification*.

Procedural rules are the second form of fundamental normative construct, either in science or political discourse. In science, concepts are defined operationally, through the experimental procedures that establish their presence or absence. It is a mistake in scientific reasoning to reify an abstraction. Similarly, the sources of law in American jurisprudence are hierarchically arranged. It is a *mistake* in legal reasoning to aver that common law precedents are superior to the "clear language" of the Constitution.

However, the logic of scientific inquiry is different from that of public policymaking in significant respects. In science, the object is verifiable knowledge and the creation of rational patterns of cognition. In policy, the goal is evaluation, the development of a reasoned basis for making an authoritative choice among alternative public projects. To put this another way, the prescriptive standards of science are a guide to inquiry. In policymaking, they are criteria for decision.

Normative constructs give structure to the scientific enterprise. They provide a basis for scholarly argument, criticism, and the development of a consensually accepted body of knowledge. Many of these prescriptive elements are well known to social scientists, for they have become part of the canonical structure of empiricism. Paradigms are model cases of the expected behavior of phenomena. Deviations from the paradigm case are problematic. Parsimony is a rule of theoretical explanation. The simpler, more elegant explanation that adequately accounts for the phenomenon is preferable. Scientific propositions are to be stated in falsifiable form. It is a mistake to present a thesis that cannot logically be proven wrong.

The logic of public policy is different. Paradigm cases do not only postulate expected behavior. They state an evaluative presumption as well. To be sure, the market ideal in liberal political economy does operate like a scientific paradigm. Deviation from the paradigm case, like oligopolistic competition, indicates phenomena that invite inquiry and explanation. However, the market mechanism is also a normative construct. More than an ideal of natural order, it is an ideal of right order. At perfect competition, prices are *appropriate*. They are *justifiable.* Any structure of prices that does not arise from competition has to be defended. The paradigm case states a standard of evaluation. It locates the burden of proof. Those who would do otherwise are those who must give reasons.

I am arguing that the logics of policymaking contain elements that are similar to those of scientific investigation. "Work incentives" and "implicit taxes" are recognized as problems in any scheme of income maintenance. Why? Because the paradigm case in liberal (as in Marxist) thought is individual self-support. Dependency on community resources has to be justified. As I suggested earlier, the central puzzle that characterizes the logic of welfare policy in almost all Western societies is defining the conditions under which the individual is legitimately exonerated from responsibility for his own maintenance. What we call "expertise" in the field of welfare policy is largely a matter of being familiar with the kinds of reasons that can plausibly override the presumption of self-support.

It is a mistake in the logic of welfare policy to argue against a scheme of income maintenance on the ground that the resulting distribution of incomes would not be perfectly equal. Absolute egalitarianism is not accepted as a presumption in this language of political discourse. For this reason, the egalitarian case, in all Western political theories, must be more cunningly contrived. For Christopher Jencks, for example, the logic of argument runs about as follows. If it is assumed that income differentials are justified if they result from differences of skill, effort, initiative, risk and so forth under conditions of equality of opportunity, and if it can be demonstrated that actual income differentials cannot be accounted for on the basis of merit—that they might be due to contacts, luck or simple randomness—then the existing distribution of income cannot be justified according to meritocratic criteria. If it can further be demonstrated that equality of education is not a sufficient condition for equality of opportunity, because education cannot obliterate certain features of early environment and nurture, then relative equality of income might be a necessary condition for realizing the norm of equality of opportunity (Jencks, 1972). The crucial normative criterion in Jencks's argument is not strict equality, but equality of opportunity, which is accepted as a pertinent ground of argument in American policy discourse. The central point is that the particular form of Jencks's argument, and the subtlety of its construction, is a function of the structure of policy evaluation accepted in this policy culture.

Of course, just as there are "scientific revolutions" in Thomas Kuhn's sense (with greater or less continuity with the past, depending on whether one accepts Kuhn or Toulmin's view) so there may be revolutions in the language of policymaking. "Normal" policymaking, like normal science, takes place within an accepted framework of political evaluation. "Revolutionary" science, like revolutionary politics, implies shifts in the fundamental logic of political appraisal.

Ideological politics has much to do with the nature of paradigm cases, the location of presumption and the burden of proof. In the economic and legal policy languages that have predominated in American history, the presumption was that natural resources should be put to productive use unless compelling reasons could be given otherwise. Today, environmentalists argue that the presumption should be reversed; that those who exploit resources bear the burden of showing that the integrity of life systems, the sustenance of vital processes of civilization and the quality of life would not be endangered by their actions.

CONCLUSION

In political science, questions of political evaluation are generally in the exclusive domain of the student of political philosophy. Empirical political scientists may be less condescending about this realm of inquiry today than they were a few years back, but the positivist insistence on a strict distinction between questions of fact and questions of value still has substantial influence in the discipline. Nonetheless, as we have seen, the logic of public policy is, at one level, no more or less than applied political philosophy. Policy evaluation can be understood as the application of classic normative constructs—public interest, right, entitlement, obligation, justice, equality, efficiency, lawfulness—to concrete cases.

Contemporary political theorists like Brian Barry, Hannah Pitkin, Thomas Connolly, J.G.A. Pocock, whose work derives from the tradition of British analytic philosophy and the ideas of the later Wittgenstein, often assert that their task is "conceptual clarification" of such basic political principles. However, in our time, the analysis of such primary political values is normally not settled by the disputations of political philosophers but by appellate courts, budget analysts, and councils of economic advisors. For the government lawyer or the public-interest advocate operating in the realm of regulatory policy, the conceptual clarification of terms like "reasonableness," "equitable," or "deceitful" (as in deceitful advertising in hearings before the FTC) is all in a day's work.

For this reason, among others, analysis of the logic of political evaluation and the act of political evaluation cannot remain totally distinct. The object of a comparative analysis of models of evaluation employed in policymaking is not merely that we might understand an interesting political phenomenon, or make predictive statements about how the system works. It is also that we might engage in criticism, clarification, and normative commentary on the way in which political judgments are in fact made in our societies. Asking what counts as a good reason for adopting a particular public policy begs the question of whether this justification is sufficient or consistent and what the implications would be of applying it as a general rule.

As we noted earlier, both scientific statements and political claims or justifications take the logical form of an argument—a case supported by reasons and evidence. The idea of "validity" in science, I think, has very much the same sense as the construct "beyond a reasonable doubt" in law. Such a case will be accepted as definitive by a jury of qualified individuals in the full exercise of their skeptical judgment. Scientific truth, Arthur Conant once observed, is that which reaches some standard.

Once we see the matter in this light, the distinction between "normative," "empirical," and "technical" analysis collapses. The social scientist's appraisal of a certain decision has no higher prima facie validity than the formal justification the policymaker offered for that action. The policymaker's assertion that he took an action to "reduce unemployment" has exactly the same logical status as the political scientist's statement that he did it to "promote mass quiescence." Both are empirical claims about the *cause* of a policy. By what standards should they be compared and evaluated by the disinterested observer?

The cogency of any normative evaluation of public policy can only be tested in a specific arena of policy discourse. We have two choices. Either we must argue that a specific analysis is a solution or a mistake (if we are operating *within* some framework of analysis) or that the wrong logic is being applied to the conception of the problem. In either event, the jury is not simply the academy of scholars and the pertinent grounds are not merely those of social science. The argument is policy-relevant, whether intended to be or not, and it is appropriately evaluated by those "engaged" in the public business. That John Rawls's theory of justice is logically inapplicable to many of the problems of distribution in contemporary industrial society says something of considerable significance about its status as a theory of justice.

In the last analysis, comparative policy analysis is condemned to be part of the argument over desirable policy. To suggest that policy evaluation is essential and inevitable in comparative policy research is not to open the door to any relaxation in the terms of scholarly rigor or to suggest the academic propriety of sheer polemic. Political argument, classically, has its own strenuous rules. We have yet to acknowledge that they apply to the enterprise of social science in precisely the same sense as they serve as a standard to guide the public debate.

REFERENCES

ANDERSON, C. W. (1975). "System and strategy in comparative policy analysis." In W. B. Gwyn and G. C. Edwards III (eds.), Perspectives on public policy-making. New Orleans: Tulane University Press.

--- (1977). "Political design and the representation of interests." Comparative Political Studies (forthcoming).

COHEN, S. (1969). Modern capitalist planning: The French model. Cambridge: Harvard University Press.

CROUCH, C. (1975). "The drive for equality: Experience of incomes policy in Britain." In L. N. Lindberg et al. (eds.) Stress and contradiction in modern capitalism. Lexington, Mass: D. C. Heath.

FREEMAN, G. (1975). British and French policies on immigration and race. Unpublished Ph.D. dissertation. University of Wisconsin–Madison.

HECLO, H. (1974). Modern social politics in Britain and Sweden. New Haven: Yale University Press.

JACKMAN, R. W. (1975). Politics and social equality: A comparative analysis. New York: John Wiley.

JENCKS, C. (1972). Inequality: A reassessment of the effect of family and schooling in America. New York: Basic Books.

JONES, A. (1973). The new inflation: The politics of prices and incomes. London: Andre Deutsch.

KUHN, T. (1962). The structure of scientific revolutions. Chicago: University of Chicago Press.

MILLER, M. L. (1976). When the center gives: The impact of the regionalization of French planning 1968-1972. Unpublished Ph.D. dissertation. University of Wisconsin–Madison.

OKUN, A. H. (1975). Equality and efficiency: The big tradeoff. Washington, D.C.: Brookings Institution.

POPPER, K. (1968). The logic of scientific discovery. New York: Harper and Row.

RIMLINGER, G. V. (1971). Welfare policy and industrialization in Europe, America and Russia. New York: John Wiley.

SHONFIELD, A. (1965). Modern capitalism. New York: Oxford University Press.

TOULMIN, S. (1961). Foresight and understanding. An enquiry into the aims of science. New York: Harper and Row.

WINCH, D. (1969). Economics and policy: A historical survey. London: Fontana.

2

A LOGIC OF COMPARATIVE POLICY ANALYSIS

HENRY TEUNE

University of Pennsylvania

The specific issue to be addressed is the improvement of predictions of the impact of particular policies. Two strategies will be suggested. The first requires the development of social science theories that are at least suggestive of specific predictions. The second requires the empirical study of policies. The latter may or may not involve theoretically informed predictions. Both would strengthen confidence in the "if . . . then" statements that are characteristic of policy predictions.

The development of social theory is an uncertain means of obtaining good predictions. Here no recipe can be offered. Certain steps, however, can be outlined to alter existing theoretical orientations such that there is a better chance of obtaining theoretical predictions, that is, those that not only state the connection between a policy and its consequences but also the reasons for and the conditions of the specific predictions. Theoretical predictions differ from extrapolations, which are predictions based on past experience without specifying the conditions.

For empirical research some "formula" or guidelines can be provided to improve confidence in policy predictions. What will be suggested is a "most similar system" design. Such a design, it will be argued, is more efficacious for strengthening policy predictions—specific predictions about specific cases—than a most different systems design. The latter is more suitable to establishing general laws, that is, those that apply to classes of systems rather than to specific cases.

The practical implications of theories to predict policy consequences or of studies of past or current policies in other systems is to shortcut the costs of direct experimentation. In research, the question is what can one system learn from another about the consequences of policies that it is considering. What could be predicted about the cost of a national health insurance program in the U.S. by studying Sweden and Canada? (Marmor et al., 1975).

Both the development of more appropriate theory and empirical research for policy predictions require comparative or cross-system research. The logic of both, focused on policy predictions, involves expanding the system variance, that is, the conditions or the social context under which particular policies have effects. Under what conditions will a universal health insurance program improve medical care for low-income groups? Only in wealthy countries, only in countries with public ownership of hospitals, or both?

Comparative policy research can serve purposes other than improving policy predictions, such as gaining insights into the nature of particular governmental systems or becoming aware of new policy alternatives or unanticipated consequences. The focus of this discussion, however, will be on predictions concerning the outcomes of policies.

THE PROBLEM OF POLICY PREDICTIONS

There are several types of public policy analyses. One is the examination of conditions that lead to the adoption of certain policies (Dye, 1972). Here certain socioeconomic factors are used to predict the nature of policies in force, such as unemployment compensation, welfare programs, increased educational expenditures. A second examines policy as indicators or manifestations of certain general structural, political, social, or economic characteristics of a system. Here, specific distributive effects of policy may be seen as reflective of power, such as favoritism of classes, interests, or regions (Cameron and Hofferbert, 1976). A third is to determine the impact or consequences—the impact of particular policies. Here, particular policy instrumentalities are analytically extracted, such as interest rates, and "if . . . then" statements made, such as if interest rates are increased, then housing construction and employment will decrease.

Impact predictions, of course, are most attractive to policymakers. They are also the most difficult from the standpoint of social science research standards. There are several reasons for the problematic nature of policy impact hypotheses. First, there are well-known measurement problems, even in such directly targeted policies as educational expenditures and literacy. Second, there is the context of the policy which can be assumed almost never to be constant across cases or time, such as the community in which schools operate. Third, almost all specific policies take place in policy "environments," some of which may be contradictory, such as educational programs to improve literacy as well as one to improve social skills.

Because of these and other confounding factors, the consequences of policies are generally ambiguous, mixed, working in some cases and not in others, and often resulting in unanticipated consequences. In addition to the social science problems there is the politics of policy evaluation. But the theoretical and empirical ambiguities are sufficient to justify adversary proceedings among different evaluators.

It is possible to conclude that not enough is known to provide scientifically acceptable policy impact statements until social science matures both theoretically and empirically. Alternatively, it is possible to admit the complexity of policy predictions and to try to reflect that complexity as variables by developing models similar to those used by econometricians. Still a third alternative is to attempt to refine empirical research by improving the controls in evaluating a policy as an experiment. The second of these increases complexity; the third impoverishes complexity by quasi-experimental controls.

It is the assumption here that policy impact statements have not been given a fair test. The problem has been that they are not theoretically informed or amenable to deaggregation in experimental form. In order to make the case for this assumption, a critique will be given of current state of affairs.

THEORETICAL MODELS

U.S. cities are one example of an attempt to model a policy problem (Forrester, 1969). A model of urban decay may include the tax base, the costs of welfare, the incentive of the poor to migrate, the disruption of the "urban style" because of migration and political demand by the poor to increase welfare. With such a model, the relationships among expenditures, taxes, and the migration of the employed to the suburbs could be charted. If the variables can be precisely specified, then relatively precise predictions can be made, including the policy predictions of "if . . . then."

The advantages of such a specification of variables and relationships, of course, are several. It explicates the complexity; it is calibrated to the case at hand (unemployment rates in Chicago); it is amenable to examining alternative assumptions. It is certainly superior to simplistic connections, such as local health clinics and the health of the population.

Substantively, such approaches to public policy fall short on several accounts. Two will be mentioned. First, at the collective level such models give little attention to policy questions concerning states of the system, matters of major importance in classical political theory–justice, equality, legitimacy. These questions cannot be transformed into indivisible "goods," such as clean air or security. Whether there are such collective values that transcend individual preferences, they, nonetheless, are part of the predictions involved in policy choice.

Second, at the individual level, most of the "goods" of public policy have been linked to divisible and allocatable material goods, despite evidence of the importance of nonmaterial incentives or values, such as dignity and respect, which are relational and thus not properties of individuals alone. Further, a subset of these values are, at least for a part of the population, preference-denying, altruistic values, which are likely to arise in policy issues addressing long-term consequences that cannot benefit the generation making those choices.

Methodologically, there are several deficiencies in such models. First, the greater the complexity of the models, the more difficult it is to appraise the role of specific sectors, such as housing, and specific variables, such as the labor cost of housing construction. The most complex form is the large econometric model of the U.S. economy, with hundreds of equations. The policy levers, however, become obscure. Simpler models provide gains in understanding at the price of potential accuracy.

Second, the greater the specificity of these models for particular cases, the less their generality for other cases. Each housing market in a city is specific, and if those specificities are incorporated into the model, then its applicability to other cases is accordingly reduced.

As a general theoretical approach to the analysis of policy, there are several additional limitations. Some of these can be overcome by a comparative or cross-national approach.

First, most public policy models are micro rather than macro. They focus on specific institutions rather than on the character of the system in which such institutions operate and how the system determines the outcomes of micro level behavior. For example, policy oriented studies of local communities in the U.S., which tend to be directed to improving their decision capacity and their efficiency in delivery of services, proceeds without examining the significance of macro system context of an open migration rule for both capital and labor. The prohibition against the imposition of political barriers to migration is a critical aspect of the consequences of local policies.

A second characteristic of this model of policy analysis is that it is, by and large, historically based rather than theoretically informed. The historical base means that the set of relationships that governed the immediate past is assumed to be constant. One example is the relationships between unemployment and inflation and the change in these relationships over time. Another is the relationships between political party identification and candidate voting and the change in these relationships in voting for chief executives.

Third, the nature of the analysis is marginal rather than structural. It deals with incremental change: altering the interest rate versus changing the structure of capital formation for housing; or a change in tax laws concerning mortgages versus the nature of legitimate access to living accommodations.

Comparative policy analysis, cross-national analysis, would move models of policy problems to the macro level to deal with differences among countries; to theoretical concerns to take into account the discontinuities in relationships both over time and across systems; and to structural analysis to analyze the obvious difference between the macro and micro levels among countries.

Although comparative policy analysis forces macro, theoretical, and structural analysis, it less clearly can remedy certain substantive deficiencies. It may do so if only because comparative analysis vastly increases the variance to be explained. This cross-national variance may include normative questions of the "states" of the system; politically initiated changes in individual preferences; cases where material abundance does not overwhelm and obscure other values; and instances of major policy successes in changing the nature of the political system.

EMPIRICAL RESEARCH

Several recent efforts have been made to improve the empirical foundations of public policy impact predictions. The thrust of these efforts has been to control the factors influencing the impacts of policy. Each of them has certain limitations.

1. "QUASI EXPERIMENTAL DESIGN"

In an influential paper, "Reforms as Experiments," Campbell (1969) presented certain correspondences between experiments and actual situations. One purpose of this paper was to elevate empirical analyses of policy impact to meet the standards of experimental design. Modifications in the logic of experimental design were indicated. One example of public reform interpreted as interrupted time series was massive enforcement of traffic regulations and the rate of accidents (Campbell, 1968).

The logic of quasi-experimental design pushes analysis to the micro-level: a relatively isolatable target population and a relatively isolatable policy action (single impact), in a comprehensibly describably context for statistical controls with specified predictions about the expected effects. The problem is that the consequences of even those policies that tend to have isomorphism with experiments, such as the impact of new teaching methods on students, have ambiguous interpretations. Applying the logic of experimental design to general institutions, such as governments, with multiple population targets, multiple policy goals, and a complex context is even more problematical. The threats to the validity of quasi-experimental analysis were set forth in detail by Campbell (1969). They include maturation effects and long-term secular trends. There also, of course, are the standard problems of experimentation, such as obtaining valid measures of "the treatment."

Since the explication of quasi-experiments, the successful cases of policy evaluation are few. The two primary conditions for meeting, even in a rough way, experimental conditions would, except under very limited circumstances, rarely obtain:

(a) that the "treatment," the policy, and the population treated are relatively isolatable from other "environmental" factors which, of course, is the primary source of the threats to the validity of the results.

(b) that the "treatment" would occur in a randomized way across social conditions.

In fact the context usually will overwhelm any particular policy treatment. Also, the adoption of particular policies is lawfully governed, not random, just as the relationship between a policy and its effects may be lawfully determined.

But even if the validity of the results of a quasi-experimental research design could be satisfactorily estimated, the language of associating policy to its results properly allowed in experimental research is uninteresting from a practical point of view. Technically, the conclusion of an experiment is a statement that there is a probability (e.g., .05) that this experiment did not disconfirm the hypothesized relationship. Such statements are hardly within range of causal connections that would be convincing for policy choices.

Quasi-experimental design in policy research runs against the logic of comparative policy analysis. The emphasis is on control and, consequently, similarities of setting and context are at a premium. Examining a policy in two or more countries would in most cases confound experimental controls.

2. THE STUDY OF SUBNATIONAL POLITICAL UNITS

One set of public policymaking units that are more amenable to ex post facto statistical control than countries for analyzing policy consequences is a large number of subnational political units, such as cities or regions, all of which share the same general political environment, but have different local policies. There are problems of controlling for local differences as alternative hypotheses to policy and of obtaining a sufficiently large range of variance in order to apply multivariate analysis (Hofferbert and Sharkansky, 1971). Is it the size of the city, its ethnic homogeneity, or the appointment of its school board that produced high per capita school expenditures?

Further, statistical relationships between policy decisions and particular kinds of results within local units are aggregative summaries of unspecified intermediate relationships. The data do not show, for example, at the U.S. state level at least, any clear relationship between capital punishment and the frequency of capital crimes. However, at the micro-level, such as the police district, there are plausible categories of evidence that there is a deterrent effect. It is simply that all other factors that intervene between the process of capital punishment and an individual crime confound the relationship between these two variables at a more macro-level.

The analysis of subnational political units is not inherently comparative. If the analysis is conducted within a single country, there are multiple policy units and variance among them to be explained, either informally or statistically. If the analysis is focused on connecting a macro-system variable, the political structure of the city, to within system differences, the attitudes of the population of the city, then the logical core of comparative analysis is present—cross-level analysis (Przeworski and Teune, 1970). Although cross-level analysis is a general form of analysis—across group and within group analysis—subnational policy analysis is highly suggestive of formal comparative analysis in that local political units are "structured" into a macro-system, the national political system.

3. MACRO-POLICY ANALYSIS

Macro-policy analysis basically can be viewed as a generalized experiment in which characteristics of systems, such as the level of decentralization of two countries, can be used to predict variance within them, such as expenditures of local governments for education (Cameron and Hofferbert, 1976). Such macro-system empirical analyses, however, are limited because of the large number of system level differences that can be used to differentiate two or more countries. Not only do they differ on their level of decentralization but also on their level of economic development, their history, their electoral system, and so forth.

The limited number of cases, the clustering of variance, and the variety of variables combine to make it unlikely that this inductive approach of examining the policy consequences of whole political systems will be productive of generalizable policy prediction (Teune, 1973). The problem of overdetermination, except in a few possible cases where there are consistent consequences of similar policies regardless of any system difference, cannot be overcome to meet the standards of formal analysis.

4. TIME SERIES ANALYSIS

Some research has examined changes related to a particular policy across several decades, involving time series analysis (Peters, 1972). An example is the adoption of social security and the relative economic status of categories of the population. Informal analysis of trends is possible. Formal time series analysis requiring at least 10 points in time and ideally 50 or more, however, limits the kinds of policies and cases that can be examined formally. A stable number of time points is a rarity. Also there is the problem of attenuated relationships between a policy in one decade and its consequences in following decades. The larger the period of time the greater the number of factors confounding the evidence for sustaining a generalization concerning policy consequence.

The major advantage of multiple time points is an increase in the number of observations. Consistency of direction across several points in time can be interpreted as a case confirming a prediction. Adding to multiple time points several countries again increases the cases for control either through matching of similarities (most similar systems design) or through the discounting of system differences (most different system design).

Time series improves the strength of the proposed general strategy for the empirical study of policy and its consequences. The strategy is to expand the controlled cases by increasing the number of cases using several levels of policy units (local governments) within systems and several points in time. Increasing the cases can improve the chances of credible generalization derived from comparative policy research.

THEORETICAL DIRECTIONS

In order to improve policy predictions, it has been argued, certain theoretical directions may be followed to determine the conditions under which policy can influence social change. This would include specifying the macro, structural factors, requiring cross-system and cross-time perspectives—a comparative approach to policy analysis. What will be done is to provide illustrations of these theoretical directions rather than to present a procedure for the construction of theories of relevance to policy.

1. CONSTRUCTING A THEORY OF THE SOCIETY AND THE POLICY

The social system and the government dynamically interact with one another and their relationships change over time. The ways in which and the degree to which "subjective factors"—governmental policies—can depart from the "objective conditions"—the state of the society—and change it can be at least theoretically indicated.

One illustration is the three sector division of a country: the society, the policy, and the economy. Although such a distinction readily allows for the influence of the political system, it is clear that not all systems have three such distinguishable sectors. It is also clear that the degree of differentiation and how the sectors are linked varies over time. In order to predict the impact of policy, it is necessary to predict the nature of the differentiation and of the integration of these sectors.

As a second illustration, it is possible to use a theory to specify the nature of the policy system. Such theory might state that as a society develops or becomes more complex, the number of decision points will increase. Hierarchy, however, is a requisite for policy. It is a structure through which one action can influence several others. With the emergence of more decision points resulting from increased complexity, there is a change in the distribution of information and influence. Thus, as a society develops or becomes more complex, the effectiveness of any single decision point will become diluted. Also, the influence of policy decision points relative to other decision points within a system becomes reduced (Teune, 1976a).

These illustrations show that the connection between policy and outcome cannot be assumed to be either universal or constant. It requires explanation. The first step toward theoretically informing policy analysis to improve predictions is to identify the nature and importance of policymaking institutions.

2. SPECIFYING MACRO-STRUCTURAL VARIABLES

Some understanding of the general conditions under which policy operates is essential to an understanding of policy impacts. These structural factors, seen in cross-national or historical perspective, become variables.

One illustration is the absence of formal authority of local communities in the U.S. to impose political constraints or incentives for migration of capital and people. Thus, the instrumentalities of cities for improving the quality of services must take place in face of individuals and organizations having the freedom to disapprove by migration.

Another illustration concerns the fragmented but strong local political power bases in the U.S. in comparison to weaker ones in Great Britain. The local power bases are often strong enough to thwart policy initiatives of higher levels of government. The extent to which this is a factor in assessing policy impact in the U.S. is, of course, a variable that varies across cities and over time.

Such theoretical insights into the policy system again call for a comparative perspective. They, at the very least, suggest modification of the "if . . . then" policy predictions to include some statement of the conditions under which the policy predictions hold. These conditions in comparative perspective become variables in the analysis of the impact of policy choice.

3. GENERATING POINT PREDICTIONS

It would be useful not only to enhance the power of the policy predictions but also to verify theories to have point predictions—specification of the values of variables over time—rather than simple directional predictions—the positive or negative relationship among variables (Meehl, 1967).

One illustration is that if it is true that the costs of density in cities increases over time and that these increased costs must be offset by increased governmental expenditures, then it should be possible to predict increases in the amount of various budget items, such as fire protection, housing, and capital projects.

A second illustration concerns the theoretical view of the fiscal crises of U.S. cities involving an inherent conflict between the pressures to spend for welfare and the need for capital formation to increase the productivity of the factories and improve urban amenities (O'Conner, 1973). If this dynamic could be specified, then it should be possible to predict levels of increased expenditures for welfare, increased taxation, and indeed, perhaps the migration of major industries out of the city (Teune, 1976b).

Point predictions are, of course, the kind of predictions required for policy impact statements. Such statements also have the advantage of allowing for more efficient verification of theories by providing several potential disconformatory statements, the value of the variables at several points in time.

RESEARCH: MOST SIMILAR SYSTEMS DESIGN

To improve the efficiency of research to test relationships hypothesized to be universal, a most different system design is indicated. For example, if it is true that increased political participation leads to increased expenditures of local governments, and if this relationship holds in both a poor and a rich country and in a capitalistic and a socialistic one, then there is a strong presumption that the relationship would hold for countries that differ on other dimensions (Przeworski and Teune, 1970). Because it is practically impossible to test hypotheses in all countries, the most different systems design has the advantage of discounting for system differences by selecting a few that are most different. In contrast, if two similar systems—Denmark and Sweden—manifest a similar relationship between class identity and voting, the generalizations are limited to similar kinds of countries—rich, small, and ethnically homogeneous. Is the similarity of the relationship because of class, the level of industrialization, or the Scandinavian culture?

The primary purpose of comparative policy research, however, is not to establish the universality of relationships. Rather it is to enhance the credibility of specific predictions about specific cases. It does not matter if the consequences are, strictly speaking, due to the policy or to the interaction of the policy with wealth or the political institutions of the country. Accordingly, a most similar system design has advantages. The question is whether this context, this country, this policy will have specific effects. Further, rather than making disconfirmation of relationships easy and then searching for likely system level variables that would explain the differences as in a most different systems design, what is important is whether a relationship found to hold in one country will be true in another. In this sense comparative policy research takes on the purpose of applied research, to get useful rather than general knowledge in the short run. What can the U.S. predict about the costs of medical care under national health insurance? Canada is a good case for comparison (Marmor, Hoffman, and Heagy, 1975). Australia would be better than France.

A CONCLUDING STATEMENT

Aside from economists, social scientists have made limited contributions to policy predictions. There are a few clear areas of success, such as in some evaluation studies. It is possible to improve on what has been done by directing theoretical concerns to macro-policy analysis and point predictions and to improve the nature of empirical research. Such improvements require a policy approach. Theoretically, such an approach would mean increasing generality to take account of more factors, especially the conditions under which policy predictions hold. Empirically, comparative policy analysis would be directed to specific cases, narrowing generality with the purpose of making the findings from one case applicable to another.

REFERENCES

CAMERON, S., and HOFFERBERT, R. (1976). "The dynamics of education finance in federal systems." Policy and Politics, 5:129-157.

CAMPBELL, D. (1968). "The Connecticut crackdown on speeding: Time series data in quasi experimental analysis." Law and Society, 3(November):33-53.

--- (1969). "Reform as experiments." American Psychologist, 24(April):409-429.

DYE, T. (1972). Understanding public policy. Englewood Cliffs, N.J.: Prentice Hall.

FORRESTER, J. (1969). Urban dynamics. Cambridge, Mass.: MIT Press.

HOFFERBERT, R., and SHARKANSKY, I. (eds., 1971). State and urban politics. Boston: Little Brown.

MARMOR, T., HEAGY, T., and HOFFMAN, W. (1975). "Canadian National Health Insurance: Policy implications for the United States." Policy Sciences, 64(December):447-466.

MEEHL, P. (1967). "Theory testing in psychology and physics: A methodological paradox." Philosophy of Science, 34(June): 105-115.

O'CONNER, J. (1973). The fiscal crisis of the state. New York: St. Martin's Press.

PETERS, B. (1972). Economic and political effects on the development of social expenditure in France, Sweden and the United Kingdom. Midwest Journal of Political Science, 41(May):225-238.

PRZEWORSKI, A., and TEUNE, H. (1970). The logic of comparative social inquiry. New York: John Wiley.

TEUNE, H. (1973). "Public policy: Macro perspectives." In G. Zaltman (ed.), Process and phenomena of social change. New York: John Wiley.

--- (1976a). "Information, control, and the governability of territorial political units." Tenth World Congress of the International Political Science Association, Edinburgh.

--- (1976b). "Macro theoretical approaches to public policy." Social Science History Association, Philadelphia.

PART II

INSTITUTIONS AND COMPARISON

3

COMPARATIVE POLITICS AND HEALTH POLICIES: NOTES ON BENEFITS, COSTS, LIMITS

THEODORE R. MARMOR,
AMY BRIDGES,
and WAYNE L. HOFFMAN

University of Chicago

Interest in the cross-national study of public policy has increased in the 1970s. Whether one uses conferences or special journal issues and books as a guide, the incidence of efforts including the words comparative and policy is greater than a decade ago.[1] Crudely, one can take a jaded or an optimistic view of these developments. One might regard this as simply the internationalization in American political science of what is called policy studies. With more resources available for policy studies, the ordinary market for academic output adjusts appropriately. The supply of efforts reflects the supply of funds. Hopefully, one can show that studying policies across nation states is intellectually interesting in its own right. More compelling justification of cross-national policy studies is what comparative policy research teaches us. This essay focuses on comparative research about health policies to illustrate the difficulties and advantages of comparative public policy research.

COMPARATIVE RESEARCH AND POLICY LEARNING

Policy research provides an additional vantage point for traditional political scientists. Consider the following questions about health policy, for example: Who benefits from alternate arrangements of publicly financed medical care services? What notions of distributive justice prevail in the distribution of access and treatment? Who dominates in the health policy subsystem? What, particularly, are the consequences of a particular administrative and fiscal structure for national health insurance and its implementation according to the social values of the political market? What stimulation does a policy alternative give to prospective group or sectoral demands on government? What will policy alternative X do to the capacity of government to govern or to change at a later date to another policy if X fails? (Lowi, 1973:61-67).

Moreover, policy studies provide a viewpoint from which to study political processes. Lowi's work (1964), for example, has focused on the political alliances which policies create. Charles Anderson's paper (in this volume) suggests that public discourse about policy alternatives serve as a key to the understanding of political culture. When we examine policies as outcomes, and look for their determinants, research focuses on the "input" side of political processes.[2]

Finally, policy research may focus on public policy itself. Here, the "input" of the political process serves to illuminate constraints on policy alternatives. Or we may want to make conditional predictions about the effects of given policy options. And politics in the broad sense will serve to explain what happens to policies during what is deceptively referred to as "implementation."

Cross-national policy studies facilitate these kinds of learning. First, they allow the researcher to weigh the social determinants of policy more carefully and especially to distinguish culturally specific from more general determinants of policies. The latter distinction suggests means for distinguishing policy–manipulable activities from those relatively immune to manipulation. Second, comparative policy analysis provides material for evaluating alternatives by looking at their probable effects. Third, comparative research helps the researcher identify the ways that institutional arrangements for implementing policy structure the politics of administration. Each of these tasks requires somewhat different research designs. The discussions which follow illustrate the kinds of learning comparative policy studies facilitate, and the difficulties in the research design for each.

DIVERSE POLITICAL SYSTEMS AND MICRO-POLICY FOCUS: THE POLITICS OF DOCTORS' PAY

Comparative policy studies, we argued above, allow the researcher to weigh the social determinants of policy and, in particular, to distinguish culturally specific from other determinants of policy outcomes. Individual country studies cannot logically test the explanatory power of hypotheses which emphasize distinctive features of individual political systems, for example, explanations which rest on "political culture." These were the arguments Marmor and Thomas (1972) addressed in a research review of Eckstein's classic *Pressure Group Politics.* Eckstein traced doctors' bargaining victories over the British government to the physicians' success in privatizing the bargaining process; this, in turn, rested on institutional arrangements specific to Britain.

Neither internal nor external evidence supports Eckstein's view that bargaining structures determine much of the British Medical Association's effectiveness. The internal evidence–remuneration disputes over time–indicates that intimacy of negotiations is not a crucial factor in accounting for BMA success on pay. External evidence is another check on this causal scheme. Three countries were chosen for intensive study–Great Britain, Sweden, and the United States–and their policy decisions about how doctors are to be paid by the state were examined: (a) the changes in methods of remuneration following the general practitioner crisis (1965-1966) in Great Britain; (b) the fee-for-service policy of the National Health Insurance Act in Sweden (1955); and (c) the Medicare "reasonable charge policy" in the United States.

We should make clear two features of this type of comparative study at the outset. First, the countries differ markedly in the setting and atmosphere of negotiations for medical remuneration.[3] Second, the policy decisions in each case are strikingly similar when measured against the intentions of the medical organizations. That is to say, methods which the respective medical organizations were known to prefer were, broadly speaking, what the government policy became in each of the three examples. Here we have a common burden on a political system–the requirement to settle physicians' remuneration in public programs–and three different decision-making structures to cope with it. The existence of a common outcome suggests that the causal factor lies in the nature of the pressure group and the resources which doctors, as opposed to other producer groups in the society, share. Why doctors in different national settings prefer different methods is a separate issue in the history and sociology of professions. For present purposes, it is enough to know that knowledge of their preferences is the single best predictor of policy decisions in this area.

The evidence gathered in the testing of this hypothesis was of two sorts. First, the pattern of payment-method decisions since World War II in three Western industrial countries—Sweden, Great Britain, and the United States—was investigated. Data from these countries include broad patterns of medical payment methods during the postwar period, as reported in the secondary literature, and Marmor and Thomas's analysis of the extraordinary controversial instances of payment-method decisions in the three societies. The second major types of data collected were secondary analyses of payment methods used in other industrial countries, notably the Netherlands, West Germany, France, Switzerland, Spain, Italy, Canada, Greece, Poland, the Soviet Union, and Israel (Abel-Smith, 1963:27-35; 1965:33-40; Glaser, 1970; Schnur and Hollenberg, 1966:111-119; Badgely and Wolfe, 1967). This evidence revealed that as producers of a crucial service in industrial countries for which governments can seldom provide short-run substitutes, physicians have sufficient political resources to influence decisions regarding payment methods quite apart from the form of bargaining their organizations employ. The hypothesis thus directly links physicians' economic and political power to public policy outcomes, asserting that intervening bargaining variables are not central in explaining public policy decisions in this area.[4]

The policy implications of these findings are important. First, the most important thing for governments to understand is both the nature of medical power and the limits on that power. We conclude that certain features of payment-method controversies are, in fact, not negotiable, however much of these disputes arise in the course of medical-government confrontations. The reason for governments' inability to control medical-payment methods emerges from the different priorities and economic power of the bargaining antagonists. That is, doctors can, by withholding services, impose higher political costs than governments are willing to pay simply to rearrange methods of paying them. The same kind of reasoning about priorities and political power will show that doctors cannot impose their will on governments in all cases—doctors almost everywhere resisted NHI, for example.[5]

Knowing what governments cannot do and what outcomes will occur is obviously important to government officials involved in controversial negotiations. In health policy, such knowledge may permit concentration on alternative means to the goals toward which traditional government payment-preferences aim. There are two alternatives to continual dispute over the choice of payment methods. One is to concede the choice of method to physicians and concentrate on administrative techniques to make these methods less undesirable. The other is to seek alternative ways to accomplish the goals which payment methods were to serve: reward of quality education, limits on excessive services, and so on.

This kind of inclusive research design, focusing on the industrial nations of the West as a group, is akin to a "most different systems" approach, although it does not strictly meet its requirements. As Przeworski and Teune (1970) suggest, use of a multination research design offers a basis for more valid results than, for example, two-nation designs. But the multination design also incurs the risk of uncontrollable complexity. Increases in "N," that is, expansion of the number of cases, involve the addition of numerous variables that ought to be controlled for a valid comparison. Only a very limited number of national cases exist for most policy comparisons. Tentatively, we suggest that multiple country designs are best used to identify the parameters or limits of social choices—invariant relationships across a variety of political structures and cultural values.

There are dangers in the kind of policy research which allows us to identify broad system characteristics as determinants of social policies. First, what exists may too drastically curtail our view of what is possible. After all, there was a time when no one had NHI. Second, the appeal of the "certainty" of this kind of knowledge may distract researchers from asking more important questions. So, for example, Newhouse (1976) shows with some certainty that per capita expenditures on medical care vary over a broad range, according to per capita GNP. Yet, since neither the quality of medical care nor the mix of medical care services is determined by per capita expenditures, it is not clear that we learn anything crucial about *medical care* when we explain per capita expenditures.

POLICY EVALUATION AND SIMILAR SYSTEMS

Comparative policy research can address the consequences as well as the constraints of policy choice. Research following a "most similar systems" approach facilitates appraisal of the effects of policy options. This paradigm requires that the nations compared share a number of features that causally relate to the policy consequences of analytic significance. More simply stated, one country may serve as a "laboratory" for another's policy choices. Deborah Stone (1976), for example, argues that the United States can learn from the German experience of regulating physicians under national health insurance, because "of all the European countries, West Germany's system is most like that of the United States" (Stone, 1976:4). Both countries use contributory public financing programs to allow individual patients to purchase care from private physicians and physicians receive pay on a fee-for-service basis. While Stone rightly argues that pure transplantation of other national policies is usually impossible, she emphasizes that cross-national examples have mostly served as negative warnings. Yet, her own work shows that we can learn from West Germany how physicians supply services when they are subject to pricing and volume restrictions; this information can make American policy planning about peer review more realistic.

Canada's current program, which resembles some leading American proposals, can serve as a "natural experiment" for the United States, a guide both to the impact of national health insurance and the reactions of policymakers and the public to this impact. The Canadian national health insurance experience is especially applicable

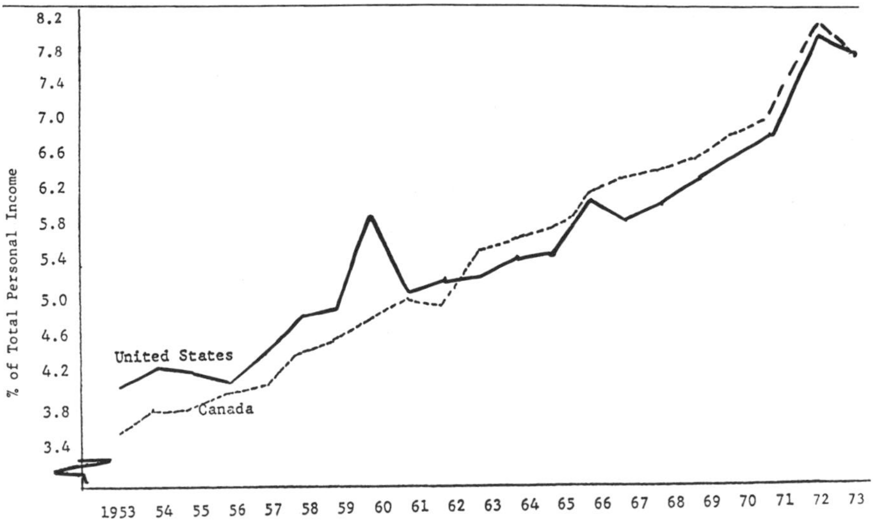

SOURCES: United States: through 1971: Reinhardt and Branson, 1974; 1972, 3: Minister of National Health and Welfare (Canada), 1975: Table 6, p. 16.

Canada: through 1971: Evans in Andreopoulos, 1975: Table 3, p. 140; 1972, 3: Minister of National Health and Welfare (Canada), 1975.

Figure 1. EXPENDITURES ON PERSONAL HEALTH CARE IN THE UNITED STATES AND CANADA, 1953-1973 (as a percent of Personal Income)

because both Canadian society and its health concerns are strikingly similar to America's (Marmor, Heagy, and Hoffman, 1975). Public officials of both countries worry about the increased proportion of national resources expended on medical care and wonder what health improvement it has bought. They also want to assure more equal access—financially, geographically, socially. A vocal minority in each country wants major reorganization of medical care providers. Finally, after many years of expansion, both Canadian and American officials are trying to reduce the use of expensive hospital service and stabilize the number of hospital beds and, to a lesser extent, physicians (Andreopoulos, 1974).

Politically, socially, economically, and culturally, the United States is closer to Canada than to any other nation.[6] Canadian

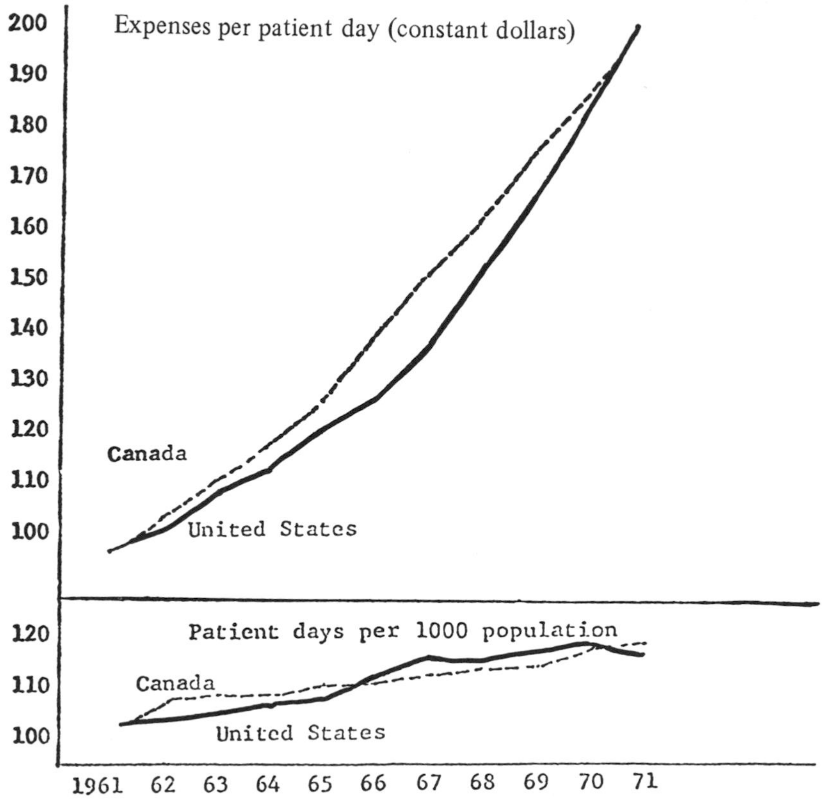

SOURCES: Unadjusted Data—Reinhardt and Branson, 1974. Bureau of Labor Statistics, U.S. Price Deflator. *Canada's Yearbook*, 1972, Canada Price Deflator.

Figure 2. COMPARISON OF TRENDS IN HOSPITAL SECTOR IN THE UNITED STATES AND CANADA, 1961-1971

political authority is decentralized. Its tradition of dispute over federal power resembles the United States. The structure of the health industry is strikingly similar, as Table 1 makes plain. American and Canadian hospitals are largely "voluntary" and physicians in both countries are still typically paid under a fee-for-service system. The two countries similarly adjusted to the growth of health insurance, which was largely private at first, becoming increasingly public in character in the postwar period.[7]

Inflation and cost-control policy is one area in which the United States may learn from Canada. Canadian and American costs have been strikingly parallel. The trends of prices, utilization, and expenditures are similar and the proportion of national resources each spent on health is almost identical[8] (see Figures 1 and 2). The late sixties witnessed severe medical inflation in both countries; while the increase in the relative cost of health care slowed somewhat in the early 1970s, in the last two years they have again escalated rapidly.[9] For simplicity's sake we will discuss Canadian hospital costs separately from physicians' services.

Table 1. SELECTED STATISTICS ON HEALTH RESOURCES, UTILIZATION, EXPENDITURES AND INFLATION IN CANADA AND THE U.S.

	Canada	*U.S.*
Resources		
Hospital beds/1,000 population, 1971	7.0	7.5
Short term hospital beds/1,000 population, 1971	5.6	4.2
Physicians/100,000 population, 1971	151.0	174.0
*Short Term Hospital Utilization**		
Percent occupancy, 1971	80.1%	76.7%
Length of stay, 1971	9.9	8.1
Patient days/1,000 population, 1971	1552.0	1199.0
Expenditures		
Per capita hospital expenditures, 1970	$132.53	$135.41
Per capita physician expenditures, 1970	48.25	70.13
Average Annual Change in Health Care Expenditures		
Total personal health care, 1965-1971	13.3%	12.3%
Total personal health care, 1969-1971	13.6	11.6
Institutional care, 1965-1971	13.6	15.0
Professional services, 1965-1971	13.8	10.5

*For U.S., data is for nonfederal short term hospitals. For Canada, data is for nonfederal, nonproprietary general hospitals.

SOURCES: *Canada Health Manpower Inventory 1973; Annual Report 1972-1973: Hospital Insurance and Diagnostic Services;* National Health Expenditures in Canada 1960-1971 with *Comparative Data for the United States,* Health and Welfare, Canada. *Statistical Abstract, 1973,* U.S. Census Bureau.

Cited in Lewin & Associates, Inc., Government Controls on the Health Care System: The Canadian Experience, p.v.

HOSPITALS

Canada and the United States proceeded in the postwar period from different starting points as to number and costs of beds; they have experienced very similar trends. Canada still has more hospital beds per capita and higher rates of hospital admissions, patient days of care, and expenditures per capita[10] (see Figure 3).

Canada has experienced a rapid increase, not in hospital *use,* but in *expenditures* for hospital services.[11] As in America, most of this increase resulted from higher expenses per patient day, not increased per capita use. From 1953 to 1971, Canadian hospital expenditures per capita (in constant dollars) increased 259% while hospital patient days per capita increased only 29% (Evans, 1974:138-142).[12] In

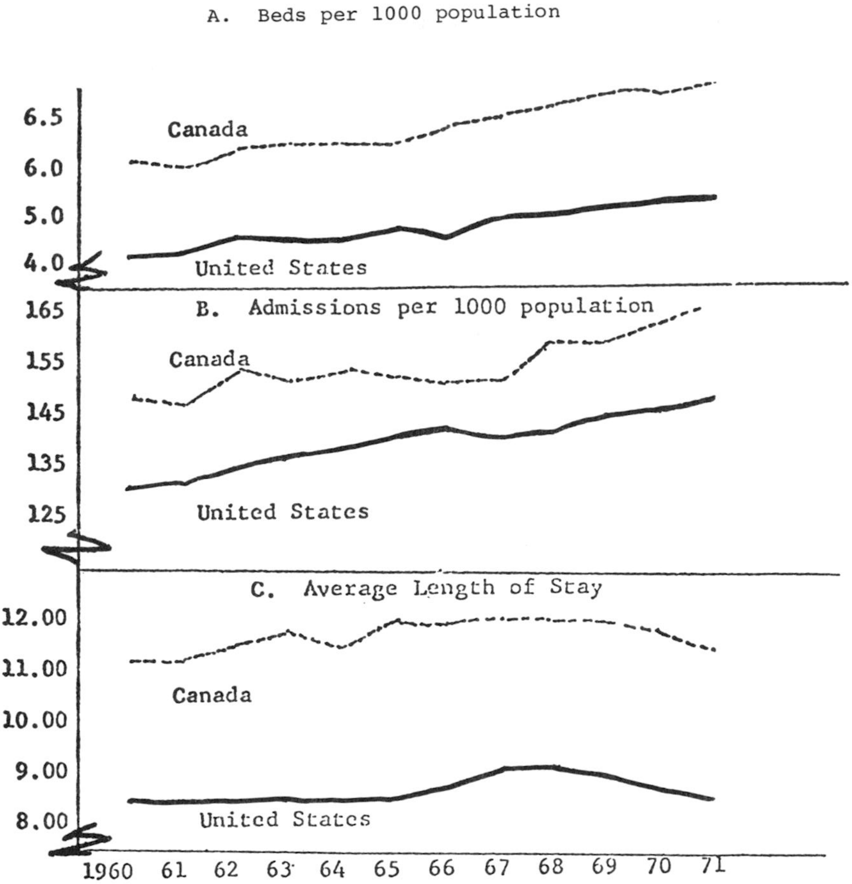

SOURCE: Reinhardt and Branson, 1974.

Figure 3. HOSPITAL UTILIZATION–CANADA AND THE UNITED STATES, 1960-1971

turn, most of these higher costs were reflected in increasing wage bills. Evans (1974:146) estimates that from 1953 to 1971, these increased 68% more than the average wage of all industrial workers and staff hours per patient day increased by 45% (Evans in Andreopoulos, 1975: 146).

Evans[13] suggests that hospital admission is not very sensitive to price; the reduction in point-of-service costs of care did not lead to a large increase in utilization. If so, co-payment requirements for patients will restrain neither use nor costs and will only redistribute costs to the hospitalized ill.[14] Cost-sharing provisions in a number of current United States national health insurance proposals seem questionable on this issue.

Canadian experiences becloud other cost-control methods proposed in the United States: detailed budget review, incentive reimbursement schemes with global (as opposed to line) budgeting, and direct bed control. Canada has employed detailed budget review for more than a decade; while apparently a good instrument for detecting fraud, it has failed to check expenditure growth. Some provinces have partially replaced it with global budgets and incentive reimbursement policies.[15] Their experience suggests that there are serious limitations to plausible reimbursement schemes. Some American authorities advocate reform of reimbursement "so that hospitals are no longer guaranteed that revenues will equal costs regardless of their productivity." They recommend an

> incentive reimbursement system . . . advocated to promote hospital efficiency and rationalize capital expenditures. Hospitals would be reimbursed on a case basis, taking account of the case mix of the hospital and its teaching program; the system would be based on a formula that assured the hospital of operating and capital costs. Deficits would force inefficient hospitals to improve their management, change the nature of their operations, or shut down. [Lave, 1974:3]

Canadian interpreters provide evidence that such a system, however theoretically appealing, is very hard to implement. For political reasons, poorly managed hospitals are rarely allowed to fail; capital funds are supplied separately from operating budgets; case mix adjustments are not well worked out; and hospital managers do not seek "profits" as much as improved services and larger budgets. The Canadian turn from fine-tuned management incentives to supply constraints is particularly revealing for American discussion (Badgely, 1974). The inadequacy of line-by-line and global budget techniques and hospital substitutes to control Canadian inflation provides a lesson for the United States. Short of direct government control over wages, few policy alternatives to bed control promise to check hospital expenditures.

PHYSICIANS

There are at least three important topics in the American health-care debate for which Canadian experience with medical insurance is strikingly relevant: complaints about the fees and incomes of physicians, the inflationary impact of their practices, and their maldistribution by location and specialty. One strategy advanced in the United States—and embodied in several national health-insurance bills—is detailed specification of fees and peer review of the appropriateness of the pattern and price of care.

The comparative data on changes in the ratio of the physicians' fee index to the consumer price index, presented in Figure 4, shows that at about the time of the introduction of medical insurance, Canadian physicians' fees started a sharp decline relative to the other prices. Figure 5 illustrates, for the same time period, that Canadian physicians' income (in constant dollars) increased.

This paradox was built into the planning for NHI, which provided physician reimbursement at 85% or 90% of established fees, but used a published fee schedule rather than an estimate of actual average fees received before national health insurance.

According to Evans (1974) "the single most prominent influence of health insurance in Canada has been to increase the earnings of health providers." This is somewhat obscured in Figure 5 because of the various dates different provinces entered the Medicare (physicians' services) program. By comparing each province's first year in the program, Table 2* shows how great the impact of national health insurance really was on physician income. The average increase in net physician income (deflated by the Canadian Consumer Price Index) was more than twice as great during the transition to national health insurance as the increase in the immediately previous period. Studies in Quebec show absolutely no increase in the number of physician visits per capita after Medicare (Castonguary, 1974:115). While comparable data are not available for other provinces, there is no reason to expect substantial differences. Thus it does not appear that the increase in physician income can be attributed to increased workloads.

---

*See page 80 for Table 2.

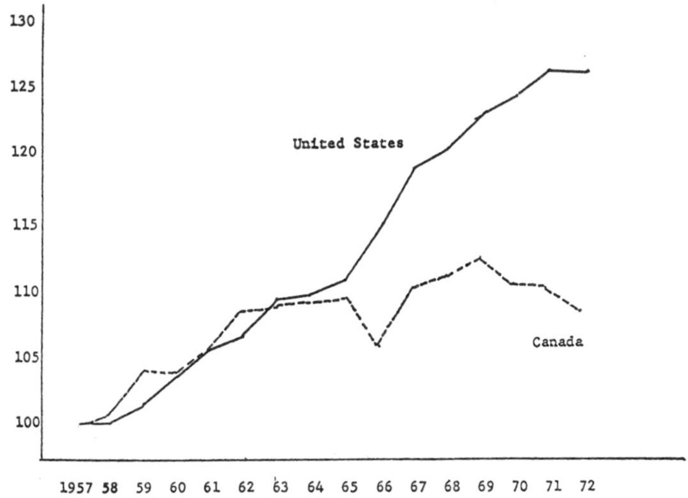

SOURCE: Reinhardt and Branson, 1974.

Figure 4. RATIO OF PHYSICIAN FEES INDEX TO THE CONSUMER PRICE INDEX IN THE UNITED STATES AND CANADA, 1957-1972 (1957 = 100)

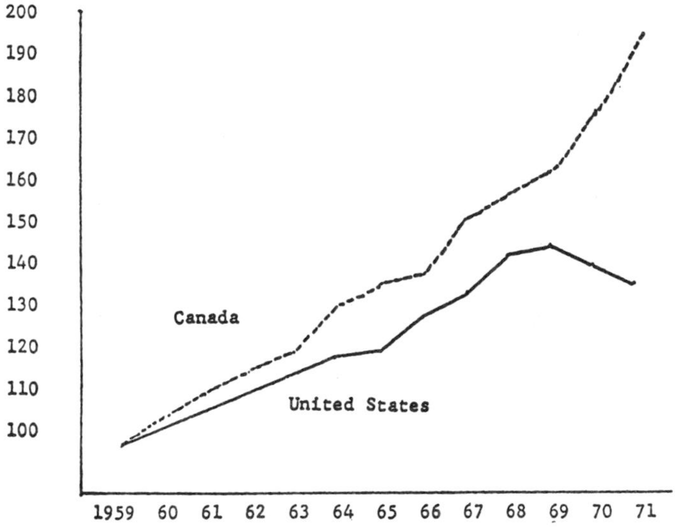

SOURCE: *Statistical Abstract of the United States.* Bureau of Labor Statistics. Evans in Andreopoulos, 1975.

Figure 5. RATIO OF PHYSICIAN NET INCOME TO CONSUMER PRICE INDEX IN THE UNITED STATES AND CANADA, 1969-1971 (1959 = 100)

Under NHI, Canadian fee-for-service reimbursement has raised physician incomes in at least two ways. The first and simplest is the reduction of bad debts and collection expenses.

A second related mechanism is the leveling-up of fees, which physicians have traditionally varied somewhat according to patients' income and insurance coverage. Under national health insurance they have tried to establish their highest rates as "customary," even though those rates are not necessarily the average, or even the most frequently asked, fee. If national health insurance reimburses at the highest rate, net earnings will increase and, just as with bad debt reduction, will not appear as official fee increases.

Clearly, average fees received, not so-called customary charges, should be the appropriate standard. But that standard requires detailed information on actual fees analyzed by specialty and region. Such information is not easily available in the United States.

Furthermore, bitter controversies in British Columbia, Ontario, Quebec, and other provinces suggest that physician incomes will be a continuous public issue, not simply a matter between the profession and the government. All American discussants are prepared for controversy over the level of fees in a national health insurance program, over variation in fees by education or location, but not over adjustment of fees for removal of bad debts and fee reductions.

Despite using the language of "natural experiment," we recognize that cross-national research seldom allows for really scientific experiments. Such designs would permit the researcher to hold some variables constant while manipulating the experimental ones. Not even two nations can be matched on all but a few policy-related factors; results thus run high risks of invalidity. One response to this difficulty is to despair of social science's capacity to produce valid results from cross-national policy research of a quasi-experimental sort (see Teune, this volume; Zaltman, 1973). This response might be termed the fallacy of comparative difference. Because we cannot have controlled experiments across nations, we cannot learn from the experiences of other nations at what Teune calls the micro-policy level. Here fascination with the natural science paradigm leads to despair. Yet we can learn by reasoned and plausible exclusion of national differences which appear distantly related to major research hypotheses. Moreover, policy options are sometimes framed such that "negative evidence" from cross-national research suffices to evaluate their probable consequences. This was the case with our discussion of the relevance of Canadian experience to incentive reimbursement policies for American hospitals. Finally, the Canadian study led to the formulation of a broad hypothesis about the relationship between levels of health expenditures and the degree of dispersal of budgetary and regulatory authority in health financing (Marmor, Wittman, and Heagy, 1976).

Cross-national research in health, then, permits awareness of new alternatives, anticipation of what might not be expected, and confirmation of relationships between policy choice, action, and consequences (Teune, this volume). It is to this last topic that we want to turn in the final section, to discuss research on the administration of health programs cross-nationally.

IMPLEMENTATION AND CROSS-NATIONAL RESEARCH IN HEALTH

There is now broad scholarly acceptance of the view that administrative implementation matters enormously in the achievement of public policy purposes. As Pressman and Wildavsky (1973) note in connection with American social policies of the 1960s, there is "widespread concern about the inability to implement governmental programs." (Pressman and Wildavsky, 1973:166) But the study of implementation is hard to do; part of the difficulty is methodological and professional. The process of implementing complex programs is unwieldly and messy, extending over long periods of time, unmarked by discrete, grand decisions or congressional roll calls or election results. The participation of pressure groups is continuous; there are fewer public hearings in which the stakes and actions of the interested parties are clear. Policy choice centralizes government action for analytic purposes; implementation disperses policy objectives, spreading the subject matter geographically, temporally, and intellectually. When the issues of policy direction are uncertain, political incentives press actors to mobilize supporters, not to design operational measures to ensure policy compliance. And when policy choices are deeply controversial—as with many health issues—implementation estimates are part of the arsenal of policy warfare, not aids to policy design.

If the task is difficult, the inclination to attempt it in health matters is nonetheless growing. And the effort to use cross-national research in the process is evident. This partly results from concern about the costs of medical care in advanced industrial countries, as expressed in a profusion of royal commissions in the 1970s seeking to structure public programs to moderate the rapid escalation of medical-care expenditures. This worry about the increased proportion of national resources going to medical care is becoming even more widespread as expenses in Sweden, Canada, the United States, and West Germany approach or exceed 8 percent of GNP. Health expenditures constitute one of the most powerful sources of strain within contemporary welfare states, making matters of change and choice both urgent and important. Increases in the proportion of public expenditures spent on social welfare policies may make a preemptive claim upon government resources or, by straining the capabilities of states to meet them, may even trigger political transformations. It is this context that lends urgency to the evident international preoccupation with the structure of public health programs.

The organizational model of medical-care delivery is at the center of reconsideration. Attempts to shift from inpatient to outpatient care are widespread, as is emphasis on preventive medicine to reduce disease and costs. Planners give attention to innovative use of existing medical manpower and to the redefinition and reallocation of professional functions. The result is widespread adoption of controls over hospitals and other health facilities (Bridgman and Roemer, 1973; Altenstetter, 1976). Despite the nationalization of medical-care financing, stringent control of the health sector has been the exception in Western Europe, with Great Britain and, to a lesser extent, Sweden atypical. In most of the continental countries, private providers continue to deliver medical services, subject to financing constraints. Changes in political regimes during the postwar period, however dramatic their impact on other sectors, have not transformed the delivery and regulation of medical care.

Two developments in this sector have dominated the cross-national research agenda. Decisions dealing with the allocation of financial resources (through third party payment, central government subsidies, or combinations) are becoming increasingly centralized (Maynard, 1975; Maxwell, 1975). At the same time, these countries are regionalizing medical institutions. This usually entails a decentralization of administrative functions from the top down and a centralization of finance from the bottom up. With decentralization has come the hope for democratization of control over medical-care delivery (Klein and Lewis, 1976).

The central research question is whether differing structural arrangements have discernible effects on health expenditures. There is some empirical support for the view that the dispersal of finance—

private-public, public-public, public with quasi-state organizations—and the separation of finance from administrative responsibility is associated with higher costs relative to other administrative structures (Marmor, Wittman, and Heagy, 1976; Evans, 1974; and Van Langendonck, n.d.).

The question is whether governments are able and willing to reshape health administration radically. Fragmentary cross-national research suggests three points. One is that it takes power at the center to produce administrative change at the periphery. Strong unitary states have a greater capacity to implement even what is unwise, weak, or ineffective than federal states. Secondly, federal states with sharing of authority—as distinguished from administrative deconcentration—are better able to share financial responsibility than to reshape administrative arrangements. Canada illustrates the ease of health revenue sharing; the German *lander* likewise adopted fiscal sharing more rapidly than federal administrative regulations (Evans, 1976; Altenstetter, 1976; Bridgman, 1976).

Corporate elements in all of these societies (local elites, medical groups, hospitals and unions) will balance or restrain unitary or federal governments' capacities. The health industry is technologically similar from industrial nation to nation, which means one finds great similarity of medical issues everywhere.

One hypothesis is that the ratio between corporate resources and resistance is higher for the medical professions at the periphery than at the center of national politics. Professionals generally seek decentralization of authority only when the scope of conflict narrows, when the professional interest groups are already in place and have paid all their organizational overhead, and when they can concentrate their marginal resources on overtaking the public authorities. At the national center the same professional groups have to deal with large mobilized political parties and mass organizations.

What can one say about governmental motivation to change administrative arrangements? We often talk about government in a very unrealistic way. We speak as if governmental behavior were always purposive. When we find governmental action—administrative reorganization, for example—we assume there must have been a large problem to which the government was directing its efforts. Or we assume that if there is a large problem out in the world, it must be the case that the government is going to do something about it (Allison, 1973). Yet a good deal of what government does pertains to the internal maintenance needs of people within it. One of the things occurring in discussions of administrative decentralization in health is that people whose job it is to run the government (or who claim to be running the government) have to find something to do. What they have to do is to shuffle back between the periphery and the center to make administrative arrangements. Administrative reorganization is thus an attractive response to bureaucratic needs. Reorganization has imprecise effects, takes much effort, and produces symbolic benefits from the appearance of action (Alford, 1976). This may have little to do with bringing medical-care needs closer to the public so that the patient can use resources more appropriately.

REFLECTIONS ON CROSS-NATIONAL POLICY RESEARCH IN HEALTH

Sometimes comparative research reveals what is possible, not what is desirable or transportable, providing illumination, not indoctrination. Sometimes such research produces seemingly transplantable policies, but the effects are so hard to disentangle from other forces that learning whether such a policy would be appropriate is difficult. This is a case of temptation without satisfaction. A third lesson is that cross-national research work is difficult, costly and time-consuming (Anderson, 1976). Only compelling, expected returns justify both the costs and the difficulty of identifying comparable circumstances and similarities. But sometimes the expected benefits are policy learning; then the issue will be whether the policy choice is clear enough to warrant the expected costs. In other cases, the benefits will be significant tests, impossible within a single nation framework, of social science theories. Cross-national research in health suggests there is a place for both types of work.

In this essay we have reviewed three types of cross-national studies in health policy politics. Several areas of research have not been discussed. Most important, although we have alluded to them, we have not discussed macro-studies of health expenditure patterns over time. In addition, we have not investigated here what effects government intervention in the health sector has had on the general problems of governance in advanced industrial societies. The current preoccupation with the fiscal strains of the welfare state has highlighted this issue as a matter of controlling health expenditures. But the political significance of that effort is not restricted to fiscal stress. Health issues are salient to citizens in all the countries discussed; government programs affect citizens' views of the capacity of public authorities to govern beyond short-run budget disputes. Finally, this essay should not be interpreted as support for the notion that there is a common politics of health across or within nations. What counts as a "health" policy, as Charles Anderson has pointed out, varies cross-culturally. What is more, there is no evidence that political disputes over health are uniform and distinctive. There are political struggles in the arena termed health, but not a politics of health. That means the arena is a microcosm of welfare-state politics, not a peculiar phenomenon. For that reason, the lessons of comparative research in health are valid for comparative policy research in general.

NOTES

1. The October 1976 Cornell conference, at which the articles of this volume were originally presented, is itself an example. In the health field, there has been a burst of cross-national interest. The Fogarty Center at the National Institutes of Health held meetings in May 1976 both on cost-control issues and on center-periphery political relations in health, with the papers forthcoming in published form. The advent of the German Marshall Foundation, among others, has increased the funds available for cross-national research among advanced industrial countries; and special issues on comparative policy studies, like *Policy Sciences* (December 1975), are just beginning, almost certainly to be increased by the efforts of the Council on European Studies' research planning groups and the Ford Foundation's sponsorship of collaborative research projects on the common problems of industrial societies.

2. See, for example, Chapter 1, Heidenheimer, Heclo, and Adams, 1975; and Clark, 1976.

3. Highly structured and regular in Great Britain and Sweden; diffuse and irregular in the United States, where consultation may take place in congressional hearings or through ad hoc meetings with executive officials responsible for public medical care programs.

4. This is simply the other side of the coin of Teune's concern with invariant policy effects.

5. In sum, the limits of physicians' power depend on the issue arena in which they are struggling. There has also been some dispute on these limits. See the symposium on Robert Alford's *Health Care Politics* in the *Journal of Health Politics, Policy and Law,* Vol. 1., No. 1, especially Flash's contribution. Heidenheimer's work has traced the relation of physicians' power to national financing of medical care services, stressing the impact of timing on the configuration of later disputes. "Public Capabilities and Health Care Effectiveness: Implications from a Comparative Perspective," Fogarty Center paper.

6. Two major differences between the American and Canadian experiences are often put forward as problematic for using Canada as a "most similar system." These are the greater constitutional and political independence of the Canadian provincial governments compared to the American states and the different route followed by Canada to national health insurance. The first means only that Canadian health insurance *had* to be decentralized. If we choose centralized insurance, we may have to rely more on European experience. But the greater the role the United States assigns to decentralized units, the more we can

learn from Canadian national standards and provincial cost control (or inability to control costs).

The second major difference is historic. Canadian national insurance began with hospital coverage in 1958, followed a decade later by full-scale coverage of physicians' charges. In contrast, the United States has been extending protection to additional segments of the population, first the aged, then the poor, and perhaps in the end to everybody. This may tell political scientists a lot about the welfare state, but it should not deter health care planners from comparison. Having converged at full coverage, Canada and the United States are facing similar choices. Cross-national comparisons of a more "macro" sort may, however, be concerned with these questions. See Heidenheimer, Heclo, and Adams, 1975; Anderson, 1972; Teune, 1973.

7. Similar does not, of course, mean identical. For some purposes, the differences in the way Canadian and American health insurance policies incrementally changed are of significance. See, for example, Evans (1975:3-4). But Evans was not placing North American patterns on continuum of advanced welfare states. Had he done so, the internal North American differences would have been minimized.

8. See, for example, *National Health Expenditures in Canada, 1960-1971 with Comparative Data for the United States,* Health Program Branch, Ottawa, (October, 1973), and the documentation presented by Stuart Altman (pp. 193-194) in Andreopoulos, 1975, a collection of papers by participants in the Sun Valley Health Forum on National Health Insurance, for the proportion of national resources expended in health.

9. The Canadian alarm was fully expressed in the *Task Force Reports on the Cost of Health Services in Canada* (Ottawa: The Queen's Printer, 1970), 3 vols. Concern about the rate of inflation in the health care field was plain as well in the Economic Council of Canada's Seventh Annual Review, *Patterns of Growth,* (September 1970). The parallel American preoccupation with rising medical care costs was perhaps best evidenced by the production in the first Nixon Administration of a "white paper" on health which catalogued familiar diagnoses of the ills of the industry.

These same concerns were apparent in the hearings on national health insurance before the Ways and Means Committee in October-November, 1971; 93rd Congress, 2nd Session, 11 volumes (Washington: Government Printing Office, 1971).

For health expenditures as a percent of GNP in the United States, see Mueller and Gibson, 1976:6. Exact comparable data is not available in published sources for Canada, but see, for example, Minister of National Health and Welfare (Canada), 1975; and the June 1975 budget, health care section.

10. See for the period 1966-1972, LeClair in Andreopoulos, 1975, Table 3; for the earlier period, see Andersen and Hull, 1969, special supplement, Table 5, p. 13; compare Altman in Andreopoulos, 1975:198 and Table 5. Canada has been and continues to be a heavier spender in the hospital sector.

11. This information is consistent with that of Anderson and Hull, 1969; and Evans in Andreopoulos, 1975.

12. The nominal data is from Evans in Andreopoulos, 1975. The price deflator is the Canadian Consumer Price Index from Statistics of Canada, *Canada's Yearbook* (1972).

13. In a letter from R. G. Evans to R. A. Berman on the subject of major issues to be highlighted for Sun Valley conference on Canada's experience with National Health Insurance.

14. The inability of increased co-payment mechanisms to restrain costs arises only partly because hospital utilization is relatively insensitive to price. Equally important is the fact that the patient's co-payment represents only a very small part of his or her total cost of hospitalization, which includes not only the direct cost of hospital services, but also physicians' fees, foregone earnings, and general inconvenience.

15. For a discussion of the reliance on detailed, line-item budget review as the mechanism of budgetary control during the first decade of Canada's national hospital insurance,

see Evans in Andreopoulos, 1975:151-155; and LeClair in Andreopoulos, 1975:57-58. For the arguments justifying less detailed budget review, see Castonguary in Andreopoulos, 1975:106-107, including an explanation on global budgeting.

REFERENCES

ABEL-SMITH, B. (1963). "Paying the family doctor." Medical Care, 1:27-35.

--- (1965). "The major pattern of financing and organization of medical services that have emerged in other countries." Medical Care, 3:33-40.

ALFORD, R. R. (1976). Health care politics. Chicago: University of Chicago Press.

ALLISON, G. T. (1973). The essence of decision. Boston: Little, Brown.

ALTENSTETTER, C. (1976). "The importance of organizational arrangements for policy performance." Paper presented at the International Conference on "Changing National-Subnational Relations in Health: Opportunities and Constraints," May 24-26, Fogarty International Center, Bethesda.

ANDERSEN, R. (1976). "A framework for cross-national comparisons of health service systems." In M. Pflanz and E. Schach (eds.), Cross-national socio-medical research: Concepts, methods, practice. Stuttgart.

ANDERSEN, R., and HULL, J. (1969). "Hospital utilization and cost trends in Canada and the United States." Medical Care, 7(6):supplement.

ANDERSON, O. W. (1972). Health care: Can there be equity? The United States, Sweden, and England. New York: Wiley-Interscience.

ANDREOPOULOS, S. (ed., 1975). National health insurance: Can we learn from Canada? New York: John Wiley.

BADGLEY, R. F., and WOLFE, S. (1967). Doctors' strike: Medical care and conflict in Saskatchewan. New York: Alberton Press.

BADGLEY, R. F. et al. (1974). The Canadian experience with universal health insurance (Third annual report). Department of Behavioral Science, University of Toronto. Unpublished manuscript.

BRIDGMAN, R. F. (1976). "Hospital regionalization in Europe: Achievements and obstacles." Paper presented at the International Conference on "Changing National-Subnational Relations in Health: Opportunities and Constraints," May 24-26, Fogarty International Center, Bethesda.

BRIDGMAN, R. F., and ROEMER, M. I. (1973). "Hospital legislation and hospital systems." World Health Organization, Public Health Paper No. 50, Geneva.

Bureau of Labor Statistics. Monthly Labor Review, various issues.

Canada Health Manpower Inventory 1973. Annual report 1972-1973: Hospital insurance and diagnostic services. National health expenditures in Canada 1960-1971 with Comparative data for the United States. Health and Welfare, Canada.

Canada's Yearbook (1972). Statistics of Canada.

CASTONGUARY, C. (1975). "The Quebec experience: Effects of accessibility." In S. Andreopoulos (ed.), National health insurance: Can we learn from Canada? New York: John Wiley.

CLARK, M. (1976). The comparative politics of birth control: Determinants of policy variation and change in the developed nations. Unpublished Ph.D. dissertation, University of Michigan.

EVANS, J. R. (1976). "Planning and evolution in Canadian health policy." In K. White and M. Henderson (eds.), Epidemiology as a fundamental science. New York: Oxford University Press.

EVANS, R. G. (1974). Personal communication to R. A. Berman, July 2.

--- (1975). "Beyond the medical marketplace: Expenditure, utilization and pricing of insured health care in Canada." In S. Andreopoulos (ed.), National health insurance: Can we learn from Canada? New York: John Wiley.

GEBERT, A. J. (1976). "Switzerland." Paper presented at the International Conference on "Changing National-Subnational Relations in Health: Opportunities and Constraints," May 24-26, Fogarty International Center, Bethesda.

GLASER, W. A. (1970). Paying the doctor, systems of remuneration and their effects. Baltimore: Johns Hopkins University Press.

Hearings before the Ways and Means Committee on national health insurance in October-November 1971, 93rd Congress, 2nd Session. 11 volumes. Washington, D.C.: U.S. Government Printing Office.

HEIDENHEIMER, A. (1976). "Public capabilities and health care effectiveness: Implications from a comparative perspective." Paper presented at the International Conference on "Changing National-Subnational Relations in Health: Opportunities and Constraints," May 24-26, Fogarty International Center, Bethesda.

HEIDENHEIMER, A., HECLO, H., and ADAMS, C. (1975). Comparative public policy: The politics of social choice in Europe and America. New York: St. Martin's Press.

KEY, V. O., Jr. (1964). Parties, politics, and pressure groups. New York: Crowell.

KLEIN, R., and LEWIS, J. (1976). The politics of consumer representation. London: Centre for Studies in Social Policy.

LAVE, J., and LAVE, L. (1974). The Hospital Construction Act: An evaluation of the Hill-Burton program, 1948-1973. Washington, D.C.: American Enterprise Institute for Public Policy Research.

LeCLAIR, M. (1975). "The Canadian health care system." In S. Andreopoulos (ed.), National health insurance: Can we learn from Canada? New York: John Wiley.

LOWI, T. J. (1964). "American business, public policy, case studies, and political theory." World Politics, 16:677-715.

--- (1973). "What political scientists don't need to ask about policy analysis." Policy Studies Journal, (autumn):61-67.

MARMOR, T. R., HEAGY, T., and HOFFMAN, W. (1975). "National health insurance: Some lessons from the Canadian experience." Policy Sciences, 6(4).

MARMOR, T. R., and THOMAS, D. (1972). "Revisiting 'Pressure group politics.'" British Journal of Political Science, (October).

MARMOR, T. R., WITTMAN, D., and HEAGY, T. (1976). "The politics of medical inflation." Journal of Health Politics, Policy and Law, 1(1).

MAXWELL, R. (1975). Health care: The growing dilemma: Needs versus resources in Western Europe, the US, and the USSR (McKinsey Survey Report, 2nd ed.). New York: McKinsey.

MAYNARD, A. (1975). Health care in the European community. Pittsburgh: University of Pittsburgh Press.

Minister of National Health and Welfare (Canada) (1975). "National health expenditures in Canada, 1960-1973." Ottawa.

MUELLER, M. S., and GIBSON, R. M. (1976). "National health expenditures, fiscal year 1975." Social Security Bulletin, 39(2):6.

National Health Expenditures in Canada, 1960-1971, with comparative data for the United States (1973). Ottawa: Health Program Branch.

NEWHOUSE, J. P. (1976). "Income and medical care expenditures across countries." Rand Paper Series No. P-5608. Santa Monica, Calif.:Rand.

PRESSMAN, J., and WILDAVSKY, A. (1973). Implementation. Berkeley: University of California Press.

PRZEWORSKI, A., and TEUNE, H. (1970). The logic of comparative social inquiry. New York: Wiley-Interscience.

REINHARDT, M., and BRANSON, M. (1974). "Preliminary tabulation of selected comparative statistics on the Canadian and U.S. health care systems." Mimeograph.

SCHNUR, J. A., and HOLLENBERG, R. D. (1966). "The Saskatchewan medical care crisis in retrospect." Medical Care, 3:33-40.

Statistical Abstract (1973). U.S. Census Bureau.

Statistical Abstract of the United States. U.S. Department of Commerce, Bureau of the Census, various issues.

STONE, D. A. (1976). "Regulation of the medical profession in West Germany and the United States: A research proposal."

Task Force Reports on the Cost of Health Services in Canada (1970). 3 volumes. Ottawa: The Queen's Printer.

TEUNE, H. (1973). "Public policy: Macro perspective." in G. Zaltman (ed.), Process and Phenomena of Social Change. New York: John Wiley.

Van LANGENDONCK, J. (1976). "Private diligence vs. public inertia?" Paper presented at the International Conference on "Changing National-Subnational Relations in Health: Opportunities and Constraints," May 24-26, Fogarty International Center, Bethesda.

ZALTMAN, G. (ed., 1973). Process and phenomena of social change. New York: John Wiley.

ZUBKOFF, M. (ed., 1976). Health: A victim or cause of inflation? New York: Prodist.

Table 2. THE EFFECT OF NATIONAL HEALTH INSURANCE ON NET PHYSICIAN EARNINGS (Divided by Consumer Price Index; Percentage Change over Two Year Periods)

Province	*First Full Year of Province's Participation in a Program Covering Physician Services*	*Period Ending with First Full Year of Province's Participation*		*Immediately Previous Period*	
Saskatchewan	1963*	32.5%	(1961-63)	2.7%	(1959-61)
British Columbia	1969	5.3	(1967-69)	16.5	(1965-67)
Newfoundland	1970	26.2	(1968-70)	21.4	(1966-68)
Nova Scotia	1970	34.4	(1968-70)	21.1	(1966-68)
Ontario	1970	12.5	(1968-70)	17.0	(1966-68)
Manitoba	1970	37.1	(1968-70)	12.3	(1966-68)
Alberta	1970	10.6	(1968-70)	26.5	(1966-68)
Quebec	1971	42.1	(1969-71)	8.2	(1967-69)
Prince Edward Island	1971	60.5	(1969-71)	1.0	(1967-69)
New Brunswick	1971	26.6	(1969-71)	10.6	(1967-69)
Average		28.8%		13.7%	

*Saskatchewan adopted a provincial health insurance plan prior to National Health Insurance.
SOURCES: Nominal Data, S. Andreopoulos (ed.), *National Health Insurance: Can We Learn from Canada?* (New York: John Wiley, 1975) p. 70. Price Deflator (Consumer Price Index), Statistics Canada, *Canada Yearbook,* 1972.

4

THE STRUCTURAL ANALYSIS OF POLICY OR INSTITUTIONS REALLY DO MATTER

DOUGLAS E. ASHFORD

Cornell University

The growth of comparative policy studies provides an opportunity to raise some fundamental problems of the modern democratic state. We begin to see such opportunities in a comparative study such as Heclo's (1974) where both historical depth and political constraints are blended to explain why two relatively similar countries would take such different courses in providing social services and benefits. Though Heclo's work is cast in the more familiar shape of the political and administrative process surrounding policy, it describes the structural characteristics that have produced very different solutions. It is the development of this idea that particularly concerns me. Do states have characteristic ways of conducting their business? Do they accommodate a variety of internal institutional and social constraints in ways that help us understand both decision making and authority itself? Is the most interesting thing about the modern state that it encounters similar conflicts and must make similar choices, or is it that it has done these things in such a variety of ways?

These questions take us beyond the familiar questions of policy analysis. Analysis of this kind will surely involve more than one policy and more than one nation. It will also depart from the prevailing economic and behavioral mode of political analysis which seems to have dominated political science for the past generation (Ashford, 1977). Comparative analysis of policy is not likely to deal with efficiency, costs, and utility, at least not in the familiar terms. This point has already been made by Eckstein (1973) in his analysis of patterns of authority. Nor will it adhere to the typologies of policy that have now begun to appear, the most widely cited being Lowi's (1970 and 1972). One of the most intriguing findings of comparative policy analysis is that what a country is doing seems to have very little association with how it does it. There is probably more similarity across policies for one country in how policies are formed and implemented than there is for the same policy across several countries.[1]

The idea that countries have characteristic ways of doing things is by no means new. We know a great deal about the behavior of the French, British, or German voter, for example, and how his behavior is influenced by party and electoral structure. What the discipline has not done is formulate such findings in a way that allows us to analyze the relation of performance to institutional differences. The policies themselves may contain better explanations of why the modern democracies perform as they do than does the aggregated individual behavior of the citizens. This is not to say that behavioral analysis does not touch on structural problems, but its methodological constraints mean that it remains difficult to generalize to the level of complex organizations and institutions.

"Structure" is a confusing and powerful term. Its most influential use is no doubt in Marxian analysis of class structure. Class structure could become a powerful idea because Marxists devised a very elaborate theory of history. But class structure is directed to social systems as a whole, not to their components. More recent neo-Marxist writing addresses both the shortcomings of the theory and the necessity to direct class analysis at a lower level than whole societies (e.g., Offe, 1974). The structural analysis of policy across states shares this change, but adds that institutions and organizations must also be considered in more concrete form if we wish to speak to real policies. In this respect, the structural analysis of policy would seem to me to be a prerequisite to testing either Marxist or liberal notions of the state. If socioeconomic equality is distorted, it would seem important to understand the institutional roots of inequality. If the marketplace has failed us as a regulator of society, it would seem important to know how institutional distortions occur. In both cases, the more abstract argument would be more persuasive if presented in terms of real policies and choices.

The structural analysis of policy may be most clearly described by noting the shortcomings of existing methods of comparing policy (e.g., Dye, 1966) depended on formulating policy as a continuous variable. In order to deal with policy change using quantitative and behavioral methods one had to construct linear models with interval variables. The close association of this attack on policy with the prevailing views on incrementalism (Lindblom, 1959) meant that the frictions and distortions introduced by decision makers or by major institutional constraints were simply omitted. More recent historical work (Binder, 1971; Tilly, 1975) casts serious doubt on the methodological assumptions of early policy research. In descriptive form this work also points to the historical circumstances and institutional configurations that influences choice in the modern state.

Second, the growth of public expenditure and increasing intervention of the modern state in day-to-day affairs has made an understanding of the institutional fabric of central concern. Policy studies probably had their origin in case studies. So long as government was a small scale operation the findings of these studies were of interest to specialists in intergovernmental relations and public administration. But the growth itself has meant that the significance of the case study has grown and they become invaluable instruments to probe the interaction of political institutions and levels of government (e.g., Piven and Cloward, 1971). The available statements to organize the structural analysis of policy around institutional features of the modern state are not very good. What is, for example, the institutional equivalent of the Prefect's role in France to other systems of local government? Structural analysis suggests that one may arrive at a better statement of his role by examining how he actually influences policies. (See Machin, 1973.)

A third characteristic of structural analysis is observation among several units of analysis. This occurs in many forms such as the various levels of government, the sectors of the economy, and, of course, in the familiar class divisions. Most economic analysis, and its associated work in politics through survey instruments, works only with individuals. There are immense difficulties aggregating such findings to larger units of organization. Analysis of the firm is an extremely sophisticated aspect of micro-economics, but its aggregation to the level of industrial structure, labor markets, or national economic policy is difficult. Likewise, voting behavior tells us much about individual perception of a specific election, but inferences about the importance of the electoral process in society are difficult to make (Key and Cummings, 1956).

Thus, structural analysis enables us to deal with social and political problems that are difficult to describe with continuous variables, that require some general statements about internal relationships of organizations and institutions, and that involve collective activity in several broadly defined institutions. Because deductive methods are unable to deal with such complexity, structural analysis also requires normative judgment. To some extent this means abandoning the goal of making politics as exact a science as economics where predictive power is purchased by making very narrow assumptions and confining oneself to directly observable phenomenon. This concession is, I think, not as crucial as many may think. The more rigorous form of empirical inquiry is replete with instances of unintended consequences, unforeseen events, and simple human failure or deception. More to the point for policy studies, as Anderson underscores in this volume, intent must be taken as meaningful in the world of real decisions. (See also Tribe, 1972.) Structural analysis takes political science out of the behavioral dilemma, but at the cost of examining leadership, institutions, and organizations in terms of their avowed aims. These are necessarily value judgments.

In the following sections I provide illustrations of the problems that the comparative analysis of policy raises. Some progress has already been made. These are stated in rather general questions about the modern democratic state. The first, inertia, raises the basic choice between growth and stability that is familiar in economics, but rarely studied in terms of implications for democratic government. The second is scale, which poses a choice between the liberal's view that small units of government enhance democratic life and the increasing awareness that individual participation has limited impact in the modern state. The third, and possibly the most promising start for comparative policy studies, is substitutability or the diverse ways that governments accomplish very similar things. Such analysis would tell us much about institutional constraints, possibly having some practical importance, but also increasing our ability to make general statements about institutional interaction in democracies in a much more concrete way than has been possible with earlier methods and theories.

INERTIA: IS THE STATE AGAINST ITSELF?

A very thoughtful paper by Jack Hayward (1975) examines institutional inertia in Britain and France. His basic argument is that in the 1960s these countries experienced a preoccupation with the stagnation or stalemate of political institutions. His implicit, if not explicit, suggestion is that we take more seriously the difficulties of changing what are often regarded as routine government activities. Many writers think that the plight of the modern state is that it has become so complex that changing performance is virtually impossible (see Crozier, 1964, 1974; Nisbet, 1970; Ionescu, 1975; O'Connor, 1973; Plantey, 1975). Policy analysis can determine if this pessimistic (others would say optimistic) view of the state is correct, and can find out how this condition is maintained, changed, and modified.

There appear to me to be two bodies of literature on the inertia question. Not surprisingly, there are important contradictions in the assumptions and findings of both. There is, first, the argument that continued growth of spending in the modern industrial state transcends ideological lines and may be irreversible.[2] A groundbreaking study at the macro-level was Pryor's investigation (1968) of public spending in both liberal and communist states (see Echols, 1975, 1976). Another was Wilensky's cross-national study (1975) of social security benefits and equality. Such studies are vitally important to policy studies, for they help us distinguish the important structural features of government associated with growth. For example, among the features they considered are the partisan nature of government, the level of solidarity of the working class, the changing demographic composition of society, and so on. Nonetheless, the overall level of state expenditure or the pursuit of specific objectives such as social security remain dependent variables in most of this work.

The opposing, or at least unreconciled, body of literature concerns decision making at the micro-level. Wildavsky has certainly been the major contributor and has stimulated much writing along these lines. The general line of reasoning is that government lacks full information and reliable (predictable) solutions for the problems it faces. Decisions are thus made in an ad hoc fashion; government seldom has time or machinery that permits it to perceive, much less utilize, any larger formulation of its objectives. This view provides the basis of a behavioral analysis of growth, but it does not help much in explaining why states have in fact grown or why they grew in the directions we can observe.[3] Nonetheless, the incrementalist position does help to solve the inertia problem, by reminding us that at the micro-level it is virtually impossible to do all things at once; even those things that are selected for change may not be thought out very well.[4]

Policy analysis could become an independent variable in the inertia problem (or its converse, the growth problem) if we could overcome the almost dogged determination to treat policy solely as a micro-level phenomena. The omission of the complexities of making and executing policies in disaggregating macro-level studies leaves these two endeavors isolated from each other. To make the link, I continually go back to a very traditional question in political science, the nature of each state's "constitution." I believe it correct to say that in each state there is a set of political institutions without which the state in its present form could not persist.[5] In the British system this is surely a strong cabinet government based on a two-party structure; for the French, a much weaker cabinet government with a multiparty structure and a strong administrative apparatus. Though this conceptualization of "constituent" elements (to use Lowi's phrase) is crude, I think that there would be considerable agreement in the literature on each country.[6] The basic hypothesis of policy analysis of politics would be that the state will not undertake those policies which tend to impair or threaten its constitutional foundations. Inertia (or growth) then consists of those activities which the state's constituent base allows it to pursue (or requires it to ignore).

The constitutional requirements of the system can be thought of as either a dependent or independent variable. Explaining constitutions by regularities of policies rather than by legal assertions, however, places policy in an independent relationship to the state. Britain can provide some examples. Looking at a variety of policy developments over the past two decades, it is remarkable how each is affected in its conception, its evaluation, and its implementation by the needs of parliamentary government. Though the Fulton Report made strong recommendations to change the elitist character of the higher civil service, changes have been slow in coming. No changes have hampered the confidential relationship between high administrators and their clients in Westminster or among privileged groups on which they rely for advice and assistance.[7] Planning remains in the Treasury, not only because of the well-known economic difficulties of planning but also because a strong planning activity would threaten the supremacy of the cabinet and prime minister (Lee, 1975). Local government reorganization has produced a system even less equipped to carry out central policymaking than the former structure, partly because the effective intervention of local political forces would endanger party discipline and cabinet authority (Ashford, 1976). Social services remain the concern of professional groups and civil servants (for example, see Thomas, 1973:143-173). A strong labor movement has complied with constitutional needs to protect the parliamentary purity of the Labour Party.

The structural analysis of policy in Britain, France, or other countries would not focus on finding out why growth occurs or who benefits from it. These are important, but secondary, questions in relation to the problem of how each country tends to solve problems in characteristic ways. If we look at a range of policies in Britain, for example, the institutions have similar structures and the governing constitutional norm is always present. A more interlocking kind of institutional structure seems to characterize many kinds of French policies and the governing norm on the constitutional level may be continuing struggle between the administrative and political definitions of the state. The kinds of hypotheses coming from a structural analysis of policy are likely to be of the following form: if country X undertakes any activity it will take the form of Y; or conversely, when we find a policy process that deviates markedly from the structure Y, we would expect that the actors and results in the policy problem greatly conflict with existing norms.

SCALE: ARE THE PARTS MORE THAN THE WHOLE?

The problem of scale in the transformation of the modern state is a particularly difficult one. We have differences over identifying the "parts" and imagining how the parts are connected. There are no easy ways of dealing with either of these issues. For some purposes the United States is conceived of as fifty states, and for others as the 80,000 odd units of local government. What does seem clear is that the two concepts derived from economic reasoning have not been very helpful. The maximizing view immediately fails because economic analysis cannot determine the correct size of subunits of government. Each function of government works best with different populations, relates somewhat differently to physical constraints of geography and distance; and policies vary in their interpretation and execution at lower levels of government. Even at the level of "rational" calculation, arranging the scale of government in relation to its subunits seems to be a "no win" proposition.[8]

Scale seems to be one of those questions where the problems of measurement have inordinately affected our analysis. In order to proceed with rigorous empirical analysis, it is necessary to select a single unit and, in most cases, to focus on the internal variations of the arbitrarily selected unit. Somewhat more satisfying is selecting a single policy area and then examining interdependencies across and among the subunits concerned with that policy.[9] Each design has its limitations. The single unit does not capture the multiplicity of decision-making units among levels of government, and the path analysis only applies to a single policy. In both, policy considerations tend to become dependent variables; that is, the effect of external socioeconomic constraints on the subunit or the uncertainties forced on the subunit in making the particular policy. Of course, controls can be introduced in both designs for such things as intergovernmental transfers, local needs, social structure, and so on. Even with adjustments, the political significance of scale is difficult to identify.

The problem of scale has been most thoroughly studied in federal systems, and in the American federal system in particular (Elazar, 1972; Diamond, 1973; Beer, 1973; D. Wright, 1975). In a recent article Douglas Rose (1973) tries to draw together both the representative role and the policy determination role of the states, rather than treat them separately (e.g., see D. Rose, 1973; Stephens, 1974, 1976). His general conclusions are more interesting than his empirically defensible ones, which still treat states as individual actors in the system. His observation that states are not small polities, but really collections of polities, reveals an important way of reconsidering the scale problem. Oddly enough, most of us who have concentrated on unitary governments would not be surprised by such a statement. We often study the subunits of government in European systems in terms of their intervention in central government. Successful intervention may depend on a wide variety of circumstances, which the legal status of the subunit by no means assures; it often depends on such distinctly political links as the mayor's network outside the city or province. (For example, see Grémion, 1976; Bequart-Leclercq, 1976; Tarrow, 1977; Thoenig, 1973.)

In order to deal with the question of scale at state level, we need not only methodological rethinking, but also reconsideration of how policy relates to politics. Many of the clues for such an inquiry have existed for some time, but have somehow fallen between the cracks in political research. For example, Froman (1967) suggested some time ago that politics have both an areal and segmental aspect. Some activities of government require a territorially defined unit, others do not. Fesler (1965) made a similar observation, noting that functional and area policies are always mixed.[10] But socioeconomic and physical properties of the policy objective determine the mix less than we have assumed, as conflicting findings suggest when trying to explain policy determinants at a single level of government. The selection of an area for research or implementation of a policy has an arbitrary quality most readily qualified by examining a number of policies in similar or dissimilar units.

Scale can easily be treated as a dependent variable. Indeed, nearly all quantified analysis of city and regional planning proceeds on such assumptions. Much planning analysis is the search for the size and composition of unit so that a particular service or need can be provided efficiently; much of the politics of planning is the contrivance of new subunits such that existing power structures are protected. But considering scale also offers intriguing possibilities of treating policy as a structural factor. How much overlap and duplication of policy implementation, for example, must exist in various systems before the government tries to bring order out of chaos? How many administratively controlled regional authorities may be created before coordination becomes an impossibility or the political dilution of locally elected authority becomes a major issue? The great debate of the 1960s over regional policy was a question of this kind.[11] The implementation of more and more policies in a wider and wider variety of territorial units has created the need for regional policies. Is there not a similarity between federal governments trying to resolve issues of fiscal federalism[12] to diminish the significance of legal territorial boundaries, and the unitary governments trying to "devolve" (England) and "deconcentrate" (France) powers to regions without breaking up the state? The study of these questions will, I think, lead to making policy an independent variable; for it is in fact the multiplication of special authorities, districts, and regions that makes government unmanageable and incomprehensible. There are so many policies being implemented and executed in different ways that both federal and unitary governments must reexamine how they handle their problems of scale.

SUBSTITUTABILITY: HOW MANY WAYS OF DOING THE SAME THING?

The notion of substitutability relating to the presumed choice among factors of production which leads to maximum production has a venerable history in economics. In different form, it also relates to the "winning" theories, which assume multiple victorious outcomes. The difference between these two concepts appears to be that the maximizing view imagines a hypothetical point where costs are minimal and seeks to reach it, while the "winning" view says there are many approaches that effectively achieve the same thing. I intuitively resist both these notions in relation to policy analysis and politics because one must then see government, particularly democratic government, as a wasteful activity. Many economists, of course, make very similar conclusions,[13] but as I have already outlined, they do not seem to do much better than political scientists in stating why and how we tolerate such inefficiencies or ineffectiveness.

In policy analysis, substitutability refers to the general question of how states often appear to be doing the same thing, but how, on closer examination, they appear to be doing it in very different ways. Much aggregate level analysis shows an overall trend toward higher levels of welfare spending, but we may exaggerate the internal uniformity of such changes.[14] Substitutability indicates institutional differences in pursuing similar objectives. Many examples come to mind. In Britain housing is delegated to the local level and, along with it, responsibility for choosing who will get public housing, how public housing will be managed and maintained, and even how the balance between private and public housing may change (Cullingworth, 1966). The French have a very different system built around a semi-public agency, only roughly corresponding to local and regional divisions and more readily brought under the influence of financial institutions (Lawson and Stevens, 1974; International Federation for Housing and Planning, 1966). There are clearly many ways to analyze this relationship: in terms of the efficiency of the two systems in building housing (maximizing); in terms of the game of politics between the center and subunits of government (winning); and in terms of the influence of institutional variations on priorities.

Until we do more analysis of various paths to similar objectives, we cannot discover methods for studying institutional equivalence. This seems to be the conclusion of Pressman and Wildavsky (1973) who warn us that "implementation must not be conceived as a process that takes place after, and independent of, the design of policy." We can see the same concern in Heclo's (1972) discussion of case studies and nondecisions. Examining how policies are transformed into state activities can lead to the unproductive study of mechanics of policy in the old-style public administration sense. It can also produce generalizations that defy empirical treatment. The key consideration in treading this narrow path between inconsequential and the transcendent is to examine more closely how states pursue similar objectives by very different means.

Explanations derived in this manner are not likely to produce causal explanations but could relate structural differences among policies, rather than among subunits as in the scale approach. Space permits only one illustration, which I have elaborated in more detail elsewhere (Ashford, 1975). Both the United States and Britain have confronted the problem of improving the quality of decision making in cities. In the United States locally generated reform movements led to the widespread adoption of city manager governments. In Britain local governments have pursued similar objectives by adopting some variation of "corporate planning," i.e., the installation of a chief executive for city government and the gradual move toward more systematic forms of planning and budgeting. There are many ways of comparing these changes, but the distinguishing structural feature is that the United States pursued a locally generated and Britain a centrally generated solution. Analysis of this change does not conflict with more general observations about local politics in the two societies (Sharpe, 1973; Newton, 1974; Curran, 1963); it enables us to compare major differences within policy areas across states.

Again, we can easily examine this question by treating the policies under examination as dependent variables. Does British housing cost more than French housing (maximizing)? Do middle-class suburbs get more favored treatment (winning)? Although we need to know these things, I would argue that we also need to know how these varying solutions to similar problems relate to political differences. For example, in both Britain and France there has been study of the possibility of relieving local government of major responsibilities.[15] There are not only questions of costs and suburban political interest, but of how such a change would restructure central/local political relationships. In this context, policy becomes a structural variable defining institutional relationships between local and national politics.

CONCLUSION: DOES POLICY DETERMINE POLITICS?

The attraction of considering policy as a result comes from many sources: the incrementalist finds it compatible with his view of the state; the classical liberal finds it a handy way to restore marketplace concepts to politics; the Marxist finds many ways to link class and capitalism to policies. What I have tried to show is that existing interpretations tend to see policy as wholly determined, precluding consideration of how policy defines the state. The analysis of politics and policy seems to swing between overdetermination and underdetermination.

I have tried to argue that we cannot analyze policy in structural terms unless we loosen the constraints of case studies and behavioral methodology. A case study can never provide more than a single observation, that is, one policy in one state. As such, case studies have difficulty raising structural or normative questions.[16] Behavioral analysis presents the same problem, for it must make arbitrary methodological judgments in order to make more general statements about policy. As I have pointed out, the techniques for doing this are based on the maximizing and winning paradigms, thereby putting policy into a dependent relationship with either individual or socioeconomic variables. To deal with larger issues of political systems, we must remove both these constraints; to do so we must convert policy analysis into a comparative enterprise.

Another way of stating the problem is to acknowledge that studying policy as a structural relationship will involve more than a single unit of analysis—that is, legislatures, administrators, field services, clientele, etc.—and more than one level of analysis—that is, the system's norms, its spatial or functional components, etc. I chose the examples I provided to illustrate these alternatives. We can study the problem of inertia or growth at the single level of the system, and with the most general unit, the state. Clearly there can be no control on such an investigation unless we use two or more states. Even so, policy does not necessarily become the independent variable, but rather a way of describing institutional complexity. There is a well-established body of literature that compares nations, with policy as the dependent variable (see Deutsch, 1961; McCrone and Cnudde, 1967; Neubauer, 1967). The craftsmanship and energy used in this research have not yet told us much about the institutional constraints or governing norms that operate in any state. If policy were treated as a structural factor in the organizational, distributional, and historical regularities of states achieving their goals, the relationship might be reversed (see Heidenheimer, Heclo, and Adams, 1975; Fraser, 1973; Roberts, 1969).

A second approach would be to examine one or more policies across many levels of a society to illuminate what I have called the problem of scale. Again, such an inquiry could present policy as a dependent variable, as does most research on planning and governmental efficiency. The institutional consequences of these studies are generally unspecified. The significance of policy changes as we find the modern state performing so many tasks on so many different levels (many of them administratively defined), that government becomes incomprehensible and possibly unmanageable. Over the past decade the major democracies have all wrestled with territorial reorganization problems. These problems are often seen as failures to find more efficient and productive solutions, or as part of the calculated self-interest of major actors. Using policies as structural factors in the analysis of scale would not answer these conventional questions, but it would help us to understand the institutional and normative changes taking place in the modern democracies.[17]

A third approach, which I have called the problem of substitution, would be to examine one policy in relation to many units of analysis. As noted above, multiple units of analysis are excluded by definition in behavioral analysis and its close corollary, micro-economic analysis. Without a single unit, most often the individual or the firm, analysis could not proceed. Such analysis invariably treats policy as an "output" or result. The problem with such inquiries is not that they may not reveal better ways to do things, which they probably do, but that they do not account for the changing meanings and content of policies over time, or their institutional effects. The simplest case of this is in the very different ways various countries do very similar things, e.g., provide education. A more complex instance is the tendency for a single policy to have very different individual salience, organizational meaning, and institutional meaning as we change the unit of analysis.[18] If we do not conceive of policy as a specific result having some kind of standardized meaning (most often economic), then we can begin to see its institutional effects across units and, in turn, how states may vary in the way they give policies importance and organize their implementation and execution. The relationship of the three kinds of policy analysis I have suggested may be summarized in Figure 1.

In policy studies, case studies and behavioral analysis are alike in that both assume that the policy has similar objectives and works through similar structures from one state to another. We rarely collect case studies in such a way that enables us to examine such assumptions so they become residual. In behavioral studies, we usually eliminate structural complications by statistical devices or by

		Policy:	
		Single	*Several*
Structure:	*Similar*	Behavior	Scale
	Different	Substitution	Inertia

Figure 1. COMPARING POLICIES ACROSS STATES

considering only the individual. Most of the applicable models of man are also extremely simplified.

As the diagram suggests, the inertia problem involves trying to deal with maximum variance across systems; that is, finding out why states adopt very different policies imbedded in very different structures. This may be the most difficult point of departure if we are to make policy studies in causal or statistical form. Substitution focuses on various levels of policy and, in its simplest form, concerns a single policy across states. Scale focuses on several policies and, in its simplest form, examines a single structure across states. Whether one wishes to treat policy as dependent or independent remains a matter of choice. But hopefully the conclusions of policy studies will take into account the structural relationships between policies and major issues of politics rather than assume such relationships are irrelevant. Such explanations will not be so tidy as those to which we have become accustomed in social science. We have no rules for establishing equivalence between French communes and British counties or between the French Association of Mayors and the British Association of Metropolitan Authorities. We can fall back into the maximizing and "winning" modes of policy analysis, but in doing so we might forego the exciting possibility of understanding the full complexity of the modern state.

NOTES

1. I have benefited immensely from discussion with Professors T. J. Pempel and Peter Katzenstein with whom I have shared a comparative policy seminar over the past three years. Professor Norman Uphoff of Cornell has also made me rethink the logical rigor of my arguments.

2. The origin of this approach may be "Wagner's Law." See Wagner (1958:108). Explanations of the growth of the state in economics are not much better than those in politics. See Steiner (1972) and also Burkhead and Minor (1971:261-278).

3. Incremental decisions can add up to rather important changes, as Douglas Rose (1973) argues in criticizing the Wildavsky view. Another criticism, raised by Cornford (1974), is that some marginal decisions may indeed have momentous impact.

4. This is surely the policy import of Wildavsky and Heclo's fascinating study of the Treasury (1974). The problem is that the book gives us no way to assess Treasury behavior vis-à-vis any objective of government, much less relate it to any general question, such as growth of government itself.

5. I see no reason why such a formulation would necessarily have a conservative bias. That power structures seek to conserve their power in all states does not appear to me to be either a very controversial or surprising assumption. Surely one can pursue policy analysis with the intention to find out how policy tends to change or preserve the state. This seems to me a value judgment that each person makes for himself or herself.

6. I am not referring to constitutions in the legal sense, though states clearly vary enormously in the extent to which the formal or informal constitutions reflect the key political institutions.

7. For example, see the virtual whitewash in the report on selection, *Report of the Ad Hoc Committee of Inquiry on the Method II System of Selection* (Davies Committee) (1969). The critical report was the Royal Commission on the Civil Service (Fulton Report, 1968).

8. The best demonstration of this problem is the extreme caution with which parties treat nearly all issues involving amalgamation or division of subunits of government. Leaving aside the delicate problems of national minorities and ethnicity, the unwillingness of parties to take clear positions on local reorganization, or even to raise the problem, indicates that scale is not a popular political issue. Perhaps the best single account of the failure of economics to provide solutions is in Harvey (1973: Ch. 2). Another example of this problem is given by Massam (1975).

9. For examples, see Lowi, this volume, and Cameron and Hofferbert (1974).

10. Note that Fesler cautions against the formal-legal definition of subunits (1965:554).

11. The debate raged most fiercely in France, but captured the imagination of policy-makers in many modern states. For a summary, see the essays in Section IV of Hayward and Watson (1975:217-294) and Plantey (1975). Not too surprisingly, there is a good economic comparison of regional policy in Hansen (1974) but no similar political treatment to my knowledge. Two studies that I think do raise policy to an independent level are Derthick (1974) and Sundquist (1975).

12. There is some excellent writing on fiscal federalism in Canada, West Germany, and the United States; for example, the annual reports of the Advisory Committee on Intergovernmental Relations for the United States, which paved the way for revenue sharing. See also Oates (1977) and May (1969).

13. For example, Burkhead and Minor (1971:292) conclude that "a federal system is expensive." Perhaps I should repeat that I do not mean to imply that governments should not try to find better ways to combine factors of production, or that they should confine themselves to pursuing only those objectives that have a high probability of success.

14. See, for example, the excellent analysis of macro-level differences by Cameron (1976). In my view, the controversy about the future of the welfare state has begun to generate more heat than light because of the failure to disaggregate to the implementation level. The liberal position appears to evade the problem by arguing for more individual control of choice without telling us much about how we are to do this (see, for example, Janowitz, 1976). The more progressive position seems to be to perfect our measures of individual needs and preferences through such devices as social indicators so that the state can formulate its own demand curves. Neither approach seems to approach directly the problem of collective choice. More recent neo-Marxist writing makes a very different and more promising attack on the problem (for example, Offe, 1974).

15. The question has arisen in the discussion of local reorganization in both countries, but the political effects of such policy changes has been neglected. See, for example, the Layfield Committee Report (1976). Though of much less significance in France, the same question has arisen in the Guichard Commission's discussion of local financial reform (1976).

16. I do not mean that a case study does not involve consideration of values or norms, but only that it provides no way for their discussion in terms of a variety of policies or a number of systems.

17. Both organizational and historical research is leading in this direction. See, for example, Grémion (1976), Becquart-Leclercq (1976), and Tarrow (1977) and compare with recent studies of administration; for example, V. Wright (1972) and Machin (1973).

18. See Marmor, this volume, for a discussion of institutional variation.

REFERENCES

ASHFORD, D. E. (1975). "Parties and participation in British local government and some American parallels." Urban Affairs Quarterly, 11(September):58-81.

--- (1976). "Reorganization of local government as a policy problem." Local Government Studies, (October):1-18.

--- (1977). "Political science and policy studies: Toward a structural solution." Journal of Policy Studies.

BECQUART-LECLERCQ, J. (1976). Paradoxes du Pouvoir Local. Paris: Presses de la Fondation Nationales des Sciences Politiques.

BEER, S. H. (1973). "The modernization of American federalism." Publius, 3(fall):49-96.

BINDER, L. (ed., 1971). Crises and sequences in political development. Princeton, N.J.: Princeton University Press.

BURKHEAD, J., and MINOR, J. (1971). Public expenditure. Chicago: Aldine.

CAMERON, D. (1976). "Inequality and the state: A political-economic comparison." Paper presented at the American Political Science Association meetings, September.

CAMERON, D., and HOFFERBERT, R. (1974). "The impact of federalism on education finance: A comparative analysis." European Journal of Political Research, 2(September);225-258.

CORNFORD, J. P. (1974). "The illusion of decision." British Journal of Political Science, 4(April):231-244.

CROZIER, M. (1964). The bureaucratic phenomenon. Chicago: University of Chicago Press.

CROZIER, M. et al. (1974). Où va l'administration française? Paris: Editions d'Organisation.

CULLINGWORTH, J. B. (1966). Housing and local government in England and Wales. London: Allen and Unwin.

CURRAN, D. J. (1963). "The metropolitan problem: Solution from within?" National Tax Journal, 16:213-223.

Davies Committee (1969). Report of the Ad Hoc Committee of Inquiry on the Method II System of Selection. Cmnd. 4156.

DERTHICK, M. (1974). Between state and nation: Regional organization of the United States. Washington, D.C.: Brookings.

DEUTSCH, K. W. (1961). "Social mobility and political development." American Political Science Review, 55(3):493-514.

DIAMOND, M. (1973). "The ends of federalism." Publius, 3(fall):129-149.

DYE, T. R. (1966). Politics, economics and the public. Chicago: Rand McNally.

ECHOLS, J. M. (1975). "Politics, budgets, and regional equality in communist and capitalist systems." Comparative Political Studies, 8(October):259-292.

--- (1976). "Does communism mean greater equality? A comparison of east and west along several major dimensions." Paper presented at the American Political Science Association meetings, September.

ECKSTEIN, H. (1973). "Authority patterns: A structural basis for political inquiry." American Political Science Review, 67(December):1142-1161.

ELAZAR, D. (1972). American federalism: A view from the states. New York: Crowell.

FESLER, J. W. (1965). "Approaches to the understanding of decentralization." Journal of Politics, 27.

FRASER, D. (1973). The evolution of the welfare state. London: Macmillan.

FROMAN, L. A. (1967). "An analysis of public policies in cities." Journal of Politics, 29:94-108.

GREMION, P. (1976). Le Pouvoir Periphérique. Paris: Editions Seuil.

Guichard Commission (1976). Le Monde, October 26, p. 13.

HANSEN, N. M. (ed., 1974). Public policy and regional economic development. Cambridge: Ballinger.

HARVEY, D. (1973). Social justice and the city. Baltimore: Johns Hopkins University Press.

HAYWARD, J. (1975). "Institutional inertia and political impetus in France and Britain." Paper delivered to the Political Studies Association, Oxford.

HAYWARD, J., and WATSON, M. (eds., 1975). Planning, politics and public policy. Cambridge: Cambridge University Press.

HECLO, H. (1972). "Policy analysis." British Journal of Political Science, 2(January): 83-108.

--- (1974). Modern social politics in Britain and Sweden. New Haven, Conn.: Yale University Press.

HEIDENHEIMER, A. J., HECLO, H., and ADAMS, C. T. (1975). Comparative public policy. New York: St. Martin's Press.

International Federation for Housing and Planning (1966). The financing of social housing in eleven European countries and in Israel. Paris: Comite Permanent International pour l'Habitat Social.

IONESCU, G. (1975). Centripedal politics: Government and the new centres of power. London: Hart-Davis, MacGibbon.

JANOWITZ, M. (1976). Social control of the welfare state. New York: Elsevier.

KEY, V. O., and CUMMINGS, M. G., Jr. (1966). The responsible electorate. Harvard: Belknap.

LAWSON, R., and STEVENS, C. (1974). "Housing allowances in West Germany and France." Journal of Social Policy, 3(July):213-214.

Layfield Committee Report (1976). Local government finance. London: HMSO.

LEE, J. M. (1975). " 'Central capability' and established practice: The changing character of the 'centre of the machine' in British Cabinet government." Pp. 162-189 in B. Chapman and A. Potter (eds.), W.J.M.M.: Political questions. Manchester: Manchester University Press.

LINDBLOM, C. E. (1959). "The science of muddling through." Public Administration Review, 19(Spring):79-88.

LOWI, T. J. (1970). "Decision making vs. policy making: Toward an antidote for technocracy." Public Administration Review, 30(May/June):314-325.

--- (1972). "Four systems of policy, politics, and choice." Public Administration Review, 32(July/August):298-310.

MACHIN, H. (1973). "Local government changes in France–The case of the 1964 reforms." Policy and Politics, 2:249-265.

MASSAM, B. (1975). Location and space in social administration. New York: Halsted (a Sage publication).

MAY, R. J. (1969). Federalism and fiscal adjustment. Oxford: Clarendon Press.

MAYHEW, D. (1974). Congress: The electoral connection. New Haven, Conn.: Yale University Press.

McCRONE, D. J., and CNUDDE, C. F. (1967). "Toward a communications theory of democratic political development." American Political Science Review, 61(1):72-79.

NEUBAUER, D. E. (1967). "Some conditions of democracy." American Political Science Review, 61(4):1002-1009.

NEWTON, K. (1974). "Community decision makers and community decision-making in England and the United States." Pp. 55-86 in T. Clark (ed.), Comparative community politics. New York: Halsted (a Sage publication).

NISBET, R. A. (1970). Social change and history: Aspects of the Western theory of development. London: Oxford University Press.

OATES, W. E. (ed., 1977). The political economy of fiscal federalism. Princeton, N.J.: Princeton University Press.

O'CONNOR, J. (1973). The fiscal crisis of the state. New York: St. Martin's Press.

OFFE, C. (1974). "Structural problems of the capitalist state: Class rule and the political system: On the selectiveness of political institutions." Pp. 31-58 in K. von Beyme (ed.), German political studies. Beverly Hills, Calif.: Sage.

PIVEN, F. F., and CLOWARD, R. A. (1971). Regulating the poor. New York: Random House.

PLANTEY, A. (1975). Prospective de l'etat. Paris: Editions de C.N.R.S.

PRESSMAN, J. L., and WILDAVSKY, A. B. (1973). Implementation: How great expectations in Washington are dashed in Oakland, or, why it's amazing that federal programs work at all. Berkeley: University of California Press.

PRYOR, F. L. (1968). Public expenditures in communist and capitalist nations. Homewood, Ill.: Irwin.

ROBERTS, D. (1969). The Victorian origins of the welfare state. New Haven, Conn.: Yale University Press.

ROSE, D. (1973). "National and local forces in state politics: The implications of multi-level policy analysis." American Political Science Review, 67(December):1162-1173.

Royal Commission on the Civil Service (1968). Fulton report, cmnd. 3638. London: HMSO.

SHARPE, L. J. (1973). "American democracy reconsidered." British Journal of Political Science, 3:1-28, 129-168.

STEINER, P. O. (1972). "The public sector and the public interest." Pp. 21-58 in R. Havenman and J. Margolis (eds.), Public expenditures and policy analysis. Chicago: Markham.

STEPHENS, G. R. (1974). "State centralization and the erosion of autonomy." Journal of Politics, 36(February):44-76.

——— (1976). "Communications." American Political Science Review, 70(March):159-174.

SUNDQUIST, J. L. (1975). Dispersing population: What America can learn from Europe. Washington, D.C.: Brookings.

TARROW, S. (1977). Between center and periphery: Grassroots politics in Italy and France. New Haven, Conn.: Yale University Press.

THOENIG, J.-C. (1973). L'Ere des Technocrates. Paris: Editions d'Organisation.

THOMAS, N. M. (1973). "The Seebohm Committee on Personal Social Services." Pp. 143-173 in R. Chapman (ed.), The role of commissions in policy making. London: Allen and Unwin.

TILLY, C. (ed., 1975). The formations of the national states in Western Europe. Princeton, N.J.: Princeton University Press.

TRIBE, L. H. (1972). "Political science and policy studies: Analysis or ideology?" Philosophy and Public Affairs, 2(fall):66-110.

WAGNER, A. (1958). "The nature of fiscal economy" (trans. by N. Cooke). In R. A. Musgrave and A. T. Peacock (eds.), Classics in the theory of public finance. London: Macmillan.

WILDAVSKY, A., and HECLO, H. (1974). The private government of public money. Berkeley: University of California Press.

WILENSKY, H. L. (1975). The welfare state and equality. Berkeley: University of California Press.

WRIGHT, D. S. (1975). "Intergovernmental relations and policy choice." Publius, 5(fall):1-24.

WRIGHT, V. (1972). "Politics and administration under the French Fifth Republic." Political Studies, 12:44-65.

5

THE USE OF SCIENCE IN POLICYMAKING: A COMPARATIVE PERSPECTIVE ON SCIENCE POLICY

ROBERT F. RICH

Princeton University

In the study of comparative policy, many apparent similarities between countries can be artifacts of the narrow range of questions asked or constraints associated with the methodologies employed. These apparent similarities mask the sometimes real differences in the policies if all their components are considered. Further, the important effects of institutional variations and intended consequences of sets of policies taken together are ignored. These problems are easily illustrated in the studies undertaken to discover the extent and methods of scientific knowledge utilization by policymakers in various countries.

Throughout much of history there has been a basic tension over the basic societal function(s) that knowledge was supposed to serve. One image (still adhered to by many scientists today) is that science produces *basic knowledge* that should serve the function of "enlightenment." In the Anglo-American tradition, this position was adhered to up to Victorian England. Another image of knowledge is represented by what some might label "vulgar Baconianism," i.e., science for use or power (see Elkana, 1976:19-25). This latter position is best presented by Max Weber who contends that "the power of all bureaucrats rests upon knowledge" (1968:941-1006). This conception of knowledge which emphasizes use or application of scientific knowledge to policymaking has evolved since the Industrial Revolution into a central concern of applied scientists.

These two images of knowledge and science have been accompanied by different trends in the funding of pure scientific research from public funds. In the latter part of the 17th century, there was practically no public support of science. With the emergence of the "Victorian philosophy" (the first half of the 18th century) science was better supported than it was in the 17th century (Elkana, 1976:19-25). This historical trend highlights one of the major debates surrounding science policy since that time: What is the appropriate mix in the allocation of public funds between basic and applied science?

GENERAL CONCERNS IN THE STUDY OF SCIENCE POLICY

From a cross-national perspective, it is clear that researchers interested in science policy have focused on the impact of scientific knowledge on public policymaking. These researchers have emphasized the relationship ("linkage") between the scientific community as the producers of knowledge and decision makers who are responsible for policy formulation on the basis of the knowledge available to them.

Those studying and making science policy (through much of history) believe that factors such as timeliness of data, objectivity, communication barriers, and cost of research play major roles in limiting levels of utilization. While some authors may stress one of these factors over another in explaining barriers to utilization and the adoption of innovations, it is presumed throughout the cross-national literature that if barriers can be overcome (i.e., if data were more timely, higher in quality, more relevant, in the proper form, more communicable, etc.), then utilization would automatically follow. In other words, researchers have concentrated on problems associated with increasing the "goodness of fit" or decreasing the "gap" between the "two communities."

By emphasizing "goodness of fit" researchers have underplayed the predominantly political functions of knowledge, i.e., knowledge for power, management, and bureaucratic reorganization. It appears that these functions have been underplayed because they focus on interinstitutional relationships within government (i.e., between bureaucracy and other parts of government) and do not include "linkages" to the scientific community.

The main argument of this essay is that researchers studying knowledge utilization and public policy in several different countries (West Germany, Austria, Colombia, and the United States) have focused on a limited set of descriptive questions, using one basic methodology (input/output analysis) with a common set of variables. This essay will be based on the recent empirical studies completed in each of these countries.

These recent empirical studies completed in Austria (Knorr, 1975), West Germany (Badura, forthcoming), Colombia (Cardonna, 1976), and the United States (Caplan et al., 1975; Rich, 1975; Weiss, 1975) have reached remarkably similar substantive conclusions:

1. In studying the application of empirically based research results and other types of policy-related information, each author found it necessary to distinguish between *instrumental* and *conceptual* utilization (Rich, 1977a). Instrumental utilization refers to cases where respondents pointed to the specific way in which information was used in policymaking (i.e., "Study X" was used in congressional testimony). Conceptual use refers to influencing a policymaker's thinking about an issue without putting discrete bits of information to any specific, documentable use.

2. To greater or lesser degrees, each study presented results on the gap between the researcher and policymaker communities as a primary independent variable in trying to explain levels and types of knowledge utilization.

In interpreting the similarity of these empirical findings, it is possible to reach one of the following conclusions: (1) the relationship between knowledge, power, and decision-making processes is strikingly similar in these different cross-national settings; (2) the findings are an artifact of the methodology used to analyze the relationship between scientific knowledge and public policymaking; and (3) the questions focused upon in these studies are very narrow and, hence, lend themselves to a common set of interpretations. This author believes that the similarity in these findings can be accounted for in terms of explanations (2) and (3) cited above.

MODELS/APPROACHES FOR MEASURING IMPACT AND USE

As already noted, much of the cross-national literature on science policy focuses on the impact of research on policymaking and the adoption of innovations. "Impact," in these cases, is conceptualized in the following manner: the documentable use of scientific knowledge (data) in the formulation and/or implementation of public policy or, more generally, in decision making. In documenting use, several approaches have been used: (1) using a survey instrument which relies upon self-reported instances of use and impact; (2) combining these interviews with linear input/output techniques, which are applied to trace information inputs directly to specific discrete outputs. If discrete bits of data (information) cannot be tied to specific decisions, then, according to these models, it is not possible to measure and document use and impact; and (3) in an interview context, presenting respondents with research abstracts and asking them if the data would be useful in a policymaking situation. In this latter case, respondents are being asked to assess the utility of information as opposed to reporting actual levels and types of utilization.

However, it is important to note that these three approaches share important characteristics in common: (1) they rely upon the ability of individual respondents to relate specific bits of information to a policymaking situation; (2) they rely upon the rationality of individual decision makers, and the decision making process. Insofar as utilization is concerned, it implies that the gathering and processing of information is oriented toward a plan and organized around a set of logically related rules and practices designed to incorporate the most useful information quickly and efficiently into policy decisions. And (3) in conceiving of the individual's ability to respond to questions concerning specific bits of information, within the context of a rational decision making process, one is asking policymakers to atomize their conception of reality. As researchers, we are asking policymakers to respond to questions which require them to take knowledge out of its context (within the policy deliberations process)—a context without which the knowledge would not have been retained in the first place.

Each of the research approaches outlined above employs procedures which attempt to trace how specific bits of knowledge have been used in decision making. These methods can be characterized as reflecting traditional input/output techniques (see Kelley, this volume, for another discussion of input/output analysis). To research utilization effectively, according to the assumptions behind these traditional measures, one must be able to explain and account for outputs in terms of the original inputs fed into the decision-making system. Implicitly, this assumes a one-to-one means/ends matching. If outputs cannot be traced to specific inputs and/or outputs are produced seemingly independent of inputs, different analytic procedures need to be introduced.

Instead, in this field, researchers have engaged in coercive means/ends matching. In the Caplan study (Caplan et al., 1975), for example, between one-fourth and one-third of the cases of use reported by upper-level policymakers in the United States were discarded because they did not involve the instrumental use of empirically based knowledge. The implications of this coding decision became clear after the responses to the following question were examined:

"On the basis of your experience in the federal government, can you think of instances where a new program, a major program alternative, a new social or administrative policy, legislative proposal or a technical innovation could be traced to the social sciences?" Eighty-two percent of the respondents replied "yes" to this item, and were then asked to provide examples of such knowledge applications. Approximately 350 examples were given. The policy areas represented ranged widely and were as likely to be technological or medical issues as the more strictly social policy issues (e.g., the decision not to build the SST, the establishment of water and sewer construction assistance programs, highway construction projects such as the Interstate System, the decision to go to an all-volunteer army, the selection of particular diseases such as sickle cell anemia and cancer for major governmental research funding, the lead-base paint prevention program, the establishment of the Environmental Protection Agency, the GI Bill, consumer information programs, major programs to "humanize" management in government operations, revenue sharing, Head Start, manpower and development programs, etc.). All of these and many more programs involving governmental actions of considerable national importance were in some way traced by his respondents to the social sciences. This question was asked in the context of searching for instances of empirically based social science utilization. Despite a series of questions and probes which attempted to limit the respondent to empirically based information, they chose to cite examples involving nonempirically derived knowledge when asked to provide the most outstanding instances of utilization known to them.

Three critical points emerged from the responses to this question: (1) policymakers did not generally provide examples of instrumental utilization; (2) the informational inputs cited did not serve to guide specific actions; and (3) critical instances of utilization of social science knowledge are passed over when they are forced into the procrustean bed of input/output analysis.

In research on knowledge utilization and public policy, it is also common for researchers to assign respondents lower "utilization scores," if they cannot cite specific bits of information that were utilized in decision making. These utilization scores are dependent upon the respondent's ability to cite details of the data they use, including its author.

Then, on the basis of utilization scores which are assigned to each respondent, impact measures are designed. Caplan, for example, employs a descriptive measure of impact which is based on the question: Does the information used apply to a policy issue affecting the nation as a whole, an issue affecting a large portion of the population, an issue affecting one segment of the population, or an issue related to the internal management of a government agency? (Caplan et al., 1975). Knorr (1975) and Weiss (1976) both try to measure impact in terms of the stage of the policymaking process in which information is used (i.e., problem definition, policy formulation, policy implementation, evaluation, etc.). Cardonna (1976) and Rich (1976) have attempted to measure impact by tracing patterns of selective use at various stages of decision making (i.e., concentrating on the form in which information is disseminated from one level of the hierarchy to another). Other descriptive, empirical measures of impact include extensive citation analyses, and budgetary analysis of the R&D expenditures of agencies over time (Caledrone, 1974). In the area of the adoption of innovations, impact is thought of as the rapidity with which an innovation spreads over time (Walker, 1971).

Each of these variations on measuring and analyzing impact focuses on the relationship between researchers and decision makers independent of other actors who contribute to and influence policymaking. Little attention has been given to the degree of centralization in government, recruitment patterns of government officials, political party affiliations of government officials, and political or bureaucratic incentives for purposely disregarded "relevant" scientific knowledge. Even the variations in institutions involved from country to country, a critical set of independent variables (see Ashford, this volume) are not considered. Only Badura (forthcoming) from West Germany and Knorr (1975) from Austria have given more attention to these variables, because they started with a theoretical orientation which leads them to explaining government policymaking (as a dependent variable) and not just patterns of utilization (as a dependent variable). If this field of research is to move beyond traditional input/output analysis, then utilization cannot be conceived as an end unto itself; it should be thought of as a means by which to reach an end; e.g., more effective policymaking, more efficient use of resources.

THE LIMITATIONS OF INPUT-OUTPUT ANALYSIS

Having studied knowledge use and policy, one learns two things very quickly: knowledge produces effect*s*, not a single effect; and policy is not made, it accumulates. Thus, the problems of locating and tracing knowledge as it flows through decision-making channels and identifying its consequences are impressive. It is almost impossible to predict when and where a specific knowledge input is likely to have an effect on policymaking. Yet, our traditional measures of utilization are based on the assumption that it is possible to predict when specific inputs will impact upon policy (outputs) (see Rich and Caplan, 1976).

If one wants to go beyond traditional input/output models, there are formidable methodological and interpretational problems to overcome. First, because knowledge accumulates and builds within organizational memories, some decisions (outputs) are made which seem to be independent of any identifiable, discrete inputs. For the analyst this poses the problem of not being able to identify the universe of inputs that have accumulated over time in order to deal with long standing issues. Thus, how is one able to judge levels of utilization and the processes affecting utilization? Second, because knowledge produces effect*s*, it is often impossible to trace outputs back to their specific inputs, even when it is possible to identify the universe of informational inputs. Thus it seems clear that input/output models are only appropriate when one is able to analyze the mechanical application of knowledge (i.e., instrumental utilization) to problem solving activities. In these cases, outputs can be traced back to specific, discrete knowledge inputs. On the other hand, it is difficult to trace the effects of conceptual utilization through the myriad of decision-making channels within problem solving organizations. Thus, from the perspective of coercive means/ends matching, researchers have been tempted to think of conceptual utilization as a failure to translate knowledge into action.

However, the recent empirical studies analyzed in this essay, from a comparative perspective, suggest that conceptual utilization may produce greater impacts (in terms of policymaking of national significance) than the more predictable and researchable instrumental uses. In any given decision-making situation, much of the relevant information under consideration is already known. Empirically derived information, past experiences, intuition, values, and other considerations all merge to form a frame of reference or perspective within which the social implications of alternative policies in a decision situation are evaluated. Our initial analyses of these data reveal the *low impact* of instrumental uses of scientific information. By contrast, conceptual utilization appeared to emerge in a vast number of different contexts. Policy formulation was determined only rarely by reliance on empirically grounded data (instrumental use).

THE EMPHASIS ON CONCEPTUAL UTILIZATION

These data suggest that more attention (from a methodological and substantive perspective) needs to be given to analyzing conceptual utilization. There are, however, formidable problems involved in changing a research agenda which has focused on instrumental utilization. From a methodological perspective, input/output analysis is easy and is the only tested method of analysis currently available (Rich and Caplan, 1976). In addition, it is relatively easy to build predictive models around this type of analysis. As already discussed, this method of analysis is inappropriate for studying the conceptual use of information. The fact that conceptual utilization cannot be studied directly does not mean that it cannot be studied. Methodological limitations need not reflect on theory building. Impact, for example, can be studied in terms of the changes produced: not necessarily from a cause/effect perspective, but, instead, from the point of view of the overall environment (context) influencing a decision, e.g., changes in agenda, organizational procedure. As researchers, we should not continue to waste time reinventing the wheel through the application of input/output models of utilization.

Knowledge utilization represents an input in the overall decision-making process; similarly it represents part of the procedures followed in considering whether or not some organization should adopt a new technique or process as part of their day-to-day operations. Thus, it is important to put the study of utilization and public policymaking in the context of the general conditions and constraints affecting problem solving. Having established this context, the priority research question becomes: what are the factors, concerns, conditions, and constraints affecting problem solving? Utilization would be seen as one concern within this context. Without studying more general problem solving procedures, researchers have missed the critical point of this type of research for two reasons: (1) one cannot say anything about the relative priority of knowledge inputs to other inputs in understanding decision making; and (2) without knowing the full range of inputs, one can only offer up incomplete explanations or analysis for patterns of utilization and nonutilization.

In addition to the limitations of the input/output approach, the research on knowledge utilization and public policy analyzed in this paper has also been constrained by the very limited, largely descriptive set of questions that it has focused on: Is a particular research study or type of analysis used; how is the information being used; what are the barriers to utilization; and how can utilization be increased? As already noted, researchers are also concerned with measures of impact.

NORMATIVE ASPECTS OF UTILIZATION RESEARCH

Beyond these descriptive measures of utilization and impact, one can also think of impact from a normative perspective. The utilization literature and the action implications flowing from it implicitly assume that the use of research results which lead to impact is of positive value (Rich, 1977b). Few policymakers or researchers have tried to assess the negative effects of utilizing social science data. Similarly, concepts of abuse, misuse, and premature utilization have also not been the subject of major investigations. The basic assumption is made that utilization of policy-related information is a priori valuable for meeting the decision-making needs of a government agency, and ultimately for promoting societal improvement (presumably, the emphasis of substantive public policymaking). Researchers and managers have become overly concerned with issues of administrative efficiency: i.e., how to facilitate the use of more scientific information? What procedures can be developed to reach this goal? It has been argued that one must concentrate on administrative procedures (i.e., creating procedures or channels that facilitate utilization) so that it will be possible to produce better policies (i.e., those that reflect the "public interest"). Implicitly, then, it has been assumed that more utilization will produce better policy.

Beyond these implicit assumptions, utilization researchers have avoided making normative judgments. From their perspective, research in this area should focus on the mechanisms and procedures that produce use and not make judgments about the quality of policies or decisions that information is contributing to. Thus, the assumption is clearly being made that information is valuable to policymakers if it is used.

From a methodological and substantive perspective, it would be a mistake to equate utilization with value without first specifying clear criteria for judging value.

In terms of trying to specify value, it should be noted from the outset that utilization studies point to the troublesome realization that agencies as well as individual decision makers can always find a use for information—especially if a budget, staff, or other resource allocation might be affected by that use. In this sense, many utilization studies have served bureaucratic interests more than they have helped to realize the "public interest." Thus, it is our conviction that, in terms of formulating criteria for judging value, most utilization studies represent unacceptable means of specifying value.

It is extremely difficult to establish an operational definition of value. Generally, within the public policymaking arena, information is of *value* if, and only if, (1) it influences or leads to policies that increase citizen well-being; (2) it is essential for answering policy questions "at hand"; and (3) it has some beneficial effects for the citizens that government service oriented agencies are supposed to be serving. In other words, it contributes to *societal improvement.* Citizen well-being and societal improvement are often viewed as general goals that "no one could disagree with." They are so general as to be trivial. However, the practices related to public policymaking as well as the methods used to study them have often emphasized bureaucratic and organizational policies. Issues of realizing the public interest have been assigned positions of secondary importance. Implicitly it has been assumed that the major output of policymaking is power, not substance.

As already discussed in this paper, utilization research has not concentrated on questions that are directly relevant to the problem of defining the concept of "information value." Actual use and measures of utilization are designed to answer questions which are of interest to those concerned with effective procedures in the decision-making environment; however, the answers to these questions only provide preliminary information in the search for specifying what is meant by "information value" in terms of producing better policy. If use cannot serve as an adequate indicator of value, researchers concerned with science policy should devote substantial resources to formulating a process which will lead to the specification of criteria for judging information value.

CONCLUSIONS

This essay began with a comparative analysis of the methodological and substantive approaches used to study science policy. More specifically, this analysis concentrated on the relationship of knowledge production and processing on the one hand, and utilization within the public policymaking context, on the other.

Research studies completed in four different countries produced remarkably similar conclusions. This essay attempted to analyze the substantive foci and methodologies employed in these studies. It was concluded that each of these studies focused on a very limited set of descriptive questions. Moreover, it was found that input/output analysis has limited utility for the kinds of questions being focused on by researchers seriously interested in science policy. From a comparative perspective, researchers need to reexamine the methodology employed in their studies and refocus the substantive questions being examined.

A commitment of this kind to understanding knowledge utilization processes would indicate the acceptance of alternative models of analysis. Conceptual utilization should not be viewed as less rewarding to study or as a failure to translate research findings into action; instead, it should be viewed as a concrete contribution to policymaking and to the general policymaking environment. This is clearly a field of research in which experimentation should take place.

In general, research strategies need to be developed which will effectively differentiate between instrumental and conceptual utilization and valuable and nonvaluable information. Coercive means/ends matching will be discouraged through the development of these new research procedures.

REFERENCES

BADURA, B. (forthcoming). The utilization of social science knowledge at the department level of the West German federal government. Knostanz, Germany.

CALEDRONE, G. E. (1974). Statistics about society: The production and use of federal data. Beverly Hills, Calif.: Sage.

CARDONNA, E. (1976). "The use of information in planning decisions in Colombia." Paper presented at an OECD conference on "Dissemination and Utilization of Economic and Social Development Research Results," University of the Andes, Bogota, Colombia, June.

CAPLAN, N., MORRISON, A., and STAMBAUGH, R. (1975). The use of social science knowledge in policy decisions at the national level. Ann Arbor, Mich.: Institute for Social Research.

ELKANA, Y. (1976). "Images of knowledge, qualitative indicators and science policy." Paper presented at the meetings of the Society for Social Studies in Science, November.

KNORR, K. (1975). "The nature of scientific consensus and the case of the social sciences." In K. D. Knorr, H. Strasser, and H. G. Zilian (eds.), Determinants and controls of scientific developments. Dordrecht, Holland.

RICH, R. F. (1975). An investigation of information gathering and handling in seven federal bureaucracies: A case study of the continuous national survey. Unpublished doctoral dissertation, University of Chicago.

--- (1976). "The impact of social science information inputs on domestic policy making at the national level." Paper presented at the Annual Meeting of the American Political Science Association.

--- (1977a). "Instrumental vs conceptual uses of social science knowledge: Knowledge for use vs knowledge for understanding." In C. Weiss (ed.), Policy uses of social science research. Lexington, Mass.: D.C. Heath.

--- (1977b). "Use as an indicator of value." Commission of Federal Paperwork.

RICH, R. F., and CAPLAN, N. (1976). "Policy uses of social science knowledge and perspectives: Means/ends matching vs. understanding." Paper presented at the OECD Conference on "Dissemination of Economic and Social Development Research Results," Bogota, Colombia, June.

WALKER, J. (1971). "Innovation in state politics." In H. Jacob and K. N. Vine (eds.), Politics in the American states. Boston: Little, Brown.

WEBER, M. (1968). Economy and society (edited by G. Roth and C. Wittich). New York: Bedminister Press.

WEISS, C. (1975). "Improving the linkage between social research and public policy." Paper presented at the Vienna Roundtable on the Market of Policy Research.

--- (1976). "Research for policy's sake." Address given at Case Western Reserve University.

PART III

ECONOMIC THEORY AND COMPARISON

6

UNIVERSAL WANTS: A DEDUCTIVE FRAMEWORK FOR COMPARATIVE POLICY ANALYSIS

PAUL PERETZ

University of Texas at Dallas

The central problem facing comparative policy analysts is the lack of a comprehensive framework within which they can evaluate the multitude of individual policy studies. In this paper I will review some current attempts to provide a suitable framework, before going on to propose a framework that presents policy analysis as the satisfaction of universal wants.

Early attempts at formulation focused on the categorizations policy-makers themselves used.[1] Froman (1968) points to a number of "traditional" categories based on substantive areas, institutions, target populations, historical eras, ideologies, values, degree of consensus, and governmental level, as typifying much of the early work in the area. Of these, categorization by substantive policy area was, and indeed still is, the most commonly used.[2] At its best this approach can yield useful insights into different ways of tackling similar problems, and it is particularly helpful in the intersystem dissemination of techniques.[3] But, as Froman points out, the traditional categories have severe weaknesses as analytical divisions in a coherent science of policy analysis. The substantive categories, for example, exemplify such diverse criteria as factors of production (labor, business, agriculture), geography (urban, interior), industries

AUTHOR'S NOTE: *This is a condensed version of a somewhat longer paper which is available from the author. I would like to thank Robert Bradley and Richard Hula for their helpful comments on an earlier draft and the other conference participants for their useful criticisms.*

(transport, housing), and type of good produced (education, defense, health). Furthermore, inductive definitions of the activities included in the different categories may vary substantially between cultures.

A second wave in the development of a distinctive comparative policy approach was the attempt, beginning in the 1960s, to construct what MacKenzie (1967) calls middle-level theories. This development led to the formulation of a number of theoretical frameworks to distinguish different kinds of policy characterized by different political processes. Some of this work developed naturally out of the case study approach typical of those using traditional categories. This approach identified features of the process leading to a particular policy and asserted they were typical of processes in that area, which was generally one of the "substantive" categories (Allison, 1969; Wildavsky, 1964, 1966). This work in turn led to a number of approaches that sought to apply inductive categorizations to the entire set of policy processes, usually with the aim of linking particular processes to particular policy categories. Froman's (1968) areal-segmental dichotomy and Edelman's (1964) division into "real" and symbolic policies are examples. The most interesting of these approaches were C. Wright Mills' (1956) use of "scope" to distinguish elite and middle-range policies and Lowi's (1964, 1970, 1972) use of "scope" and "coercion" to divide policies into distributive, redistributive, regulatory and constituent categories. In this collection, this approach is represented in the papers of Lowi and Ashford.[4]

Although these attempts to construct middle-range policy theories are a distinct advance, they suffer from a number of defects that limit their usefulness in explaining policy-related phenomena; both within and between systems. As Froman (1968) points out, most of these approaches have considerable difficulty arriving at adequate categorizations and specifications of the policies to be explained, although this is clearly part of the price that must be paid for increased generality and meaningfulness. More important, there is a distinct tendency for the definition of the policy types to be partly derived from the policy processes that are meant to characterize them, with some of the approaches only narrowly avoiding tautology. Furthermore, the essentially inductive method through which the categories were made limits their usefulness in comparative policy analysis, owing to the effects of cultural, developmental, geographical, and structural variables on policy definitions and policy processes in different systems.[5]

Partly in response to the perceived lack of progress of this middle-range approach, writers oriented toward the public choice literature or economics have sought to produce more deductive theories of policy. Usually they advocate variants of a market exchange approach and stress production constraints, indifference curves, externalities, and maximization. Typically they work with a vision of man as rational; most of the current work tends to assume perfect or near perfect information (Olson, 1965; Dahl and Lindblom, 1953; Buchanan and Tullock, 1962). They generally assume that demands properly represent interests and see the task of policy analysis in showing how market imperfections can be corrected. This approach resembles more traditional ones in its emphasis on prescribing policy (Wade and Curry, 1970); in contrast to middle-range theories it is less concerned to explain actual policy differences. Though this approach's precision, theoretical power, and potential for comparison are attractive, it is not without its problems, many of which Ashford details in his paper. In particular these writers tend to overstate both the information available to the individual and the rationality with which it is applied, as well as to understate the lag effects of political structures.

In this paper I seek to build such an approach. I start with the essentially tautological proposition that social mechanisms produce policy in order to satisfy human wants, given technological/informational constraints, and go on to postulate that whereas traditional behaviorists sought to describe a universal structure that would operate irrespective of the particular policy, policy analysts are concerned with structures as more or less efficient satisfiers of wants. Given this, it becomes necessary, if one is to do comparative policy analysis, to assume wants as constant across systems. In this paper I propose a hierarchical Maslowian need model as a first approximation to a constant want structure. I then examine how adoption of this approach can give some current work a much needed baseline before suggesting why it should be fruitful in generating new research.

WHY A UNIVERSAL WANTS APPROACH?

There are only two bases upon which we can build a science of politics. Using one we can look at the structures of government in their most general sense: the ways in which societies allocate values. With the other we can examine the manifold wants that people have and see how these wants are satisfied. If the researcher had access to all information about the system and could properly analyze it–if, in other words, he could perform a complete general equilibrium analysis of social behavior–it would not matter where he started. Since in fact such an analysis is impossible, at least for the foreseeable future, it makes a great difference where one starts.

As we have seen, political analysts have proceeded mainly by comparing the structures of decision making in a given society. This is as true of behavioral as of institutional or legal analysis, and is equally true of the so-called post-behavioral approach. Whether the researcher looks at structures supposed to exist, or at some subset of those that actually do exist, the questions he or she examines concern which structures should deal with problems, which structures cope with which problems, how they solve them, which structure is most important in solving a given problem, and whether a structure could become more efficient in terms of some criteria.

If we look at it from this perspective, it should be apparent that the distinctive feature of public policy analysis is that it has as its implicit foundation the satisfaction of wants. Policy analysts, generally adopting the later stages of the Eastonian demand-satisfaction model (though generally failing to note that demands are different from wants), essentially question how people in societies satisfy their wants, whether this want satisfaction is efficient, and what the feedback effects of inefficient want satisfaction are (though they generally ignore the feedback effects of efficient want satisfaction).

Before proceeding further we should note that we must proceed from one or the other base if we are to do comparative social research or do more than deliver nonaggregatable particular studies. If we do not assume either that different structures satisfy similar wants or that similar structures are dealing with similar wants, no comparative analysis is possible. For unless one element of an analytical system is the same as one in the system which it describes, we have no way to evaluate or compare the other elements of the systems. Although much public policy work makes no explicit mention of needs or wants, they are invariably implicitly assumed. Indeed, one answer to the question of why we should proceed from an explicitly need-oriented basis is that it makes available for examination and improvement a set of criteria that has always been used.

If wants are to be used as the basis of comparative public policy, an immediate problem arises. Human wants are many and various. In one social system there might be a demand for hula hoops and in another a demand for chess sets. Wants, it is generally agreed, are not the same across systems nor, indeed, within systems. But, if comparative policy analysts demand that wants be the same, is this not to say that such analysis is impossible? This question forces us to a redefinition of the relation between wants and comparative policy analysis.

> Comparative policy analysis is the study of the way that societies satisfy those wants which are similar across systems.

Furthermore,

> A science of policy analysis is the study of the most efficient satisfaction of universal human wants (needs).

Although these definitions do not imply that every individual everywhere has identical wants,they do imply that scientific comparative policy analysis is possible only to the extent that some of the wants of individuals in different societies are the same or can be reduced to similar underlying wants. Otherwise no scientific *comparative* policy analysis is possible and we are left with plausible empirical generalizations true under unknown conditions. But do individuals in different societies have some similar wants? To answer this question we must turn to the field of psychology.

PSYCHOLOGICAL THEORY AND NEEDS

There are two schools of thought on human motivation in psychology today. One school has a mechanistic conception of human motivation and sees behavior as a stimulus-response mechanism which can be explained most profitably without recourse to cognition. B. F. Skinner and his followers are the most fervent exponents of this approach (Skinner, 1953; Dews, 1970). The other school holds that it is impossible to explain behavior fully without recourse to cognitive factors. They contend that the two-stage stimulus-response model must be replaced by a three-stage stimulus–best goal attainment mechanism–response model. Although Atkinson's name is most often associated with this approach, Fromm is probably its most extreme proponent (Atkinson, 1964:275; Fromm, 1941).

The mechanistic school thinks of man as being in one sense a highly evolved species and in another sense very close to other animals. Like other animals, humans can be trained to respond to stimuli; the resulting stimulus-response mechanisms can be studied without introducing cognitive variables. Unlike other animals, humans are at the top of a pylon hierarchy defined in terms of evolution from instinctual responses at the lower end, to blank-slate, learned responses at the upper end. Thus, unlike other animals, humans have only weak preferences and can be easily trained away from these; but as with other animals, it is not necessary to hypothesize cognitive intervening variables in order to explain behavior. Most mechanists do, however, infer at least some human drives, if only physiological, partly because without them there is no motive for adaptive behavior (Hull, 1951; Miller, 1959; Spence, 1956).

The cognitive school tends to reverse these positions. They see humans as being like other animals in that they have inborn structured response patterns, but unlike them in that these structures are cognitive rather than instinctual. Following Kant, they see the human mind as innately structured. This means both that certain goals are inherently more important than others whatever the societal socialization mechanism, and that certain means toward these ends seem more attractive than others prior to learning (see, for example, Atkinson, 1964; McClelland, 1971; Heider, 1946, 1958).

In recent years, for reasons Weiner (1972) has explained in some detail, the trend has been toward the cognitive approach, with recognition of the suitability of the mechanistic approach for some limited problems. Our approach is quite explicitly cognitive. Following Atkinson (Atkinson, 1957; Atkinson and Cartwright, 1964; Weiner, 1970), I assume both that humans have innate needs and that they can consciously plan strategies to attain those needs. Because of this I hold that humans can manipulate many factors in the "field" (for field theory, see Lewin, 1935, 1951), but that normally they find it best to regard most of these factors as fixed in the short term.

DEFINING UNDERLYING WANT STRUCTURES

Up to this point we have defined universal human wants eclectically. Particularly when we examine short-term change in policies, this will be as far as we can go. Thus it may often be useful to select such wants as a clean environment (Enloe, 1975) and medical care (Heidenheimer, 1975) and see how different nations and political systems provide them. We should look at such things as the degree of coverage, the cost-benefit ratio and the kind of structures that satisfy wants. On the macro-level, we also need to find independent measures of the public's relative preferences among wants and compare these with actual spending to construct indices of strain or democracy that we can use across nations.

It seems worthwhile, however, to investigate a somewhat more ambitious solution to the problem of specifying the universal wants whose provision policy work analyzes. Psychologists have long explored the possibility that subconscious basic needs underlie the consciously felt wants of people. If we could reduce the diverse and almost infinite number of wants to a few more basic needs, this would obviously facilitate comparative policy analysis. Under these circumstances, different countries would differ only in the environmental and structural constraints on the achievement of essentially constant human needs.

A convenient starting point for a useful theory of universal wants is the work of A. H. Maslow (1943, 1970). Maslow defines a hierarchy of needs starting with physiological needs, then moving upwards to safety needs, love needs, esteem needs, and the need for self-actualization. He perceives these as lying along a Guttman scale similar to Figure 1, such that satisfaction of the prior needs is a necessary precondition for the emergence of the later ones. Underlying Maslow's model is an optimistic developmental view of human nature similar in many respects to that of Fromm (1941) and Erikson (1964). In a deprived condition, lower-level needs are primary. But a fully developed human being is one who has satisfied and integrated the lower-level needs and is now primarily concerned with the satisfaction of the need for self-actualization.

As Maslow partly recognizes (1943:165-172), his view, though suggestive, is not without its problems. At the individual level are problems of sorting manifold wants into Maslowian categories, of

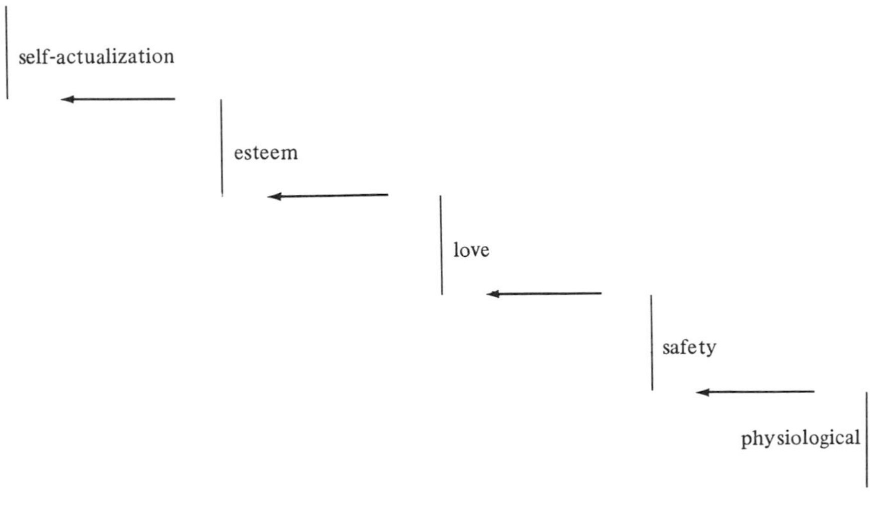

Figure 1: A DIAGRAMMATIC REPRESENTATION OF A MASLOW NEED HIERARCHY

deciding whether each category has finite upper bounds, of defining self-actualization, of accounting for individuals who seem to exhibit contrary priorities and of proving that men are more complete when pursuing "higher" needs. At the social level there are problems in fitting ordinary language policy categories into Maslow's divisions,[6] of showing the aggregation rules for those whose wants are satisfied, of specifying the degree to which societies can ignore the needs of most of their members and still survive, and of the usefulness of this categorization in explaining short-term policy change. In addition, there are problems of specifying the ceteris paribus conditions and excluding the effects of other variables on policy outputs.

The model I will propose is partially illustrated in Figure 2. While it retains the Maslow design's hierarchical ordering and categories, it differs in a number of significant respects. These changes are intended to solve some of the problems outlined above and make the model more useful in analyzing public policy. It recognizes that every individual will not always fall into the hierarchical Guttman scale, but thinks it sufficient if the broad mass of people do.[7] Thus the vast majority of the members of a given society should fall along the scale even though, owing to the effects of exogenous variables, some individuals will not. Next, it asserts that the achievement of wants will increase their value. Thus people will see an attempt to take away a satisfied want as worse than the failure to assuage unsatisfied wants.[8] It is also assumed that the various wants (as shown in Figure 2) overlap, with the result that given individuals will balance increasingly more marginal primary wants against the core parts of new secondary wants. The model posits that needs are only universal wants, i.e., that there is no special status for primary wants other than their primacy. Finally, at the social level, the model does

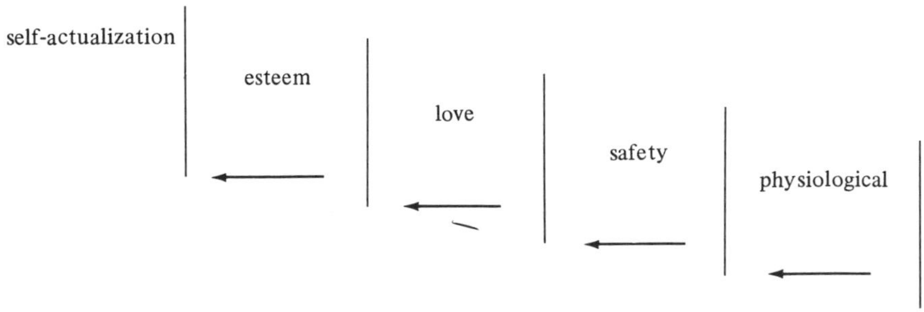

Figure 2: A MODIFIED DIAGRAMMATIC REPRESENTATION SHOWING OVERLAPPING HIERARCHICAL WANTS

not assume that all members of a society are satisfied to the same extent; but it does assume that technological and artificial structures constrain the achievement of wants both by individuals and by society as a whole.

Thus the revised theory postulates three types of constraints on policy outcomes: the want hierarchy, the degree to which the broadly defined technological level of the society permits satisfaction, and the shape of the structures which satisfy those wants in given social systems.[9] The want hierarchy is assumed to be constant for individuals and society.[10] The technological base—the potential resources available to achieve the given want structure—can differ between systems, individuals, and groups. The policy delivery structure, conceived of as the organizations responsible for satisfying individuals' wants in societies, represents the means of converting technological potential into want satisfaction. The degree of efficiency with which it does this is the central question for comparative policy analysis.

Given these three constraints, it follows that improvements in either technology or the policy delivery structure should move societies up the want hierarchy,[11] leading to potentially predictable changes in social policy preferences and outputs.

UNIVERSAL WANTS AND TRADITIONAL POLICY CATEGORIES

Most current policy analysis is still done in areas of traditional policy categorization, such as defense and education. How do these relate to a categorization by universal want? The answer is that there is a rough correspondence, though not one that we should overstate. Within each of the traditional categories, policymaking includes most of the basic wants to some degree. Nonetheless, the categorization of policy has generally followed a want formulation. In naming the traditional categories, analysts have generally given primary consideration to the basic wants which that policy area is supposed to satisfy.

We can see this more clearly by looking at the categories employed in the best-selling policy making text to use the traditional system of classification, Thomas Dye's *Understanding Public Policy* (1975). Three of the categories—poverty, welfare, and urban—are primarily concerned with the *distribution* of basic physiological wants for food, shelter, and clothing. Categories such as agriculture, commerce, interior, and labor, not used in Dye but represented in the U.S. Cabinet, are the categories within which *production* of goods to satisfy physiological wants is regulated. Three of Dye's other categories—health, crime, and defense—are primarily concerned with the provision of security from illness, internal attacks on property or person, and external attack. The other three policy areas Dye mentions are somewhat less specialized in serving basic wants. Nonetheless, civil rights seems primarily concerned with correcting "private" mechanisms for satisfying need for achievement and power; lower education with training people to satisfy physiological needs; and higher education with the need for self-actualization. Dye's last category, budgetary policy, is the highest level mechanism available for ensuring monetized need satisfaction. It is supposed to meet social indifference curves between the different basic wants.

UNIVERSAL WANTS AND EASTONIAN ANALYSIS

Although essentially generated by mechanistic behavioralism, the Eastonian heuristic system (1953, 1965) owes much of its attractiveness to its basic neutrality on the nature of man. It does not matter if the individual is initially a blank slate or whether he is "biased." In either case one can use the framework Easton provided to order data. This is one reason why the Eastonian system has been so attractive to so many policy analysts. But it is also why the use of the system has yielded very few new insights. A framework that does not make some assumption as to human nature can be expected to lead to sterile analysis.

In particular, two criticisms of the Eastonian system continually surface: (1) that the system does not explain what the individual's response will be to a government decision, and (2) that it does not allow for system change. These criticisms have arisen because the general interpretation of Easton, as for example in Almond et al. (1960, 1966) has been in terms of a homeostatic system comparing individuals with fixed, environmentally determined wants, subject only to technological constraints. This interpretation inevitably leads to a static conception of government where, as long as individuals' environmentally determined wants are met, there is no reason to change government. As long as communication channels remain open, there is no internal reason for change and all change therefore must come from outside the system. In addition, as the wants are not specified or ranked, it is generally not possible to see which wants have to be satisfied and which are optimal.

The adoption of the hierarchical wants structure proposed here has the effect of rejuvenating the Eastonian schema. It allows us to compare governments according to their efficiency in satisfying wants, gives a criteria for comparing alternative policies and makes the model dynamic. The satisfaction of lower level wants can be expected to lead to demands for higher level wants rather than quiescence. Thus a political system specialized so as to deliver only lower level wants might be expected to be overthrown, not when it fails to satisfy those wants, but when it succeeds.

Such a formulation makes it unnecessary to introduce an extraneous expectations variable to explain changing response within a given system (Deutsch, 1963). It would also provide a firmer theoretical base for theorists of revolutions who argue, like Tocqueville (Tocqueville, 1955; Davies, 1962), that a system's success, particularly if followed by a temporary setback, may lead to its demise.

UNIVERSAL WANTS AND FUNCTIONALISM

The relation of a universal want approach to functionalism has to be discussed for two reasons. First it is necessary to point out the differences in the two approaches, to escape charges that a want approach is just functionalism revised. Second, I would claim that a want approach helps to explain both the attractiveness and the limitations of functional theory.

What is the difference between a want approach and functionalism? One is in the unit from which the approaches start. There was a (rapidly discarded) functional theory in psychology in the first two decades of the 20th century (John Dewey was its main proponent); but functionalism as it is found today in sociology (Davis and Moore, 1945) and political science (Almond and Coleman, 1960) discusses the necessary functions that a social mechanism must perform if it is to survive in the long run (Parsons, 1936). Thus the unit of analysis is society and the question posed is: what must social mechanisms do to ensure survival? A universal want approach deals with the degree to which individual wants are satisfied. The basic unit of analysis is the individual and it asks when social mechanisms should be changed to ensure individual satisfaction.

Turning to an examination of functional theory in regard to the wants approach, I would contend that the wants approach helps to explain why functionalism has continued to seem attractive despite continued attack and why those attacks seem so effective against particular examples of the theory. First, many of the functionalist propositions are tautological in the wider sense of that word; they assert that systems have to maintain themselves if they are to remain in being. Second, and more important, functionalism implicitly asserts that systems that fail to satisfy some set of basic wants are not performing properly and may not survive, while simultaneously asserting that the ways that systems satisfy these wants may not be obvious. This combination explains much of the attraction of functional theory.

But the confusion involved can also explain functional theory's vulnerability to attack. First, the implicit wants are attached to the social organism rather than to individuals within it, leading to questions on the relations between the social organism and the individual, and whether society is in fact organic. Next, the confusion between the needs of the social mechanism and the wants of individuals often leads to the unjustified assumption that a mechanism performing the function necessary for its survival is also optimizing the utility of most members of that society. In particular, the bias toward those wants best satisfied by social mechanisms often obscures negative effects on more "private" needs. Finally, the same confusion leads functional theorists generally to have a conservative bias, because their lack of an explicit need framework makes it difficult to separate social mechanisms successfully ensuring their own survival from social mechanisms maximizing want satisfaction. Because of this, it is often difficult to advocate replacement of any existing social mechanism.

It should be noted further that the differences between a want approach and a "pure" functional approach depend on one's view of the good citizen. The functional approach leads to an idea of the citizen as manipulated by his societal imperatives or as owing loyalty to a well-functioning state. The ideal citizen in the want approach is much more of a balancer and calculator, willing to support a social system that optimizes need satisfaction but careful to lend it no more support than is necessary for base survival. He does this to prevent the structure from developing an independent ability to maintain itself when another structure could more successfully maximize wants.

USES OF THE UNIVERSAL WANT APPROACH

We have seen that the universal want approach is useful in providing a single touchstone whereby we can fruitfully evaluate most of the commonly used comparative theories within a unified framework. But good approaches do not merely unify previous theory; they provide new ways of approaching central problems. There is not space here to develop a complete application of the approach to the field of comparative public policy. I will, however, indicate a few of the ways that this approach can consider comparative policy questions that existing theories neglect.

One advantage of a universal wants approach is that it immediately points to a more comprehensive view of government. Although political scientists fully quote Easton's definition of government as the "authoritative allocation of values," only rarely do they take it at face value to claim that value satisfying mechanisms, whether "public" or "private," are government. Much more often they unthinkingly adopt the ordinary language definition, with government being the activity of "governmental institutions." With want satisfaction as the criterion, political scientists must examine a much wider range of social mechanisms, making the distinction between public and private policy in terms of the scope and salience of the policy in question (McConnell, 1966). This should have the beneficial result of redirecting policy inquiry toward more important decisions. It should also assist in cross-social inquiry by forcing the investigator to look at both "public" and "private" want satisfaction mechanisms, obviously beneficial when one country fulfills wants through a "private" mechanism and another country through a "public" mechanism. This should, in turn, be particularly helpful in seeking to discover whether different societies satisfy their wants through democratic, oligarchic, or dictatorial political structures.

As well as providing the investigator with a more comprehensive and accurate view of government, the adaptation of the universal want approach also gives him a consistent evaluation schema that he can apply across societies with widely different social mechanisms. First, as noted in the section on development theory, societies that satisfy all wants at a higher level can be judged as more advanced (though their citizens need not be more content), facilitating an ordinal ranking of societies. Second, since we have assumed that the underlying indifference curves between wants are the same in all societies, observation of the actual trade-offs among wants should allow structural categorization of differently shaped production possibility curves, holding the level of technology constant. In addition, social structures could be categorized according to whether they tend to satisfy the higher-level wants of a few or the lower-level wants of the many. For example, the major differences between communist and capitalist nations would be that communist government's policies aim to satisfy lower-level wants of the many and physiological wants at the expense of wants such as power and self-actualization. Finally, the adoption of an explicit want hierarchy points the researcher toward hidden trade-offs between and within want categories. In particular, most comparative work measures structures in terms of their ability to satisfy physiological and esteem wants. Work showing how policies that maximize want satisfaction in these areas have had difficulty satisfying other wants has been lacking; it could be encouraged by the explicit adoption of a wants approach.

Another advantage of the universal wants approach is that considering the different wants affected by a policy decision may give new insights into probable feedback. Thus, as Kurth (1971) points out, it is impossible to understand weapons procurement without looking at the effects of procurement policies on people's physiological as well as their security wants. Or, as my own research indicates, one cannot fully understand the public's continued hostility to mild inflation, which has little long-term effect on their incomes, without seeing it in the context of their desire for security.

Finally, the universal wants approach provides a new way of classifying policy outcomes across nations, which is useful for many purposes in itself. In many cases we would not want to take the general equilibrium approach and examine how societies satisfy all wants, but would rather want to take a partial equilibrium approach, comparing the satisfaction of a given want across societies. We could thus compare the degree to which the want was satisfied, the structures which satisfied it, the alternative method of satisfying the want, and the interactions between structure and technology that change the way societies satisfy wants. We could take a want like hunger and connect the degree of satisfaction with the mechanisms used to satisfy it.

SUMMARY

Most people who write on public policy and comparative politics take an essentially inductive approach. In this brief essay, I have attempted to illustrate the advantages of taking a more deductive approach. In the first part of the essay, I showed that political inquiry has to take as its base either wants or the structures used to satisfy those wants, with the former being the proper foundation for policy analysis. Furthermore, I showed that comparative public policy analysis has to take as its province the way that universal human wants are satisfied under different conditions. With this as a basis, I proposed that we adopt a modified version of the Maslow need hierarchy as a first approximation. Then I showed the degree to which such an approach can unify many of the approaches currently used in comparative inquiry. Finally, I attempted to illustrate a few of the ways that the adoption of a universal wants approach could yield new insights.

I must conclude by pointing out that the adoption of a universal wants approach is not without problems–in specifying the steps in the hierarchy, discovering the wants satisfied by given decisions, deciding to what degree the want hierarchy is temporally symmetric or asymmetric, and converting ordinary language policy categories into a universal want form.

Yet these problems are not, I feel, insurmountable. The concern with patterns of behavior has dominated comparative social inquiry for too long. It is time to change the underlying assumptions behind our endeavor.

NOTES

1. See C. Anderson (this volume) for a cogent defense of this approach. Using policymakers' public categories and rationales, as opposed to their private categories or subconscious motivations has some advantages and may be particularly helpful in explaining the form, as opposed to the substance, of policies. Its usefulness for comparative policy analysis depends, however, on an isomorphism between real and public explanations and on similar public definitions across systems. It is far from obvious that either of these conditions holds.

2. See Heidenheimer et al. (1975) and the papers by Marmor and Hoffman and by Friedland, Alford, and Piven in this collection, for recent examples.

3. This is particularly true in the manpower training area, with the dissemination of Swedish techniques, such as regional spending, retraining, employment services, and a variety of devices to encourage interarea migration to a wide variety of countries, including the United States. The manpower area also illustrates the dangers of such an approach, with techniques that worked in the context of Swedish policy delivery structures often failing when tried elsewhere. For examples see Lloyd Ulman (1973), Roger Davidson (1972), and Sar E. Levitan and Robert Taggart (1971).

4. Another development, represented here in Friedland, Alford, and Piven, is the attempt to expand the existing Marxist, elitist or pluralist approaches to explain the differences between the processes associated with different policies. Many of the middle-

range theories discussed above can be seen in this light. For a discussion of some of these theories as examples of broader approaches, see Prewitt and Stone (1973).

5. This should not, however, be overstated. We can see some similarities in different systems and it is useful, for reasons explained later, to chart both similarities and differences in the processes associated with similar policies in different systems. This would enable us to test the extent to which wants led to similar demands in different systems. We could also correlate satisfaction of different wants with the respondents' characteristics. Thus we could compare satisfaction of physiological wants with such things as housing and diet, and security wants with such things as victimization rates and marital status. Such research conducted across systems might uncover universal want-satisfaction mechanisms, show which policy outputs would do most to satisfy wants, and yield evidence on whether want satisfaction is a relative or an absolute phenomenon.

6. As Froman (1968) points out, this is a common problem in theoretically meaningful categorizations. It has, for example, frequently been pointed out as a major drawback in the categories developed by C. Wright Mills, Edelman, and Lowi. It would seem likely that a universal want approach would have as much (or as little) interobserver reliability as these if random observers were used. The way out of the problem would seem to lie in the development of psychological scales to measure wants and their use as Weberian ideal-type ordinal scales which could characterize an ordinary language "policy" to a greater or lesser extent.

7. As with a great many other social science hypotheses, this is primarily because of the difficulty of specifying for every case the ceteris paribus conditions under which the generalization holds.

8. This assertion, which is generally contrary to Maslow's position (1970), is made primarily because of the combination of risk aversion and the information differential between knowledge of the effects of established and new policies.

9. It should be noted that I see structures in societies as a series of policy delivery systems, which include information distribution as part of the systems but see the production of information as part of the technological constraints at a given time.

10. The reasons for making this crucial assumption have been given earlier. Here it should be noted that it would be sufficient for our purposes if this were true for the broad majority of individuals and the distributions were similar in the systems being compared. I should further point out that it is a central part of the theory that demands, whether explicitly or in the form of Truman's latent groups, do not equate with the want structure.

11. This is not necessarily true. As C. Geertz points out in *Agricultural Involution*(1963), it is possible for negative interaction to take place between technology and the policy delivery structure. I would contend however that the normal interaction between the two is positive, with technological improvements making policy delivery structures more efficient and vice versa.

REFERENCES

ALLISON, G. T. (1969). "Conceptual models and the Cuban Missile Crisis." American Political Science Review, 63(3):689-718.

ALMOND, G., and COLEMAN, J. (1960). The politics of the developing areas. Princeton, N.J.: Princeton University Press.

ALMOND, G., and POWELL, B. (1966). Comparative politics: A developmental approach. Boston: Little Brown.

ATKINSON, J. W. (1957). "Motivational determinants of risk-taking behavior." Psychological review, 64:359-372.

--- (1964). Introduction to motivation. Princeton, N.J.: Van Nostrand.

ATKINSON, J. W., and CARTWRIGHT, D. (1964). "Some neglected variables in contemporary conceptions of decision and performance." Psychology Reports, 14:575-590.
BINDER, L., and LAPOLOMBARA, J. (eds., 1974). Crises and sequences in political development. Princeton, N.J.: Princeton University Press.
BRADBURN, N. M. (1969). Structure of psychological well-being. New York: Aldine.
BRAYBROOKE, D. (1968). Three tests for democracy: Personal rights, human welfare, collective preference. New York: Random House.
BUCHANAN, J. M., and TULLOCK, G. (1962). The calculus of consent: Logical foundations of constitutional democracy. Ann Arbor: University of Michigan Press.
DAHL, R. A., and LINDBLOM, C. E. (1953). Politics, economics and welfare. New York: Harper and Row.
DAVIDSON, R. (1972). The politics of comprehensive manpower legislation. Baltimore: Johns Hopkins University Press.
DAVIES, J. C. (1962). "Toward a theory of revolution." American Sociological Review, 27(1):5-19.
DAVIS, K., and MOORE, W. (1945). "Some Principles of stratification." American Sociological Review, 10(2):242-249.
De TOCQUEVILLE, A. (1955). Old regime and the French Revolution. New York: Doubleday.
DEUTSCH, K. (1963). "Social mobilisation and political development." In H. Eckstein and D. Apter (eds.), Comparative politics. New York: Free Press.
DEWS, P. B. (1970). Festschrift for B. F. Skinner. New York: Irvington.
DOWNS, A. (1972). "Up and down with ecology, the 'Issue Attention Cycle.'" Public Interest, 26-29(summer):38-50.
DYE, T. (1975). Understanding public policy. Englewood Cliffs, N.J.: Prentice Hall.
EASTON, D. (1953). The political system. New York: Knopf.
--- (1965). A systems analysis of political life. New York: John Wiley.
EDELMAN, M. (1964). The symbolic uses of politics. Chicago: University of Illinois Press.
EDELMAN, M., and FLEMING, R. W. (1965). The politics of wage-price decisions, a four country analysis. Urbana: University of Illinois Press.
ENLOE, C. H. (1975). The politics of pollution in comparative perspective. New York: David McKay.
ERIKSON, E. (1964). Childhood and society (rev. ed.). New York: Norton.
FROMAN, L. (1968). "The categorisation of policy contents." In A. Ranney (ed.), Political science and public policy. Chicago: Markham.
FROMM, E. (1941). Escape from freedom. New York: Farrar and Rinehart.
GEERTZ, C. (1963). Agricultural involution: The processes of ecological change in Indonesia. Berkeley: University of California Press.
HECLO, H. (1974). Modern social politics in Britain and Sweden: From relief to income maintenance. New Haven, Conn.: Yale University Press.
HEIDENHEIMER, A. et al. (1975). Comparative public policy: Policies of social choice in Europe and America. New York: St. Martin's Press.
HEIDER, F. (1946). "Attitudes and cognitive organisation." Journal of Psychology, 21:107-112.
--- (1958). The psychology of interpersonal relations. New York: John Wiley.
HULL, C. L. (1951). Essentials of behavior. New Haven, Conn.: Yale University Press.
KURTH, J. (1971). "A widening gyre: The logic of American weapons procurement." Public Policy, 19(summer):373-404.
LEVITAN, S. A., and TAGGART, R. (1971). Social experimentation and manpower policy: The rhetoric and the reality. Baltimore: Johns Hopkins University Press.
LEWIN, K. (1935). A dynamic theory of personality. New York: McGraw Hill.
--- (1951). Field theory in social science. New York: Harper.
LINDBLOM, C. (1959). "The science of muddling through." Public Administration Review, (spring):79-88.

LOWI, T. (1964). "American business, public policy, case studies and political theory." World Politics, (July):677-715.

——— (1970). "Decision making vs policy making: Toward an antidote for technocracy." Public Administration Review, (May-June):314-325.

——— (1972). "Four systems of policy, politics and choice." Public Administration Review, (July-August):298-310.

MacINTYRE, A. (1972). Is a science of comparative politics possible. Unpublished paper.

MacKENZIE, W. J. M. (1967). Politics and social science. Baltimore: Penguin.

MASLOW, A. H. (1943). "Theory of human motivation." Psychological Review, (50):370-396. Reprinted in R. J. Lowry (ed.), Dominance, self esteem, self actualization: Germinal papers of A. H. Maslow. Belmont, Calif.: Wadsworth, 1973.

——— (1970). Motivation and personality (2nd ed.). New York: Harper and Row.

McCLELLAND, D. (1971). Assessing human motivation. New York: General Learning Press.

McCONNELL, G. (1966). Private power and American democracy. New York: Random House.

MILLER, N. (1959). "Liberalisation of basic S-R concepts: Extensions to conflict behavior, motivation and social learning." In S. Koch (ed.), Psychology: A study of science (vol. 2). New York: McGraw-Hill.

MILLS, C. W. (1956). The power elite. New York: Oxford University Press.

OLSON, M. (1965). The logic of collective action. Cambridge, Mass.: Harvard University Press.

PARSONS, T. (1936). Structure of social action. New York: Free Press.

PECHMAN, J., and TIMPANE, M. (eds., 1975). Work incentives and income guarantees: The New Jersey negative income tax experiment. Washington, D.C.: Brookings.

PREWITT, K., and STONE, A. (1973). The ruling elites. New York: Harper and Row.

RAE, D., and TAYLOR, M. (1971). "Decision rules and policy outcomes." British Journal of Political Science, 1(January):71-90.

RUDOLPH, L., and RUDOLPH, S. (1967). The modernity of tradition. Chicago: University of Chicago Press.

SKINNER, B. F. (1953). Science and human behavior. New York: Free Press.

——— (1974). About behaviorism. New York: Knopf.

SPENCE, K. (1956). Behavior theory and conditioning. New Haven, Conn.: Yale University Press.

ULMAN, L. (1973). Manpower problems in the policy mix. Baltimore: Johns Hopkins University Press.

WADE, L. L., and CURRY, R. L. (1970). A logic of public policy: Aspects of political economy. Belmont, Calif.: Wadsworth.

WEINER, B. (1970). "New conceptions in the study of achievement motivation." In B. A. Maher, Progress in experimental personality research (vol. 5). New York: Academic Press.

——— (1972). Theories of motivation: From mechanism to cognition. Chicago: Markham.

WILDAVSKY, A. (1964). The politics of the budgetary process. Boston: Little Brown.

WILDAVSKY, A., DAVIS, O., and DEMPSTER, M.A.H. (1966). "A theory of budgetary process." American Political Science Review, 60(3):529-547.

7

UNIVERSAL NEEDS: AN INDUCTIVE FRAMEWORK FOR COMPARATIVE POLICY ANALYSIS

E. W. KELLEY

Cornell University

The central problem facing comparative public policy, or any comparative endeavor for that matter, is not the difficulty in making comparisons; instead it is to know what comparisons to make and for what purposes. We can iterate the activities of committees in national legislatures in several industrial democracies; we can state what health policy is—at least in part—in Britain, France, and the United States; we can provide analyses of public expenditures on welfare as a (difference equation) function of change in state income and other readily measurable properties; offer typologies of policy types; or cite key neglected variables. All this is to what end? Surely we do not want the compilation of facts, the charted typologies, or the equations for themselves. At first approximation, we want some understanding of why particular public policies[1] exist and what their consequences are. Additionally some of us would like to be able to evaluate the intended and unintended consequences of such policies.

Such understanding and evaluation eventually lead us to explanation and prediction, which in turn lead us to generalization and, always, explicit or implicit comparison. For such comparisons, explanations, and predictions to be part of our shared knowledge, its terms or concepts must have shared referent. For such knowledge to cumulate, it must eventually assume aspects of a deductive system. In the end, then, we are looking for deductively connected sets of hypotheses which will allow us to explain and possibly predict aspects of at least selected public policies. Here we agree with Peretz (this volume). However, we insist that any such deductions be rigorous and be from true premises. Both these conditions require that the referents of the concepts in such premises be exact and shared. A common mistake in the policy sciences is to assume that the higher the level of generality of a statement in a deductive system, the less exacting are the requirements for precisely defined terms. Any logician would point out that nothing could be further from the truth. Indeed, if one wants to make deductions at all, all concepts must have clear, shared referent.

We are looking for statements like: "under conditions XYZ, if more of A then more of B," or "under conditions XYZ, if A increases by 1 unit, B increases by C units," concisely expressed as $\Delta B = C\Delta A$; where A might be something like the number of different sources of payment for a service and B might be percent of net national income spent on the service. The aspects of policies we seek to explain might be qualitative or quantitative; hence the principles—hypotheses—we might use can reference qualitative conditions, even the presence of political or social institutions, or they may be difference equations. Such statements are presumed to be such that when the antecedent conditions are met, the subsequent condition-aspect of policy or consequence of policy obtains. These statements, then, are always comparative; they are relevant wherever and whenever the antecedent conditions occur.

APPROACHES TO COMPARATIVE POLICY

Approaches to comparative policy usually either express a point of view about what is important in studying policy or tell us how to obtain understanding. Presumably, importance is eventually judged in terms of the benchmark of understanding we have laid out. We do not need approaches to iterate either policies or institutional variations across countries. Hence, an approach must either produce hypotheses that are not simply guesses about facts or give us some systematic insight into what would be included in such hypotheses.

Some approaches to comparative public policy fall under the rubric of input-output analysis, a particularly simple version of the systemic approach. By input-output analysis, we refer to approaches in which some combination of demands or citizen needs, along with economic resources, determine changes in the policies of government. The intervening stages of the systemic approach are bypassed (Easton, 1953, esp. Chapter 7). In case studies of policy changes, this approach is often implicitly assumed. The policy changed may be the distribution or enforcement, or public expenditures to secure a right or privilege (i.e., voting, integrating schools) or a literal distribution (ADC funds). In some way a coalition of individuals and interests able to impose bother and cost on others (though this is rarely mentioned) and having some shared need or demand secures public resources for its private end. Such a descriptive picture does not explain which groups, which ends, when it succeeds, and what resources impact on what political institutions to impel a policy change. What we have is a redescription of a policy change using somewhat more global, vaguer terms; in other words, we have what social scientists usually have when they think they have a system.

Often input-output analysis of policy changes confine inputs to quantitative attributes, i.e., level of party competition and, particularly, changing tax and resource base and total personal and/or corporate income. This practice is common when one has 48-50 cases and something like SPSS at hand (e.g., Sharkansky, Hofferbert). The subsequent analysis is deficient on two counts. First, to our knowledge, a greater resource base is not followed by any particular kind of policy change. One need only look at economic growth and relative stagnation of public support for education in the South in the early sixties to see that the effects of resource changes is mediated through institutions (and their internal structures), rules, and belief systems as well as, in some cases, the game of competitive electoral politics. Cross-sectionally (and irrelevantly), levels of public expenditures for various types of public services in Alabama counties are simply not related in any simpleminded, mechanical way to differences in resource bases (Sanders, 1977).

Even if there were some sort of direct "relationship" between resource changes and policy changes, such could not easily be found by those doing quantitative policy studies. Of course a nonrandom association obtains, so such analysis always gives a result—with enough cases, a significant result. However, one or more difference equations mechanically arrived at never correctly describe the (possibly contextually lawful) association of various changes in resource base and the amount of change in the provision of a public good or service. We simply introduce more cases and set different coefficients anyway, even when such studies are done within the confines of similar political and bureaucratic structures (i.e., states with the United States). If a difference equation described the lawful association between a particular resource and an aspect of policy, the equation could not be found using the sort of averaging of contingent and interaction effects, both empirical and statistical, that result from the use of partials in regression and other multivariate econometric techniques. Not only is physical partitioning of data usually essential to testing hypotheses in the form of difference equations, but even then, unless one has a closed, complete set of lawfully connected properties and instances of same, such analysis will not bear directly on the relevant difference equation(s) (Kelley, 1972).

More frequently, however, what we really hypothesize about resource and policy changes is likely to be something of the form: given the presence of Y and Z, then if more of X and less of V, then more of Q, ceteris paribus. Nothing in an econometric analysis is relevant to testing such a hypothesis (nor is anything in SPSS). Such a hypothesis lends itself to a best test, but only when the hypothesis is specified in advance. Although there is no mechanical way to test a hypothesis before knowing what it is, when once stated, if we take its grammatical format seriously, we can always maneuver the data in the proper way. Simple versions of programs which will do this now exist and will be improved and extended to test more complicated grammatical formulations involving complex comparisons relevant to testing hypotheses of the above comparative form. Again, though the proof is in what is found, we would not bet on simple connections between resource and policy change unmediated by institutions and rules for reasons that will become clear later.

Like input-output analysis, typologies of policy types and/or governmental functions have had long standing in comparative politics and public policy. Unlike input-output analysis, typologies usually involve qualitative properties and policies—the presence or absence of socialized medicine, a regulatory body, and so forth. The advantages and difficulties involved in using such typologies in explaining and/or predicting anything have been well documented elsewhere (Hempel, 1965). Clearly though, the entries in such typologies must be mutually exclusive. To use Lowi's (1965) example, if span of control is always greater (smaller) in bureaus that implement policy type X than in policy type Y, we cannot have any policies that are both types X and Y at the same time. To insure such exclusion, the policy types must be well defined. Such must also be true, if the policy types are to be generally useful, in explanations of anything. One advocates use of a particular typology (as contrasted to the huge number of others that could be formulated), because some things are (lawfully) true of one type that are not true or are less true of the others. To know this, one must be publicly clear as to what would constitute falsifying evidence; otherwise, what we call true and what we say we explain would depend on our sleight-of-hand facility with language, rather than evidence from the world.

Sometimes policy types are said to be related to "marginals," two of which give a fourfold table, three of which give an eightfold, and so on. Presumably such claims are meant to be hypotheses and the same stringent requirements for exact shared definition of terms obtain. Hence words like "coercive," "generalized," "aggregated," "decentralized" found on the marginals of various typologies must be carefully used and what it means for each not to be exemplified must be clear and unambiguous. Again, the literal, logical consistency of our linguistic expressions of hypotheses and observations, not our linguistic cleverness, must govern what we call true in comparative public policy.

Finally, we must be clear about the aspects of any policy a typology is about. Are we referencing the public law(s) that eventually lies behind the policy—what the statute says or delegates? Are we referencing that part of the statute that names what is to be done or delegated, or that part which gives administrative organization or procedure? The difference is important, given the propensity of what are (say, in congressional or parliamentary debate) viewed and stated as being partial redistributions (parts of ESEA, 1969, council housing in Britain, reallocation of public school funding and students) to become principal distributions through the character or timing of administrative activity. Possibly different lawmakers view a policy as being of different types (ESEA, Title I). Differences among the substance of a law, the attached administration of its provisions, or different views of its intent or consequences can lead to the same policy being differently placed in any typology. Any such placement, by any criteria, however clearly given, is useful only if it is used to test some hypothesis systematically covering more than the cases or policies in hand.[2] Alternatively, such categorization in any particular typology must be shown to lend to such hypotheses an empirical claim in itself.

Approaches to comparative policy sometimes center around advocacy for using particular types of concepts as independent variables in one's analysis. Presently some authors push the notion that similarities and differences in public institutions (types of legislatures, separation of powers, federalism, etc.) or rules are critically important in explaining policy similarities and differences (Ashford, this volume).

There is no reason that the hypotheses that would be used to explain policy similarities and differences could not contain properties of the institutions that make policy, electoral laws, bases of representation, party discipline, and changes in same. We would agree with Ashford, that to exclude such properties would be difficult. However this is not to say that such institutions, rules, and the like have the same "functions." Particular institutions do many things and have many descriptive properties. Those "institutional" properties that might be lawfully related to aspects of health care in one country might not be lawfully related to the same or even any aspects of health care in another country. However, to say that we must use institutions in explaining policy is like saying that we must explain the product of a machine by citing its structural features like its height and weight. Such may or may not be true.

We are emphasizing that we cannot force form on the world or policy in spite of the evidence (even though we often do not get to the latter). No structure or institution need have the same function, do the same things, or be instituted or organized for the same purposes; no function, policy, desire or whatever is necessarily caused by the same things. To say that hypotheses or laws must have a particular content or form without qualification is silly and probably untrue. Yet at the same time we want to emphasize that explanations of aspects of policies or their changes are likely to include properties of rules and institutions, unlike most of the statements made in the input-output approach.

Such hypotheses are not likely to successfully explain every aspect of what we call a policy. No set of hypotheses is likely to do this. In particular, we need not undertake the burden of explaining historical development or initial conditions. Someday we may be able to do so with respect to some properties, but there is no reason this will prove any easier than the use of laws of relativistic physics to explain the original singularity as contrasted to explaining *changes* in *relative* momentum or position. Further every hypotheses involving change in some aspect of a policy need not be comparatively relevant to each country or state, or indeed to any right now. If the antecedent conditions are not exemplified, a hypothesis is irrelevant to the case in hand; the truth functional of hypotheses and laws is that of nominological, not material, implication. Further, it is probable that such hypotheses in comparative policy are more likely to be about policy changes, rather than policies or their administration per se, at least initially.

Finally we note that the many problems of making cross-cultural comparisons are not really problems of policy comparison. First, the problem often arises of how can we be sure that this question, when translated into that language, means the same thing. There is no reason to believe it does; chairs are different things connotatively to different people. Yet what is true about chairs publicly is not in dispute. Further we would not use a paper-pencil questionnaire because the responses are unlikely to be lawfully related to anything even within one culture. If we were to persist, however, our difficulty could be that of finding the different causes of some apparently similar behavior (checks in an answer has, say) for people in different cultures. If all people in several cultures did X and then did Y, that would be so even if X meant different things to people in the different cultures. This leads to a second point: unlike what is sometimes thought, the use of words–their meaning–for those of us trying to pose and check guesses about laws need not be the same as the usage by the people whose behavior or institutions we might be dealing with. This is not to say that the latter is unimportant, if indeed not vital, to know in order to test some hypotheses.

All this is not to say there is not extreme and relevant cultural diversity in the world. Particular inhabitants in Southeast Asia may not view Western political and bureaucratic forms as at all involving "real" politics or power even as they participate in such processes. This is totally different from the challenges to legitimacy and authority offered by separatist groups like the Basque, various Celtic groups, or even revolutionary movements like Castro's. These were not challenges to the fact of bureaucracy and other "Western" institutions. They were disputes over particular bureaucratic personnel, centralized control and policymaking, and the policies themselves. This suggests that most hypotheses are likely to be true under carefully stated boundary conditions–for example, conditions that would *not* name, but would include either the Basque or Indonesia but *not both*–if the hypotheses were about the administration of delivery of medical care or legal aid.

HYPOTHESES

There are actually very few carefully formulated hypotheses in the social sciences. Some of those that exist, and are probably true under strictly specified (and never perfectly actualized) boundary conditions, involve the nonincreasing slope of the demand curve and the nondecreasing slope of the supply curve in economics. The difficulty in these cases is not in giving the two hypotheses involving price and quantity but the detailing of the many and complex boundary conditions. It is likely that the nonextinguishing effects of intermittent reinforcement extends across a wide variety of boundary conditions.

There are many more hypotheses of other sorts—plural descriptions and vague organizing principles or pictures. Examples of the latter are Easton's work on political systems or Parsons' general theory of action (Easton, 1953; Parsons, 1949). Examples of the former would be the guess that most retailers in Sweden or car dealers in New York State will resist the establishment of new outlets or franchises. The latter may be particular applications of some hypothesis in our sense, but, taken alone, are guesses about what the facts are.

There are even ways to make predictions relevant to comparative policy without using hypotheses. Econometric estimations are a case in point. Whether the derived difference equations be normal or structural, no one would pretend they are lawful statements, yet they are useful in making predictions relevant for planning economic policy. We often make use of the commonsense underpinnings of such techniques to make more qualitative predictions in the area of public policy. This underpinning is essentially an extension of one of Mill's principles—"same cause(s), same effect(s)"—to which it added the observations that many independent variables change very little or systematically in the short run. Such rules or methods do not work for discontinuous changes in effects, like the predicting of stock market crashes or particular technological discoveries. When we encounter these, our common sense and policy science is surprised.[3]

Hypotheses can be extensions and corrections of knowledge about policies we already imperfectly hold. We sense, see, and even state a number of almost regularities relating institutions and interests to laws and policies. Indeed, politics itself could scarcely function if we did not have regular expectations of the needs of organized groups, some knowledge of the regular functioning of representative institutions in passing laws, and of the consequences of such laws for bureaucracies and the private groups. Notice that unlike Peretz (this volume), we consider well defined groups with particular interests; in this way our claims can be checked.

If we start with Marmor, Bridges, and Hoffman's information (this volume) about medical care, we can quickly offer two statements: As the market power of those receiving medical payments (doctors, hospitals) is (becomes) greater relative to the market power of those who make such payments (individuals, insurance companies, levels of government), the proportion of net national income spent on medical care is greater (increases). The same is true of the average real income of those who provide the service relative to those who provide other services or compared to their own average real income at an earlier time. By market power of providers is meant the extent to which they are organized in noncompeting groups to bypass the risk of market mechanisms. Payers obtain market power as sources become fewer in number, down to the extreme of one, usually the state. Here are four hypotheses: two involving changes in real income; two involving changes in percent of net national income spent on medical care. Within each group one hypotheses refers to temporal changes in market power of groups within a country; the other refers to differences in comparisons of relative market power of payers and payees taken across countries cross-sectionally. There is no reason to confine these hypotheses to the provision of medical services. Let us hypothesize that such are true for the provision of any service within a state. We may possibly wish to add as a boundary condition that the service must be at least privately organized as contrasted to being totally privatized. Even a shift from the latter to the former condition involves an increase in market power and may have results consistent with our hypotheses, making the condition unnecessary.

Notice that the same aspect of a policy or an institution need not be involved in these hypotheses across states in the same way. The service profession with the most market power vis-à-vis payees may be architects in Britain and doctors in the U.S. The institutions that involve the state in payments, if at all, in any one service area across countries may be quite different. Further, the force of our argument and examples is directed toward their form and characterization. If they are not true, or must be modified to fit evidence unknown to us, they simply suffer the fate that afflicts all hypotheses in science at some point. In their modification and correction, however, we come to assertions that bear the weight of current, relevant evidence better.

As another example of the kind of knowledge we are seeking, consider what factors might prompt consolidation (in the state) of payments for a service, or even the control of distribution and availability of a service. Possibly there are many sets of sufficient conditions for the state to exercise each sort of activity/control. A necessary condition for any such activity/control, however, appears to be prior *direct* involvement in the selection of those to be trained to perform the service or prior *direct* (e.g., not through loan guarantees, etc.) subsidy of individuals in the process of training. Additionally, a necessary condition for even this state activity is the prior private organization of many of those rendering the service (possibly even on local levels, but noncompetitively).

Pictorially, trade associations are like professional associations, particularly in their attempts to control free riding, to avoid market risks, and to externalize the cost of both, usually to the state. (A crude hypothesis itself.) At the same time our political lore suggests that regulated industrial sectors benefit from such regulation, which itself is heavily symbolic (Edelman, 1964). These benefits are extended at times of economic crisis and movement from regulation to syndication or even under threat of foreign competition (Perna, 1975, also MacLennan, Forsythe, and Denton, 1968:275-278). With a number of intermediary considerations, we are led to hypothesize that the state only regulates, nominally or otherwise, industrial sectors that already have trade associations. Costs of setting markets, prices, and risk are transferred to the public sector, as in the case of service professions in return for the claimed public benefits of regulation.

So far we have assumed that we are dealing with somewhat industrialized states with elected legislatures (in the elections two or more parties compete). The basis of representation is areal, not functional. We will now express more of our point of view about what is important about public policy and political institutions in such states. These comments might be called the background to our hypotheses. In the explication of this background, cryptic mention will be made of other hypotheses, not yet fully formed. Alternatively, one may regard what follows as our "approach" to comparative policy. First it is important to note that political life derived from the economically well off (even in Aristotle) who shared concern and interest for the well-being and protection of the state and economy, but who were differentially better or worse off depending on exactly what collective policies were pursued. As soon as competition is with votes, a new profession is born–electoral politics. This new game, superimposed upon the patterns of economic interests is an initial boundary condition for our discussion of comparative policy. We are concerned with policies in countries and subunits of same in which policy is nominally made by elected legislatures and indirectly or directly electorally responsible executives. We want competition; one party states are excluded to begin with (though they and mixed regimes like Brazil can be brought back into the boundary conditions of many likely hypotheses). The rules people make for their politics are not neutral. Though particularized benefits are not so common, knowledge of what will generally benefit people like one's self, rather than some veil of ignorance and/or rule utilitarianism govern much of what one says in actual or implicit constitutions. Hence some structural basis is made for facilitating and trading off anticipated interests among organized minorities. At the same time, that collective activity which benefits most organized interests without imposing external cost is mandated: Adam Smith's view that government should do what facilitates organized business and not interfere in the decisions of business is clearly expressed in Article I of the U.S. Constitution. Collective action, even just securing contracts and providing for commerce and national defense, while possibly helping everybody some, helps some more than others. Collective action in general, because of economies of scale, the partial public feature of some goods and services, and differing capacities to impose external economies and diseconomies may benefit many but some more than others. Those who benefit more are generally those making the rules of politics, the initial rules internal to political institutions, and trying to insure appropriate government action (inaction) into the future. In representative bodies, those playing the game of politics try, among other things, to maximize benefit (called incumbency) and its entailments and to minimize costs. This is done by minimizing the sum of information, decision, and external costs while obtaining benefits relevant to reelection. The resultant organization of a legislature is tricky as it depends upon the effective representational base of the politician. Where parties, particularly the selection of candidates is local, something like the House committee system results. Individuals specialize in what is attributable to them in part and is, at the same time, useful to organized constituents. Reciprocity of passage of such benefits is a cornerstone of legislative activity even more important than seniority (Bensel, 1977). Alternately, where selection of local candidates results from national influence control, costs are reduced in party structures, which is also where benefits are packaged. As might be guessed, those policies that are actually considered in detail legislatively (both tax breaks and expenditures) are those that benefit interests that are organized best at the level at which party candidates are actually selected. Others are sent to regulatory bodies, commissions and the like. This is consistent with relevant cost reduction to legislators (and politicians in general). They do not deal much with what will not help them.

In the United States Congress, transportation is a no-win issue. If busses and truckers are helped, railroads are hurt. The former have gained much from public funding of a highway system (although they pay taxes, these by themselves would not begin to support the interstate highway system), but have rates set in a body that includes other transportation interests. The result of this is the reduction of market risk, principally by making price competition illegal, but also by regulating entry. Prices are set so that all sectors stay in business. When this is impossible, the public purse is used to buy somewhat unproductive fixed assets as to run an economically inefficient service. The control over price entry and the like was carried to greater extremes, particularly in terms of number of economic sectors affected. Under NRA and in Sweden in the sixties (Sandburg, 1965) control of labor pricing, production, distribution, and product and service pricing was set in councils in which labor, producer, and retailer were all represented. This contrasts to the Gaulist sector-by-sector syndicatilization of French industry in the 1960s in which labor was excluded from the planning process. This contrast may be due to factors close to those expressed in one of our hypotheses concerning income and market power for service areas. French labor organization is more fragmented within economic sectors and can impose fewer costs sector-wide if disposed to do so than is the case in Sweden.

All redistributions of rights, resources, and opportunities, particularly as much of the public shares the view that such redistribution is going on, cannot work to the benefit of all incumbent politicians simultaneously. Hence not only is taxing separated from spending so that apparent benefits can be passed around and/or costs saved, visible redistribution is seldom directly attempted. This does not mean that areal or functional redistribution does not go on throughout the state. Indeed, we could say the less the extent that fiscal equivalence obtains, the more such state activity. In particular, if taxpayers view taxes as centrally collected and the rates as varying little and see spending at the local or district level clearly, locally selected legislators who decide how to spend national taxes locally will spend more. They will also organize themselves to pass the political benefits of such district-by-district spending to almost all members (Mayhew, 1976). Additionally, apparent redistribution is avoided by localizing the distribution of the benefit side of national redistributions (note that a large part of all state spending involves redistribution areally, by interest or economic sector or even, sometimes, by income). Nationally funded public housing or urban renewal is distributed locally, by locals, even though the tax base is national. The mechanisms differ, but the benefits and onus of distribution are always placed on local housing councils (as in Britain) or local political officials (as in the U.S.). Even the redistribution of rights and obligations in representative, industrial systems is slowed. When the law commands redistribution (i.e., affirmative action) the bureaucracy set up by the law almost always has the effect of drastically extending the time over which the activity takes place. If judicial systems are involved, the privatization of cost-bearing for claiming a right and the narrow scope of consequence of each judicial decision have the same effect.

Clearly the problem with the preceding points are their lack of specificity, our inability to falsify them. That is why we include them under "approaches" and not hypotheses. They follow out of a view of the relationship between private interests and the state when there is a lawmaking body popularly elected from constituencies that are areal, not functional. We have viewed the location of policy-making as following, at least in part, from the resources politicians and parties need to succeed in their arena game. Hence, the effective areal level at which candidate selection occurs is important. What interests want is surprisingly common across such states. Roughly put, each would like (1) market power, (2) reduction of the risks attendant to the actions of the market, other interests, or the state, and the externalization of costs (particularly of the manner in which 1 and 2 are obtained) beyond themselves and, in some cases, beyond the consumers of their goods and services. At the same time, they would prefer all this to interfere with the private or bureaucratic discretion in the allocation of productive resources, services, and remuneration where possible.[4]

The public institutions through which they must operate vary across countries, depending in part on where they started. This was determined in part by the sort of institutions that would facilitate the needs of those interests organized at the time institutions began or changed (see the powers of Congress, article one, section 7,8 of the U.S. Constitution for an example), the introduction of new interests with different specific needs, and beliefs that placed limits on the character of institutions (the representative character of legislatures as contrasted to particular representational formulae). With thought and data, we would hope to pose more readily testable hypotheses relating interests and institutions to policies, and even about the internal organization of institutions themselves. About the latter, we already have a few which follow naturally out of this approach. Similarly, we have a few testable hypotheses in the area of parties, party systems, coalitions, electoral laws, and the structure of bureaus as they relate to changes in policies (like Lowi). All these will be the subject of other work, however. There and here, the value of an approach to the comparative study of politics or policy is determined, in the end, by the readily testable hypotheses that follow from it. In such testing, relevant data rather than verbal forensics must be the arbiter.

NOTES

1. Public policy is used as a chapter heading word. It is any policy, whether directly involving the state or political subunits or not, behind which the coercive sanctions of the state lie. Hence the actions of county medical associations in the U.S. are often public policies. Any such policy can have many aspects, only some of which we may be able to explain or predict.

2. Another way of saying this is that the hypothesis must support a hypothetical or counterfactual subjunctive. See Carl Hempel, 1965.

3. It is claimed (Thom, 1974) that catastrophe theory—a corner of applied typology—can be used for these cases. This claim is erroneous; in fact catastophe theory is closer to the pictorial qualities of an Eastonian system than to those of a set of structural equations. See E. W. Kelley, 1977.

4. We are implicitly saying that some of our hypotheses and approaches in general are not altered when interests and/or the producers of goods or services are brought within the bureaucracy of the state. The mechanics for influencing government, particularly funding levels, change, but the intent and consequences of doing so do not, with one principle exception. Usually greater economic inefficiency in the allocation of all factors of production or service is introduced; for this is traded greater control (equity) in the level and distribution of the good or service and its greater use as a resource to those in politics. Hence, Schumpeter's view that the introduction of nominal state socialism alters the relation between interests, citizens, and government is not the case in any fundamental sense.

REFERENCES

ANDERSON, J. E. (1962). The emergence of the modern regulatory state. Washington, D.C.: Public Affairs Press.

BENSEL, R. (1977). Reciprocal behavior and rules in the House of Representatives. Ph.D. dissertation, Cornell University.

EASTON, D. (1953). The political system. New York: Knopf.

EDELMAN, M. (1964). The symbolic uses of politics. Urbana: University of Illinois Press.

HAMLIN, S. (1930). The menace of overpopulation. New York: John Wiley.

HEMPEL, C. G. (ed., 1965). Aspects of scientific explanation. New York: Free Press.

HOFFERBERT, R. (1966). "Public policy and structural and environmental variables." American Political Science Review, (March).

KELLEY, E. W. (1972). "The methodology of hypothesis testing." Unpublished manuscript.

--- (1977). "Problems in policy analysis." Revised paper delivered to the annual meetings of AAAS, Denver.

--- (forthcoming). Doing political science.

KOONTZ, H., and GABLE, R. W. (1956). Public control of economic enterprise. New York: McGraw-Hill.

LOWI, T. J. (1965). "Review of Bauer, Pool, Dexter 'American business and public policy.' " World Politics.

MacLENNAN, M. et al. (1968). Economic planning and policies in Britain, France and Germany. New York: Praeger.

MAYHEW, D. (1976). Congress. New Haven, Conn.: Yale University Press.

PARSONS, T. (1949). The structure of social action. New York: Glencoe.

PERNA, F. (1975). "The politics of the NIRA." Unpublished manuscript.

SANDBURG, L. G. (1965). "Antitrust policy in Sweden." Antitrust Bulletin, pp. 535-558.

SHARKANSKY, I. (1968). "Economic development, regionalism and state political systems." Midwest Journal of Political Science, (February):41-61.

THOM, R. (1974). Structural stability and morphogenesis. Reading, Mass.: W. A. Benjamin.

PART IV

POLICY AS THE DETERMINANT OF POLITICS

8

COMPARING SOCIAL POLICY ACROSS LEVELS OF GOVERNMENT, COUNTRIES, AND TIME: BELGIUM AND SWEDEN SINCE 1870

MARTIN O. HEISLER

University of Maryland

B. GUY PETERS

University of Delaware

Even a cursory glance at the formation, implementation, and consequences of social policies in advanced industrial Western democracies is likely to reveal some serious problems. Policy formulation is not always consistent with the basic criteria of legitimacy operating in the regime. Such policies are very costly—increasingly and perhaps unsupportably so. They often do not yield the results initially expected of them; and they are difficult or impossible to control or

AUTHORS' NOTE: *Earlier drafts of this paper were presented at the 1976 Annual Meeting of the American Political Science Association, Chicago, Illinois, and at the First Annual Meeting of the Social Science History Association, October, 1976, Philadelphia, Pennsylvania. The authors gratefully acknowledge the critical comments and constructive suggestions of Professors Carolyn T. Adams, Douglas E. Ashford and James W. Bjorkman on the earlier drafts. Heisler wishes to thank the General Research Board and the Computer Science Center at the University of Maryland for support in the collection and analysis of the Belgian data and, for research assistance, Paul Robinson. Peters acknowledges the support of the Ford Foundation for financial assistance in the collection of the Swedish data.*

redirect through the political means that had been used to launch them.

This situation is distressing for several reasons. First, the citizens of these democratic welfare states are paying more and more for results that satisfy them less and less. Neither the mounting costs nor the erosion of citizen satisfaction can be borne indefinitely. In some countries, imminent public insolvency and/or citizen disaffection are sufficiently serious to jeopardize the regime's legitimacy. Second, virtually no one–not citizens, not students of politics and public policy, nor, for that matter, policymakers–can see what constructive steps might be taken to manage these increasingly exacerbated problems.

These problems and the realization that the conceptual and theoretical approaches currently in evidence do not hold much promise for identifying and controlling the relationships between politics and social policy led to the work adumbrated in this paper. Our aims are, first, to transcend the unidimensional and rather static qualities of the major approaches currently used for the consideration of such relationships, and, second, to consider the relative importance, form, and locus of politics in the structures and processes of social policy formation and implementation. A multidimensional, dynamic framework is proposed, one that permits more nuanced analyses–perhaps more nuanced than available data will allow in the near future. This is followed by the presentation and analysis of illustrative data on the relationships between politics and social policy at the national and municipal levels in Belgium and Sweden–two countries typical of a class of advanced industrial societies in many respects.

I. POLITICS AND SOCIAL POLICY: CURRENT WORK AND SOME OF ITS LIMITATIONS

During the past 10 to 15 years, students of industrialized Western democracies have been confronted by three important bodies of work, each advancing the argument that politics has become relatively unimportant in the formation of public policies and the determination of policy outcomes. At the national level, this position has been articulated through both verbal theory and propositions based upon quantitative analyses. At the level of local and intermediate governments, most of the work has been based on sophisticated analyses of quantified data.

Much of this work followed from the belief that policy formulation in advanced industrial societies had been freed from the ideological conflicts that characterized it in the late 19th century and the first half of the 20th. In this view, policy was made increasingly through technical, routinized processes rather than through the partisan political clashes that had been so important in the earlier period. With the institutionalization of the welfare state and the erosion of programmatic opposition to it, or so the "decline of ideology" writers argued, the period since the end of World War II has been relatively free of political conflict over major social policy questions (Bell, 1960; Myrdal, 1960; Rejai, 1971). Viewed in this light, the "decline of ideology" or "depoliticization" thesis is tantamount to saying that conflicts between socioeconomic class based parties are no longer salient in the politics of advanced industrial societies.

This limited view of "depoliticization" is in fact supported by many inquiries into the influences that shape policy, especially at the national level (Peters, 1974; Peters and Hennessey, 1975; Jackman, 1975; Peters et al., 1977). But it can be quite misleading if it is not carefully specified and qualified. In fact, the evidence and hindsight now at our disposal indicate that where "depoliticization" was manifested, it meant fewer and less intense ideological clashes on social and the economic issues in legislatures; but it did not necessarily signal the end of the importance of socioeconomic classes in the entire domain of public policy (LaPalombara, 1966; Westergaard and Resler, 1975.).

Class distinctions may remain important in the allocation of material goods and burdens, as well as status, and in the way in which various social policies are implemented. Further, public reactions to differential allocations may also reflect class distinctions, even in systems in which the clash of class-based parties is no longer a major factor in shaping policy decisions in parliament or cabinet. Rather, as the data and analyses presented below show, *the relative importance and significance of these and similar political processes associated with policy formation vary with the polity's developmental stage and the level of government at which politics and policy come into play.* [1]

At about the same time that the "decline of ideology" thesis was first advanced, several social scientists sought to identify relationships between political and socioeconomic conditions through empirical analysis. While strong indications of coincidence between high levels of development and democratic politics were found, causal relationships have proved much more elusive. And later studies of the linkage between policy outputs and political variables at the national level have tended to conclude that, again, the factor accounting for most of the variation is socioeconomic development and not politics.

In brief, we see a direct relationship between the historic mobilization of large segments of populations and the politicization of particular socioeconomic and political issues on the one hand and the subsequent adoption of redistributive policies that benefit the newly mobilized groups. This phase, termed the "transitional stage" by Peters (1972:278), has generally involved the substantial broadening of the franchise, the organization of workers, and the politicization of such social policy issues as workmen's compensation insurance, the extension of educational opportunities to the children of classes previously excluded from schooling, and so on. In the next section some of these processes and structural shifts are discussed, with illustrations from Belgium and Sweden.

Following from the political upheaval of the transitional stage, the "modern" or "postindustrial" stage is characterized by a broad consensus on social policy goals and there are widely extended opportunities for political participation (Myrdal, 1960:72, 77; Heisler and Kvavik, 1974:38-63). This stage coincides with the decline of ideology. Political variables take a backseat to socioeconomic or simply economic variables in shaping social policy outputs (cf. Jackman, 1975). Alternatively, political variables may play important roles in the policy process, but different roles or in different arenas.

A substantial body of analytic literature has developed dealing with the relationships of politics and policy outputs at the national level, but the best known literature of this genre is based on data from intermediate and local levels of government. An extensive discussion of that literature will not be provided (since that task has been performed by others so well), but, some of the findings reported in it—indicating that both politics and policy are dependent on socioeconomic resources—will be noted.

THREE MODELS IN SEARCH OF A THEORY

These shifts in the role of partisan politics suggest three simple models; and, in fact, much of the literature in public policy studies fits into these models. The models can be identified in terms of the factor each advances as the likely explanatory variable(s) for variations in the dependent variables (operationalized as expenditures–outputs–and as performance or impacts–outcomes): (1) (partisan) *politics*; (2) *needs* or environmental and demographic loads; and (3) economic circumstances or available *resources*. Most writers acknowledge overlaps across two or all three of the models. That is, social policy is generally seen as the product of some combination of political, "needs," and "resources" factors. However, it is probably fair to say that to date the theories of students of social policy formulation have accorded a pivotal position to one or another of the three forces.

First, the political model posits an influence or explanatory power of political variables–in the form of inputs or structural features on policy outputs and, in the work of a few scholars, on policy outcomes (Fried, 1975:307ff.). Thus, following this model, one might hypothesize that the rise of left-of-center parties in a political system would tend to be followed by redistributive income policies; or, it might be suggested that political stability or political violence affect social policy outputs or outcomes in predictable and theoretically meaningful ways (e.g., Lipset, 1959; Cutright, 1963; but cf. Jackman, 1975: chap. 5). Still in this vein, in the late 1950s and through the 1960s, a number of writers suggested that there was a strong and probably causal association between political democracy on the one hand and socioeconomic democracy–egalitarian distributions of income and wealth (see the writers cited immediately above).

It is probably indicative of the relatively weak position of this model, particularly among students of local level policy outputs, that it is often advanced in defensive tones. Thus, in a recent study of policy outputs in nearly 200 Belgian municipalities, the authors present their main conclusion in the following terms:

> At minimum . . . these results suggest that political factors should not be dismissed. We conclude that it may be a bit premature to sound the death knell of the impact of the political process on public policy. [Aiken and Depré, 1974:24. See also Fried, 1976; Fry and Winters, 1970.]

Second, the "needs" model has received a considerable amount of play, particularly from students of local or urban policy (Sharkansky, 1971; Alford, 1969; Boaden, 1971). It posits a direct relationship between demographic and ecological pressures or "needs," broadly conceived, and the magnitude of policy outputs in the issue or functional areas associated with the needs. Policy outputs are seen as almost automatic—rather than directly politically chosen, specific—responses to the objective needs confronted by the system. For, if outputs are directly tied to the levels of needs, then policy responses might not require specific allocative decisions in each instance. It might be the case that some political choices in the past have institutionalized a "formula" policy response on the basis of levels or indices of needs. (Thus, for instance, it might be argued that the size of the school-age population is the most powerful predictor of educational expenditures.)

The needs model would seem to follow the political, if these two patterns of policy formulation are considered through a developmental logic. For, a part of many "decline of ideology" or "depoliticization" arguments is the notion that once ideologically motivated political clashes cease to be a significant feature of policymaking, outputs can be produced through previously routinized procedures. The agreement on the values underlying such policymaking procedures is likely to be the product of political conflicts, of course; and it can be eroded by such changing circumstances as economic decline or the rise of new political forces.[2]

Finally, the "resources" model posits a direct relationship between the relative level of socioeconomic resources and levels of expenditures. Like the "needs" model and unlike that focusing on politics, the resources model also entails an essentially mechanistic notion, arguing that governments that command greater resources are more likely to spend greater amounts (and perhaps also greater proportions) on social policy. Taken to a broader level, this model leads to the hypothesis that richer or economically more developed societies will develop more extensive social programs.[3] Perhaps the most outspoken advocate of this model has been Thomas Dye (1966).

During the past decade much of the effort in empirical policy studies at both the national and the local levels has been devoted to advancing the case of one or another of these models in competition with the others. A particularly vigorous debate has been engaged in local policy output studies between those who see economic or "needs" variables as the major influences on expenditures and those who argue that political variables are more important.[4] While in the early stages of empirical exploration and the pursuit of theoretical points of departure this dialogue may have been justified, the continuation of the debate does not seem worthwhile.

TOWARD A COMPREHENSIVE FRAMEWORK

Were the fundamental hypotheses indwelling any or each of these models validated, it is difficult to see what the net theoretical gain would be. Political allocations are made on the basis of estimates of resources and needs; and, consequently, were the political model to be supported by research findings, it would not show much more than a particular value or priority schedule superimposed on estimates of resources and needs. Indeed, the identification of needs and the marshalling of resources—in the context of any of the models—is substantially a value-determined process. Thus, situations in which levels of needs or resources seem to explain policy outputs better than political variables do (e.g., in Belgium and Sweden in the post-World War II period at the national level) may be showing nothing more than the outcomes of earlier political balances. (This possibility is perhaps the strongest argument in favor of incorporating a cross-time or developmental dimension in policy analysis.)

Instead of pitting these models against each other, it seems more constructive to ascertain their utilities and limitations in the context of coherent theoretical frameworks. Thus, in seeking to understand the dynamics of public policy, it may prove helpful to know under what circumstances the relative importance of certain political variables in shaping policy outputs and outcomes has risen or fallen. The importance may vary by time, level of government, political system, and policy area.

The compelling argument in favor of such analyses is that existing public policy models tend to be rather simple, unidimensional and static, while the processes and structures involved in policymaking are very complex and dynamic. Thus, attempts to identify the "key" variables or "the best" model in a universalistic quest for general theory seem less useful at this time than the establishment of conditional relationships (Fried, 1975:320). Surprisingly, until recently, relatively few students of policy outputs have sought more complex, multidimensional models. Alford (1969) and Boaden (1971) suggested that needs, resources, and political commitments ("dispositions to act") were all instrumental in shaping policies at the local level. But even they did not fully integrate into their more complex framework two of the dimensions we deem crucial: time and multiple levels of government.

Most comparative studies of policy outputs and outcomes are cross-sectional (Fried, 1975:330), and, consequently, they do not contribute much to our understanding of the processes of change. Most comparative studies of policy outputs and outcomes are restricted to one level of government, although only a foolhardy student of policy at any level would assume that other levels can be held constant for any significant substantive or theoretical purpose. What is called for is not an all-encompassing design (since that would probably render multi-case studies unmanageable and unwieldy), but, rather, a design that keeps before the investigator more interested in one level the intervening or contextual potentials of other levels, and a design that permits the pursuit of both empirical and theoretical possibilities across levels.

Since in public policy studies as well as in most of the cognate disciplines, cross-national comparison is now widely regarded as essentially another facet of systematic social scientific inquiry (Lijphart, 1971), it seems unnecessary to stress the need for introducing this dimension into the study of social policy.[5] Nor does it seem necessary to enter a plea for a fourth dimension of comparative policy analysis—comparison across issue or policy areas. Recent literature, indicates that this dimension is likely to be covered even more in the future than it has been to date (Rose, 1973; Heidenheimer, Heclo, and Adams, 1975).

It is feasible to develop relatively broad, integrated frameworks—frameworks that will help to discern the relative importance of political and other influences on social policy at different levels of government, in different developmental phases within advanced industrial societies. Concomitantly, the different forms taken by social policies and the political consequences of the operations of such policies over time can be identified. In this way, we should become more adept at identifying the import of politics for social policy in particular settings; and we should also become more sensitive to the varied and often indirect political responses triggered by operating social policies.

Finally, it seems necessary to remind students of public policy that policy outputs and outcomes are quite different things and that the influences shaping the former do not necessarily have commensurate importance for determining the latter. Converting laws, rules, decisions, regulations, and even authorized expenditures or budget items into consequences for or impacts upon the society or any other targets of policy (e.g., the environment, another polity, etc.) is neither a routine process nor one free of politics (see, for instance, Heisler and Kvavik, 1974; Peters, 1977). Indeed, one of the interesting developments over time in the role of politics in public policy in countries like Belgium and Sweden (advanced, highly industrialized societies) is that it seems to have moved from the portion of the system in which inputs were converted into outputs to the segment where outputs are being converted into outcomes. Put into simpler terms, the decline of ideology in partisan, legislative politics may have been followed by the rise of politics in the implementation of policies—administration.

Sketching a comprehensive framework and translating it into an operational or testable model are two different things. Thus, at a highly abstract level, it is both desirable and possible to ask for designs of policy studies to include time-series analyses that permit developmental insights, the estimation of rates, and directions of change, etc.; to test the relative explanatory power of a variety of independent variables, and to analyze these through cross-lagging with the dependent variables; to compare policy formulation, outputs and outcomes in several countries, at more than one level of policymaking, and for several issue areas; and so on. In practice, researchers are not likely to have the resources—funds, time, human skills, or, for that matter, extant or obtainable data—to undertake such a study. Minimally, what is necessary is a conscious, active concern with the cross-time, cross-level and cross-national dimensions of policy analysis; and, as several writers have recently reminded us, it is useful to compare across policy areas as well.

At present, only some aspects of social policy in Belgium and Sweden and Brussels and Stockholm can be analyzed with data. A broad developmental hypothesis has been tested through the systematic analysis of quantitative input, output, and some performance data at the national level for the two countries for the past century. Some of these findings, as well as analyses for Brussels and Stockholm for the period since World War II are presented below.

It is not yet possible to demonstrate any dynamic links between the national and local levels of policy development, but this gap can be filled within a short time with fairly straightforward analyses of data already in hand. A much more difficult problem is presented by the need to provide a positive analysis of the policymaking process and policy outputs at the national level. For, while it is possible to demonstrate the null hypothesis that political variables do not explain a significant proportion of the variance in redistributive policy outputs at that level, data for testing the hypothesis that those outputs are currently produced by regulatory and self-regulatory means are not likely to be available in the near future. This is because these await measures of administrative outputs; and the operational indicators for those are proving very elusive.

The next two sections of the paper present in summary form findings on the influences that shape social policy at the national level in Belgium, Sweden, and their capitals. In order to maintain conceptual and theoretical contact with the existing literature in the field, the discussion is presented in terms of the familiar constructs of policy output types introduced by Lowi (1964) and refined by Salisbury (1968) and Salisbury and Heinz (1970) and in terms of the three putative explanatory models of policy—"politics," "resources," and "needs"—reviewed above.

II. STRUCTURES OF SOCIAL POLICY OUTPUTS IN BELGIUM AND SWEDEN

Social policy processes and structures in Western European countries in general and in systems like Belgium and Sweden in particular exhibited clear-cut patterns of massive redistribution during a very long and important period in their modern histories. Redistributive demands, the advent of mass parties, and widespread electoral participation and unionization were concurrent with the development of massive bureaucracies designed to implement central policies, to channel information to the central policymaking subsystem and to assess the impacts of redistributive policies.

This period also coincided with the expansion of resources and increased demographic and environmental loads. Thus, it is difficult to make a clear-cut case for any one of the three models from a simple overview of the data. Nevertheless, both formal and informal

Table 1. MOBILIZATION IN BELGIUM AND SWEDEN

Belgium				*Sweden*			
Year	*Population (000)*	*Eligible Voters (000)*	*Union Rate (%)*	*Year*	*Population (000)*	*Eligible Voters (000)*	*Union Rate (%)*
1870	5,031	79	1.0	1870	4,164	201	0
1913	7,530	1,746	19.0	1905	5,278	432	6.0
1919	7,600	1,989	30.0				
1947	8,512	2,620*	58.0	1936	6,259	3,925	28.0
1974	9,710	6,322*	70.0	1974	8,144	5,557	84.0

*Women were enfranchised in 1949.

Table 2. RESOURCES AND STRUCTURAL CAPABILITIES

Belgium			Sweden		
Year	NI/Capita*	Civil Servants (/1,000 pop.)	Year	GNP/Capita**	Civil Servants (/1,000 pop.)
1870	274	3.5	1870	172	5.2
1913	863	7.0	1905	394	9.9
1919	NA	8.6			
1947	25,611	14.2	1936	1,096	20.1
1974	222,063	26.7	1974	26,113	36.7

*In current Belgian francs. (In order to retain consistency of data over time, the values reported approximate national income/capita more closely than GNP/capita.)
**In current Swedish kr.

analyses yield the impression that, from the mid-19th century to the mid-20th, both the Belgian and the Swedish systems passed through three distinct phases of social policy formation. Peters has discussed this pattern of development in numerous works (listed in the References); and Heisler has indicated a parallel development in Belgium, as traced through its cleavage structure (Heisler, 1974a).

THREE PATTERNS IN POLICY FORMATION: A SET OF DEVELOPMENTAL HYPOTHESES

Since the middle of the 19th century, three relatively distinct phases can be identified in the development of social policies at the national level: (1) a traditional phase, lasting from 1865 to 1906 in Sweden and from the 1840s until the first or second decade of the 20th century in Belgium; (2) a transitional stage, from about 1907 to 1935 in Sweden and from the first World War to the second in Belgium; and (3) a modern stage, from the closing dates of the transitional period to the present. Before proceeding to the analysis of our data, it seems worthwhile to present brief developmental sketches of the countries under examination.

The traditional phase was characterized by small public sectors and low levels of mobilization. The level of resources (measured by GNP or surrogate indicators)[6] was the best predictor of outputs at the national level in such social policy areas as education, welfare, health, pensions, and labor benefits.

In both Belgium and Sweden, the last years of the 19th century were characterized by massive social, political, and economic change. A rapidly mobilizing population was already beginning to articulate its needs. Equally significant was the structural impact of mobilization in this period: unions and working-class mass parties were created and rose within a generation to important positions in the political system. Thus, even though these organizations were not yet in positions of formal authority in the second phase (which terminated approximately 10 years earlier in Sweden than in Belgium), they represented a sufficiently important constituency to push the much more conservative governing parties toward the implementation of social policies that were most directly in the interests of the lower-middle and working classes.

During the transitional period such political variables as unionization and the strength of parties of the left (the Socialists or Social Democrats) and such political structural variables as the size of the civil service were the most powerful predictors of social policy outputs. In both countries, the political party and labor organization variables were indicative of the dominant role that had been assumed by the central government in the first decades of the 20th century. The expansion of the civil service and of the share of the growing wealth commanded by the central government are indications of this importance. This was the period in which the modal response to newly raised or dramatized social issues was the extension of the public sector to subsume those issue areas under new central government programs.

The demands addressed to the central government involved the redistribution of status and goods, as had been the case in the last decades of the traditional stage. However, while in the earlier period some of the most important demands made of the government could be managed through redistributions of status—e.g., the right to vote, the right to organize for collective bargaining—the demands most important in the second stage involved redistribution of income and wealth. They were characterized by demands for large-scale and costly services, such as the expansion of educational opportunities and social insurance.

It is significant for an understanding of the relative distribution of public tasks between central and municipal governments in the type of system under discussion that during the crucial transitional phase—and particularly between the two world wars—the types of demands to which the central governments had to respond were most appropriately or only addressed to it rather than to intermediate or local governments. Large-scale, programmatic redistribution was best undertaken at the most comprehensive level, because the tapping of higher incomes and greater wealth that was necessary if the redistributive goals were to be achieved was most efficiently accomplished at and by the level of government with the most extensive domain. Disparities of wealth and income tended to be lower within municipal or provincial domains than at the national level; and, consequently, both the opportunities and the support for such redistribution were focused at that level. The parallel expansion of the scope and functions of the central authority, the civil service, and the central government's share of the national income established a pattern of response and channelled expectations to the capital.

The modern phase has been treated elsewhere in these terms (see, for instance, Heisler and Kvavik, 1974; Heisler, 1974a; Peters, 1974). It is not necessary, therefore, to delve into it here. Briefly, it has often been characterized as a period of relatively low ideological intensity in which the broadly—perhaps even consensually—based welfare state allocates public resources on the basis of "objective needs," produces satisficing outcomes within the limits of its resources and often operates through logrolling.

Except for the difference in its beginning dates, the modern stage has been remarkably similar in the two countries. If the "resources" model is the most accurate reflection of the first, traditional stage and the "politics" model best captures the transitional phase, then the "needs" and "resources" models most effectively characterize the current, modern period at the national level. Politics, understood in terms of such conventionally used indicators as the strength of parties of the left, coalition composition, and the coalition's share of parliamentary seats, seems to make little or no difference for expenditures in most social policy areas we investigated.

TESTS AT THE NATIONAL LEVEL

On the basis of these summary sketches, which can be used as informal hypotheses, it is now possible to turn to our illustrative data. Nation-level aggregate, time-series data were analyzed for the two countries for the period 1870-1974. The time-series were broken into three periods, corresponding to the three developmental stages identified above for each country. Regressions were run for each country. In each case sectoral expenditures for a major social policy function—education, health, welfare—constituted the dependent variable, and tests were conducted for the predictive power of independent variables that represented "political," "resources," and "needs" influences.[7]

Table 3. EXPLANATIONS OF SECTORAL SPENDING–NATIONAL LEVEL (correlation coefficients)

	Sweden				
	Political		*Resources*	*Needs*	
	Left-Voting	*Civil Service*	*GNP*	*Age*[a]	*Unemployment*
First Period (1870-1905)					
Education	.03	.22*	.41*	.22*	–
Health	.10	.17	.37*	.11	–
Welfare	.09	.19	.50*	.08	.13
Second Period (1906-1935)					
Education	.33*	.59*	–.26*	.19	–
Health	.61*	.50*	.04	.02	–
Welfare	.44*	.72*	–.06	.11	.61*
Third Period (1936-1974)					
Education	.02	.56*	.62*	.52*	–
Health	.04	–.06	–.08	.09	–
Welfare	.05	–.03	–.28	.30*	.019
	Belgium				
	Left Seats				
First Period (1870-1913)					
Education	–.11	–.07	.40*	–.06*	
Health	.34*	–.32*	–.36*	–.20*	
Welfare	NA	NA	NA	NA	
Second Period (1919-1946)					
Education	.28*	–.83*	–.76*	.71*	–
Health	.36*	–.13	–.17	.00	–
Welfare	.02	–.06	–.01	.04	–.13
Third Period (1947-1974)					
Education	–.39*	.17	.83*	.95*	–
Health	–.28*	.21*	.19	.33*	–
Welfare	.45*	–.23*	–.61*	–.76*	.08

a. For education, population aged 5-14; for health and welfare, population 65+.
*Correlation significant at .05 level.

The level of central government expenditures in the traditional stage was most strongly predicted by the level of available resources (GNP for Sweden, energy consumption for Belgium) for all three policy areas examined in Sweden and for one of the two for which data were available in Belgium. A closer examination of the correlation coefficients for the traditional period shows that the Swedish case provides very strong support for the proposition that the level of resources was a more important influence than electoral politics on social policy outputs.

The findings for education expenditures in Belgium in the traditional phase also show the primacy of the level of resources available in the system; but there is a marked divergence from the prediction with regard to health expenditures. Here the political variable is the only one positively associated with the dependent variable; and there is a significant negative relationship between the resource indicator and expenditures by the central government for public health and hygiene. There is no satisfactory theoretical explanation for this finding. It may be an artifact either of the nature of the Belgian health expenditure data for this early period (representing such sanitation activities as sewer construction, road and field drainage, etc.), or of the heavy concentration of responsibility for health at the local level, or possibly the coding of parties for the first half of the "traditional" period when the moderately conservative Catholic Party occupied the "left" segment of the political spectrum on socioeconomic issues. Most likely, the disappointing findings come from some combination of these.

Our hypothesis posits the primacy of political factors in determining levels of social policy outputs in the transitional period; this is indeed the finding for both countries—again, more unambiguously for Sweden than for Belgium. The growing strength of the socialist parties and, in Sweden, the increasing size and influence of the civil service substantially explain the increases in central government expenditures for the social policy areas examined. Welfare expenditures are not effectively traceable through Belgium's central government budget. This may explain the weakness of all of the relationships tested for this dependent variable in this period. It can be seen in Table 2 that the Belgian civil service grew less rapidly and was appreciably smaller in this period than its Swedish counterpart. This may account for the absence of positive relationships between that political structural variable and the policy outputs investigated for the transitional phase.

For the modern period, the level of central government spending for education in Sweden is most strongly predicted by the Gross National Product; the second independent variable to enter the regression was the number of school-age children in the population—an indication of needs to be satisfied. The "resources" and "needs" variables were substantially more significant predictors of educational expenditures than were the political variables. The national government's expenditures for health were not influenced significantly by any of the variables with which they were tested, perhaps because of their intimate connection with *lan* activity. Finally, central governmental expenditures for welfare in Sweden showed the influence of the "needs" variable—in this case, the population over age 65—and the share of the votes received by parties of the left did not explain an appreciable part of the variance.

For Belgium, the findings for education and health outputs in the modern period strongly support the hypothesized positive relationship between "needs" and "resources" on the one hand and expenditure levels on the other. However, neither the strong negative relationship between parliamentary seats held by parties of the left and education and health outputs nor the even more anomalous findings for the welfare sector can be explained at this time.

While these findings do not provide complete validation of our general hypothesis concerning national level social policy outputs in the class of systems represented by Belgium and Sweden, they warrant optimism regarding continued investigation along these lines. As more cases and more direct indicators of both the independent and dependent variables are added to the data sets, it will be possible to test the hypothesis more fully and more rigorously. However, from the type of data accumulated to date, it is difficult or impossible to address an interesting and important question regarding the role of politics in the shaping of social policies at the national level in advanced industrial societies. This is the problem of the absence of direct measures of politics in administration.

In a number of places above it was suggested that one of the most important arenas for political activity in modern or advanced industrial societies is the "output side" of the political system: the politics of converting outputs into outcomes. Particularly where outputs take the form of regulatory policies—and they often do in Belgium and Sweden—such political activity may have significant consequences for the ultimate allocation of benefits and burdens, for differential access to public goods, and for the opportunity to influence policy application and evaluation. In the absence of indications that traditionally conceptualized political influence plays an important part in policymaking, it is reasonable to hypothesize that different forms of political influence might be at play in other segments of the political system. Regrettably, this hypothesis is not directly testable at this time.

III. POLITICS AND SOCIAL POLICY AT THE LOCAL LEVEL

An alternative hypothesis for locating the political in the modern period is that at least some of the classic style political activity has shifted to the municipal level in at least some advanced industrial societies. A part of this argument has already been presented. During the lengthy period in which major redistributive policies were generated, people shifted their expectations to the central government. This kept loads on local governments relatively low. The types of demands directed toward the central government were, as noted, more effectively managed through central policymaking and relatively centralized administration. Demands and expectations involving the local setting–e.g., housing, street paving and maintenance, proximate medical care facilities, and the like–rose to the fore only after the demands for the involvement of the central government in vast areas of what had previously been the private sector had received response and had moved toward institutionalization.

If politics, here conceptualized as mass political behavior and as partisan control of various decision-making institutions, is ceasing to have a crucial impact in determining national policies, this does not appear to be true for subnational governments, especially when viewed from a longitudinal perspective. A good deal of evidence coming from studies of the American states, as well as from other subnational governments, might seem to contradict this statement (Dye, 1966; Sharkansky, 1971).[8] However, these findings, as important as they are, are greatly weakened by their cross-sectional nature. In a developmental perspective, significant consequences can be expected from changes in political composition and behavior within a subnational political unit on the priorities of spending and on the implementation of those priorities.

Perhaps the most important difference between the national and subnational levels of government indicative of the differences in their current politics is the differential rate at which public expenditures have increased. While national expenditures seem at once both stimulated and constrained by the growth of needs and resources, and consequently have increased steadily if not especially rapidly during recent years, local expenditures have climbed at very steep rates. For example, while national expenditures in Sweden have increased from 23% to 29% of GNP, subnational spending has risen from 13% to 33% of GNP. This differential rate of spending has not been so dramatic in Belgium, but it is also evident there. These simple facts would appear to indicate that, while policymaking at the national level is restrained both by the greater awareness of socioeconomic trends and by routines of politics forcing out incremental expenditure growth, local expenditure patterns are more responsive to conscious political choices to spend more money.

Why should it be that local politics should be more subject to political influences? The same forces of "postindustrialism" that have affected national politics might be expected to be just as strong at the subnational level, so that the same sort of declining impact of partisan politics on policy might be expected there as well.

The first crucial difference between the levels of government is the tasks they are usually assigned. Much of what local governments do is the provision of services that might be classified as distributive, i.e., they provide goods that are highly divisible among individuals and geographic areas and can be handed out differentially to various groups. Likewise, they are frequently involved in the implementation of programs developed at the national level, and they must often convert broad policies into specific actions and into effects on individuals (Pressman and Wildavsky, 1974). This necessity of local governments to differentiate among individuals, groups and neighborhoods makes them more susceptible to political pressures than national level decision makers tend to be. There are always individuals affected, and, therefore, individuals have direct, personal reasons to organize politically and to try to bring pressure to bear on the local politicians and administrators. Another way of saying this is that the roles of the individual as voter and as consumer of public goods and services are less separated at the local level than at the national.

This characteristic is especially important in light of a second aspect of local governments, which is, simply, that they are smaller and therefore they provide greater opportunities for both individual influence over policy and individual involvement in politics—independent of institutionalized political forces. The role of local notables is more pronounced in Belgium than in Sweden, but it is an important factor in local politics in almost all political systems. Local politics is frequently highly personalized, with the voter knowing the candidate personally.[9] In turn, the politician is also expected to react to the voter—or the seeker of services—personally. It is through the development of personal contacts and the use of personal patronage that much local politics is conducted. As a consequence, it is difficult for a local politician to claim impersonal forces, such as macroeconomic constraints, as reasons for not providing services or jobs.

Local government, then, is open to the types of political inputs that, at the national level, would be sorted out by political parties or pressure groups long before they could be taken up directly by policymakers. These types of inputs are difficult to quantify, but, inasmuch as different political parties are likely to have supporters who seek different types of benefits from government, the political composition of a local government can be expected to have bearing on policy outputs.

Another function of the smaller scale of local governments is that they are much more likely to be politically homogeneous than most national governments are, especially in the smaller European democracies, where central governments are customarily heterogeneous coalitions. Single party cabinets are quite common at the municipal level (Aiken and Depré, 1974:7).

Associated with the greater openness of local governments to political inputs is a relatively lower level of institutionalization of decision making at the local level. While there are certainly stable institutional bodies involved in making decisions on expenditures in all local governments, they generally lack the degree of development, professionalization, and insulation possessed by their national counterparts. Likewise, the legislative bodies that consider local expenditure decisions tend to have less adequate institutional apparatuses for policy advice; they are likely to be more transitory, and, therefore, to make decisions out of the mold of previous decisions. Further, as noted, they will be subject to political pressures that may be irresistible.

Finally, local governments do not face as heavy a decision-making load as national governments must handle. This is true not only because popular expectations for the good life have come to be focused on central governments, but also because of the threat of "politics" and political conflict to the regime in many national systems. Since most subnational governments are ethnically more homogeneous, potential conflicts are removed from the forefront of political relationships, and partisan differences can surface with less risk.

A major exception is Brussels. Its status as the national capital, its precarious constitutional position, artificially rigid boundaries between it and its natural suburbs, and its legally bilingual position all contribute to the likelihood that its political problems will spill over into the national arena (Heisler, 1974b; Heisler, forthcoming). Even in Sweden, which lacks the ethnic cleavage of Belgium, national politics can easily upset the balance of interests among various subnationally active economic groups, thereby upsetting the stability of local systems. Yet, in general, the risk of politics and political conflict is less at the local level, and one might, therefore, expect less depoliticization and more impact of politics on policy at that level.

This general assessment parallels the findings of the authors of the most thorough and detailed data-based study of policy outputs and outcomes in Belgian municipalities (Aiken and Depré, 1974). On the basis of a broad range of variables and with expenditure data drawn from 1965-1966 for nearly 200 cities (all those with populations of 10,000 or more), they found that patterns of expenditures

> imply . . . that past and present decision-makers in these cities–i.e., the mayor, aldermen, and other members of the city council–have evidently responded rationally to needs for . . . "basic" services, although politics still makes some difference in such choices. However, it is in decisions about public assistance; arts, popular education, and leisure; and public education that the form and content of the political structure seem to make the greatest difference. In other words, it is in certain more socially sensitive policy areas that the nature of the political process seems to have the greatest effect. [Aiken and Depré, 1974:22]

These characteristics of subnational government as compared to national government lead rather obviously to a conclusion that politics are more likely to make a difference at the local level. Consequently, one would not expect to find the lack of partisan political influence in shaping policy outputs that has come to characterize the national arena in modern times. Local politics can, on the contrary, be expected to remain a significant factor in determining policy outputs and of influencing the manner in which people live.

INFLUENCES ON LOCAL POLICY OUTPUTS: BRUSSELS AND STOCKHOLM IN THE POST-WORLD WAR II PERIOD

As the analysis in Part II above has shown, the "decline of ideology" and the decline of political impacts on policy arguments have some validity at the national level during the period since World War II. Indicators of the salience of political, "resources," and "needs" factors in explaining the levels of social policy expenditures in the capitals of Belgium and Sweden will be tested in this section, using time-series data for Stockholm for the years 1946 and 1972 and data for the 19 boroughs of Brussels, arranged in cross-sectional form with observations at five time-points between 1952 and 1972.

Given the preceding discussion of the differences between national and local governments and policy processes, the findings can be expected to differ noticeably from those obtained for the national level.

The analysis of the municipal data sets is complicated by several factors. First, it was not possible to collect fully comparable data for the two cities. Thus, some of the more direct indicators used for Stockholm are not available for Brussels, and in some cases it proved difficult to find good surrogate indicators. Second, Brussels consists of 19 largely autonomous boroughs, each with its own school system, police department, welfare and health programs, etc. Until 1974 it possessed virtually no metropolitan umbrella structures and fiscal mechanisms, and most municipal functions–including those indicated by our dependent variables–remain decentralized. Finally, both time-series analysis and the use of aggregates and means for Brussels pose some problems. The former has been managed by the use of sectoral expenditures as the dependent variables, so that the effects of time will be less proncunced than they would be with per capita measures. Also, for Stockholm, the findings were checked by using first-differences, which tends to remove the confounding effects of time in the analysis. The latter was checked through both cross-sectional and time-series (for as many as 14 time points for some variables) and was also found to be manageable.

The results of the tests of our hypotheses are presented in Table 4. Keeping in mind that they must be interpreted warily, since they are difficult to compare because of the differences in the composition of the cities and the possible intrusion of extraneous variance through time-series analysis, the results do appear to give some support to our hypothesis that there are more substantial relationships between political variables and social policy outputs at the local level than at the national in the period since World War II. These relationships hold for politics conceptualized as a mass behavior phenomenon–as reflected in electoral outcomes and cabinet composition–and when it is viewed in more institutional terms, through the indicator of the size of the municipal civil service, for instance.

The general finding that politics makes more of a difference in determining local policy outputs in the modern period than it does in shaping national level expenditures in the same policy areas needs to be refined and qualified before it can lead to useful theoretical insights. Thus, it is noteworthy that there are distinct patterns between the findings for health and education expenditures on the

Table 4. RELATIONSHIPS BETWEEN POLITICAL, RESOURCES, AND NEEDS INDICATORS AND SECTORAL SPENDING AT THE LOCAL LEVEL (correlation coefficients)

	Political		*Resources*	*Needs*		
Policy Area	*Cabinet Composition*[a]	*Civil Service*	*Median Income*	*Age Composition*[b]	*Total Population*	*Unemployment*
Stockholm 1946-1972[c]						
Welfare	.42*	.51*	.41*	.20	.31*	.61*
Health	.44*	.22	.61	.36*	.44*	.14
Public works	.61*	.67*	.26	–	.37*	.27
Education	.22	.20	.33*	.57*	.19	.11
Brussels, 1952-1972[d]						
Welfare	.37*		–.25	.34		
Health	–.08		–.03	–.07		
Public works	–.26		.34*	–		
Education	.01		–.26	.20		

a. Percent Socialists or Social Democrats in municipal government.
b. As in Table 3, for education, population aged 5-14; for health and welfare, population 65+.
c. Time-series analysis.
d. Means of five observations for 19 boroughs.
*Correlation significant at the .05 level.

one hand and public works and welfare on the other. The former are policy areas that have now reached the status—especially in Sweden—of virtually universal, guaranteed benefits. Thus, partisan political differences are less likely to yield substantially different levels of expenditures in these areas. While it is true that these functions are heavily subsidized and controlled from central and intermediate levels of government (except for health in Belgium), there remains considerable latitude for local decisions in setting patterns and levels of expenditures. This latitude, however, is apparently not exercised as a function of the political characteristics of the decision makers or the degree of local bureaucratic strength, but, rather, more as a function of the needs for the services and the availability of resources. It would appear that the manner in which these social policies are provided conforms to our earlier supposition regarding universalistic benefits for which expenditures are determined largely by nonpolitical forces but where politics may remain significant in the making of decisions not directly involving expenditure levels.

In contrast, welfare and public works expenditures show more significant relationships with political variables. It seems that expenditures and services that are not essentially universal, that can be disaggregated, are more likely to be strongly influenced by partisan politics. However, in Stockholm for welfare and in Brussels for public works, the levels of outputs in these policy areas are also affected significantly by available resources and needs. This is as one would expect in welfare states.

The measure of economic resources had more predictive power in Stockholm than in Brussels; and the strength of political variables was somewhat greater there as well than in the Belgian capital. These differences may be accounted for by the greater degree of institutionalization of Swedish parties at the local level and by the number of personalistic local governments in Brussels. In addition, the realignment of Belgian parties—particularly in Brussels—along ethnic and/or linguistic lines has substantially blurred classic "left-right" distinctions. In fact, it is interesting and somewhat surprising to note that time-series analyses for particular boroughs has shown substantial continuity with regard to the two policy areas deemed particularly sensitive to partisan politics: welfare and public works. In several boroughs with long-lived Socialist municipal governments welfare expenditures have remained very high and have responded to changes in the Socialists' fortunes. In others, a fairly consistent pattern emerges between the strength of conservative parties (particularly the pro-business classical Liberals) and expenditures for public works. Richer and more conservative boroughs consistently outspend their less affluent, more moderate neighbors, just as the latter spend much more on welfare.

SUMMARY

These findings, coupled with those reported earlier for the national level, provide some support for our assumptions concerning the evolution of social policy formation in advanced industrial societies. Politics does make a difference, but it does so more at the local level than at the national in the present phase of development, and more with respect to some policy areas than others. These findings, then, reinforce our conviction that it is necessary to locate policy processes within certain contexts of time and space in order to be able to make meaningful statements concerning the impacts of environmental conditions and internal structural characteristics on policy outputs.

IV. CONCLUSIONS

This paper has raised at least as many questions as it has answered. The ideas involving the extension of policy-focused studies across time and across systems are not in themselves particularly novel, but their relationship to other bodies of literature and to events in advanced industrial societies today makes the pleas for more detailed and multidimensional analyses more compelling than they might otherwise be. Our conclusions, instead of merely summarizing what has already been said, will add to the confusion that already exists by pointing out several additional lines of research that can be mapped—ideas that are in part derivative from the concerns voiced in this paper.

First, there is the question of the nature of redistributive politics in the advanced industrial societies of today. It seems that at the national level there is little political activity directed toward those ends. At the same time, it is apparent that a massive amount of political activity is occurring. It appears that the redistributive issues of today are of a different sort than those evident in the period in which the welfare state was created. They are frequently not class based now, but, instead, they seem to be based on regional or ascriptive alignments. This is true even in countries such as the United Kingdom, which had been regarded until recently as both ethnically homogeneous and as displaying class-based politics. These issues concern redistribution from producers to consumers, or from some to all. Some examples of issues of this type are consumer protection, conservation, and environmental protection. Further, although local politics seem viable even in mass democracies, there is a tendency toward nationalization of local politics. Many of the crucial issues of our time, such as those mentioned above, become more apparent in some localities than in others and are frequently the stimulus for local political activity. However, because of problems of financing and of spillovers, there is a need to shift the decisions to the national level. Also, the very tendency of local governments to spend money more rapidly than central governments means that central authorities have been forced to seek means for controlling public expenditures more effectively, and, as a consequence, they have been compelled to take local issues and politics into the national arena.

Finally, as was discussed in part in the body of this paper, there is a need to conceptualize more fully and to understand better the process of policy implementation as a fundamental *political* process. In a bureaucratic polity, this is of necessity one of the more important loci of political choice. It is, at the same time, the one which is least understood by most students of public policy. Likewise, it is the one which is least amenable to research, given tools presently available.

If we return to the idea of the "decline of ideology" where much of this discussion began, it would appear that ideology of one sort has declined, but the resurgence of another type—in fact, a number of different types—should be expected. The issues currently politicized in many advanced industrial societies are not essentially those of class-based divisions of goods and services. They are considerably more complex. They involve a number of cross-cutting allegiances and interests, so that politics tends to be less predictable and at times rather confusing. For example, labor unions and industrialists may find themselves allied in opposition to environmentalists seeking to close a plant that pollutes. Similarly, many social issues—such as abortion—often cut across stable political groups organized around "old" ideological questions. Our task, then, is not only to keep track of the sides, but also to develop some theoretical and analytical means for dealing with the changes in political issues and with the changes in politics.

NOTES

1. The specific policy or issue area may also be a crucial dimension for comparative analysis. While it is touched upon in the reports of our findings, below, it is not developed in this paper. (For a good treatment, see Heidenheimer, Heclo, and Adams, 1975.)

2. A decline in one form of political activity relative to policy does not necessarily signal a net decline in the politics of policy, as some of the discussion below shows.

3. In a recent study based on cross-sectional data for 60 countries, it was strongly suggested that while the overall level of economic development was the best predictor of social equality, the relationship is curvilinear: the richest countries begin to exhibit a drop-off in socioeconomic equality (Jackman, 1975.)

4. Dawson and Robinson (1963) and Dye (1966) can be identified as the principal champions of the "economic primacy" school. But for a large number of scholars (e.g., Sharkansky, 1967; Lineberry and Fowler, 1967; Clark, 1968; Aiken and Alford, 1970; Fry and Winters, 1970) political variables remain crucial. For a general review of the local level policy literature, see Fried (1975).

5. A case for cross-level comparison in cross-national comparative studies can be found in Przeworski and Teune (1970).

6. For the traditional period, only sporadic national income estimates exist for Belgium. (No gross national product data are available at this time for the 19th century.) Consequently, a surrogate indicator—the consumption of energy in the form of coal—was used. In Belgium in later periods as well as in those countries for which both national income and

energy consumption data are available the correlation of energy consumption and national income is uniformly high. For Belgium during the period 1913-1960, for instance, it is .95.

7. The independent variables were selected from large data sets containing many variables on the basis of theoretically informed judgments and experience. Subsequently, factor analysis was used to sort through larger sets of variables, and the initial selections were confirmed by this technique.

8. But our position parallels that taken by Aiken and Depré (1974).

9. Consider, for instance, the city of Brussels. For most of its more than one million inhabitants, the most important and functionally most comprehensive governmental and political arena has been, until now, the commune or borough. The city has 19 of these, with a mean population of slightly more than 50,000. Thus, in partisan politics, in relating to public services and goods–for most public business–the citizen of Brussels has been accustomed to dealing with the government and politics of a medium sized town. Personalist politics have been the rule in the boroughs.

REFERENCES

AIKEN, M., and ALFORD, R. R. (1970). "Community structure and innovation: The case of urban renewal." American Sociological Review, 35(August):650-654.

AIKEN, M., and DEPRE, R. (1974). "Politics and policy outputs: A study of city expenditures among 196 Belgian cities." Paper presented at the 8th World Congress of the International Sociological Association, Toronto, August 20.

ALFORD, R. R. (1969). "Explanatory variables in the comparative study of urban administration and politics." In R. T. Daland (ed.), Comparative urban research: The administration and politics of cities. Beverly Hills, Calif.: Sage.

BELL, D. (1960). The end of ideology. Glencoe, Ill.: Free Press.

BOADEN, N. (1971). Urban policy-making. Cambridge: Cambridge University Press.

CLARK, T. N. (1968). "Community structure, decision-making, budget expenditures and urban renewal in 51 American communities." American Sociological Review, 33(August):576-593.

CUTRIGHT, P. (1963). "National political development: Measurement and analysis." American Sociological Review, 28:253-264.

DAWSON, R. E., and ROBINSON, J. A. (1963). "Inter-party competition, economic variables, and welfare policies in the American states." Journal of Politics, 25(May):265-289.

DYE, T. R. (1966). Politics, economics, and the public: Policy outcomes in the American states. Chicago: Rand McNally.

FRIED, R. C. (1975). "Comparing urban policy and performance." Chapter 6 in F. I. Greenstein and N. W. Polsby (eds.), Handbook of political science: Vol. 6: Policies and policymaking. Reading, Mass.: Addison-Wesley.

--- (1976). "Party and policy in West German cities." American Political Science Review, 70:11-24.

FRY, B. R., and WINTERS, R. F. (1970). "The politics of redistribution." American Political Science Review, 64:508-522.

HEIDENHEIMER, A. J., HECLO, H., and ADAMS, C. T. (1975). Comparative public policy: The politics of social choice in Europe and America. New York: St. Martin's Press.

HEISLER, M. O. (1974a). "Institutionalizing societal cleavages in a cooptive polity: The growing importance of the output side in Belgium." In M. O. Heisler (ed.), Politics in Europe: Structures and processes in some postindustrial democracies. New York: David McKay.

--- (1974b). "Politicized ethnicity and the making of public policy in the city: The case of Brussels." Paper presented at the Annual Meeting of the American Political Science

Association, Chicago, September.
--- (forthcoming). Brussels-Capital: Government and politics at the heart of a divided country.
HEISLER, M. O., with KVAVIK, R. B. (1974). "Patterns of European politics: The 'European Polity' model." Chapter 2 in Politics in Europe.
JACKMAN, R. W. (1975). Politics and social equality: A comparative analysis. New York: John Wiley.
LaPALOMBARA, J. (1966). "Decline of ideology: A dissent and an interpretation." American Political Science Review, 60:5-16.
LIJPHART, A. (1971). "Comparative politics and the comparative method." American Political Science Review, 65:682-693.
LINEBERRY, R. L., and FOWLER, E. P. (1967). "Reformism and public policies in American cities." American Political Science Review, 61(September):701-716.
LIPSET, S. M. (1959). "Some social requisites of democracy: Economic development and political legitimacy." American Political Science Review, 53:69-105.
--- (1960). Political man. Garden City, N.Y.: Doubleday.
LOWI, T. J. (1964). "American business, public policy, case-studies, and political theory." World Politics, 16:677-715.
MYRDAL, G. (1960). Beyond the welfare state. New Haven, Conn.: Yale University Press.
PETERS, B. G. (1972). "Public policy, socioeconomic conditions and the political system: A developmental analysis." Polity, 5:277-284.
--- (1974). "The development of social policy in France, Sweden, and the United Kingdom: 1850-1965." Chapter 7 in Politics in Europe.
--- (1977). The politics of bureaucracy: A comparative perspective. New York: David Longman.
PETERS, B. G., and HENNESSEY, T. M. (1975). "Political development and public policy in Sweden: 1865-1967." Chapter 5 in C. Liske, W. Loehr, and J. McCamant (eds.), Comparative public policy: Issues, theories, and methods. New York: Halsted Press (a Sage publication).
PETERS, B. G. et al. (1977). "Types of political systems and types of public policy: A comparative examination." Comparative Politics, April.
PRESSMAN, J. L., and WILDAVSKY, A. (1974). Implementation. Berkeley, Calif.: University of California Press.
PRZEWORSKI, A., and TEUNE, H. (1970). The logic of comparative social inquiry. New York: Wiley-Interscience.
REJAI, M. (ed., 1971). Decline of ideology? Chicago and New York: Aldine/Atherton.
ROSE, R. (1973). "Comparing public policy—An overview." European Journal of Political Research, 1:67-93.
SALISBURY, R. H. (1968). "The analysis of public policy: A search for theories and roles." Pp. 151-175 in A. Ranney (ed.), Political science and public policy. Chicago: Markham.
SALISBURY, R. H., and HEINZ, J. (1970). "A theory of policy analysis and some preliminary applications." Pp. 39-60 in I. Sharkansky (ed.), Policy analysis in political science. Chicago: Markham.
SHARKANSKY, I. (1967). "Economic and political correlates of state government expenditures: General tendencies and deviant cases." Midwest Journal of Political Science, (May):173-192.
--- (1971). "Economic theories of public policy: Resource-policy and need-policy linkages between income and welfare benefits." Midwest Journal of Political Science, 15:722-740.
STIEFBOLD, R. P. (1974). "Segmented pluralism and consociational democracy in Austria." Chapter 4 in Politics in Europe.
TINGSTEN, H. (1955). "Stability and vitality in Swedish democracy." Political Quarterly, 26:145-167.
WESTERGAARD, J., and RESLER, H. (1975). Class in a capitalist society. New York: Basic Books.

9

PUBLIC POLICY AND BUREAUCRACY IN THE UNITED STATES AND FRANCE

THEODORE J. LOWI

Center for Advanced Studies in the Behavioral Sciences
Stanford, California

Max Weber may be the founding father of contemporary study of bureaucracy, but he is also the source of some important imbalances in the empirical study of the phenomenon. Despite Weber's own admonition that his "ideal–typical model" of bureaucracy was a "one-sider accentuation," many social scientists view bureaucracy as though the ideal model were the empirical reality–a unitary social force without variety or variation. Their concept is bureaucracy, not bureaucracies.

A variant of the unitary model is a culturally particular model, in which bureaucracy realizes itself in different forms from country to country because it is considered a culturally determined phenomenon. Nevertheless it is treated as a unitary social force for its own sake. Real agencies and organizations tend to get lost in the process.

The advantage of treating bureaucracies as a unitary phenomenon is that it need not be treated at all. Bureaucracy can be the given. As context within which social list takes place, divisions are made or values are allocated. The culturally particular approach has the added value of appearing to be comparative when actually it only allows the analyst to redescribe the conventional wisdom about the culture in question. In neither case is our understanding of bureaucracy advanced—quite the contrary, since both approaches contradict common experience that real bureaucracies differ from one another in some fundamental ways. One of the prime motivations of administrative reform for two hundred years has been the persistent variation among public agencies and the urge to bring them into a closer fit with some general organizational norms. In brief, the effort has been to make unitary that which is virtually by nature not unitary.

The advantages of a Weberian understanding can be maintained and the disadvantages minimized by rejecting the idea of the unitary model of bureaucra*cy* in favor of a concept of bureaucra*cies* as specific, mission-oriented organizations. All bureaucracies have characteristics in common. Nevertheless, each has a distinctive set of tasks to perform and the requisites for carrying these out will shape each organization and its basic characteristics. Such at least is the point of view of this essay: (1) There are several universal characteristics of bureaucracy, but each of these should be treated as a political variable whose incidence may vary from bureaucracy to bureaucracy, according to the immediate and predictable influences of the tasks each organization must perform. (2) This process whereby the mission influences the bureaucracy will occur in any country at any time, and it will occur despite the social, cultural, and general political context that may uniformly affect all bureaucracies in that country. Finally, (3) among public or governmental bureaucracies (the exclusive forms for this essay), the mission of each is the formal public policy or policies delegated to it by some higher authority.

THE POLICY CONTEXT OF BUREAUCRACY

The general perspective here is that "policies cause politics." Politics, including bureaucratic structures, takes its shape from the functions the state performs, and these functions can be understood and observed concretely by the formal policies of government. My argument is that each type of policy, when properly classified, will tend to be associated with a distinctive "arena of power" with its own characteristic political process and power structure.[1]

Figure 1 is an effort to develop a classification of public policies according to a basic consideration of state power. Since the state is basically a coercive force, the starting distinctions in the figure are distinctions among types of coercion. Each cell in the fourfold table contains a public policy category drawn logically from a cross-

	Applicability of Coercion	
	Coercion Works Through:	
	Individual Conduct	*Environment of Conduct*
Likelihood of Coercion Remote (indirect)	*Distributive*–These statutes embody *no rule,* only authorize a process or designate privilege. E.g.: Public works Ag. extension services Patronage 19th century U.S. land policies	*Constituent*–These statutes embody *rules about rules,* or *rules about powers.* E.g.: Creating an agency or other administrative reform Budgeting and other overhead Most elections laws
Likelihood of Coercion Immediate (direct)	*Regulative*–These statutes embody *rules of conduct,* with sanctions. E.g.: Public health laws Industrial safety laws Antitrust laws Food and drug laws	*Redistributive*–These statutes embody *rules of classification* or *categorization.* E.g.: Social security Graduated income tax Monetary policy Low interest loan programs

Figure 1. CATEGORIZATION OF PUBLIC POLICIES

tabulation of the parameters at the margins. A few concrete examples and other materials are included to show the reader the basis of classification and the way these distinctions can be brought into actual statutes and agency documents to categorize the type of policy involved. Not nearly enough material is provided here to enable the reader to classify the policies with ease or consistency. However, the figure and the materials therein will give the reader some sense of the logic of the analysis. Table 1 provides a number of examples of the results of applying these considerations to actual agencies.[2]

It should be apparent that this approach to classification expresses a particular view of public policy and what it represents. Not all government actions emanate from policy; some are sporadic, haphazard, nonrational. But many, probably most, actions of government do derive from government policies. Probably the most fundamental government actions are policies—actions that are repetitive, relatively consistent, and derived from some formally expressed value, goal, or intention. Policies are a rational exercise of political authority expressed as guidelines which seek to bring the actions of agents into some accord with the intentions of the governing elite.

This is a deliberately formalistic definition of policy, which makes use of the formal and legal language of laws and decrees that set up agencies. Granted, some important aspects of public policy are eliminated from the definition; we all know that policies are shaped from beginning to end every time they are implemented. However, the advantages of a formalistic definition of policies far outweigh the disadvantages.

1. This kind of definition reduces variation from one country to another. If we define policies as any and all authoritative actions, then it becomes a major research task just to identify what the policy is in a given context. The actual policy source will vary tremendously from one context to another. In contrast, there tend to be very few sources of formal policy, especially in developed countries, and these are at the highest levels of formal authority.

2. A second important advantage is that it can be a priori. By definition, formal policies exist before agencies and programs. A more informal definition of policy, even if it appears to capture reality, requires a long stretch of time before one can know what the realities are. If agency realities and policy impacts are part of the political process we would like to be able to predict and explain. It is wrong to include them in the very definition of policy itself.

3. The formal definition of public policy is directly relevant to bureaucratic agencies and their missions without being a statement or rationalization offered by the agency itself. At the level of the actual operating agencies—the first level below head-of-department or minister, usually called "the bureau level" in the U.S. and the *direction* in France—each agency tends to work under one organic statute or decree as amended. Agency heads and assistants usually write documents of various sorts, interpreting and implementing the organic statute; these certainly refine the mission. Nevertheless, the mission of the agency as stated in the organic statute or decree is the source of authority for the agency as well as the primary source of guidelines for agency jurisdiction and action. Once the organic statute has been classified within the fourfold scheme, the agency has also been classified.

4. Within this approach, empirical findings on specific political patterns never stray too far from a theory of the state. If the state, or political authority, is maintained as the context for policy *and* for politics, then there ought to be a common logic running through both. There ought not to be two separate realities with two separate theories—one for policy and one for politics. To propose that "policy causes politics" is to identify a direction of flow; but it means a flow of logic and argument from state to policy to politics, just as it implies a hypothesis about the direction of causation. Discrete empirical findings can be logically related and cumulative within this common context.

This essay explores variations in the structure and composition of bureaucracies and the meaning of these variations within the context of the state and public policy. Once the categorization of policies has been accomplished, the empirical task is relatively simple. Since each statute fits within one of the four categories of public policy, and since each statute defines the mission of an agency, each agency is thereby placed within one of the four categories. Following that process, any differences in the distribution of characteristics from agencies in one policy category to those in another can be attributed to their policy or mission. The data are mainly characteristics and attitudes of personnel employed in the upper management levels of United States and French agencies at the bureau or *direction* level.

FRENCH BUREAUCRACY–THE CASE OF THE CORPS

Perhaps it is best to begin with France because of its tradition of a strong central state authority, its unitary (versus federal) composition, and the longevity of its central bureaucracies, which pre-date industrialization, modern interest groups, and modern political parties, reputedly the source of pluralism and governmental fragmentation in the United States. The French are also an interesting contrast to the United States because their code places great stress upon national uniformity of laws, procedures, and structures. In France the state has been brought to every corner of the country by the maintenance of large field staffs *(services extérieurs)* even at the expense of the Paris headquarters. The prefectoral corps is one of the most prestigious governmental agencies in France; it is expected to provide administrative unity in face of the highly fragmented character of French national society.

The *corps*–a wholly French concept of training and recruitment for the civil service–is a means of gaining continuity within diversity.[3] However, diversity tends to outweigh uniformity. Despite the institution of the single *concours* throughout the civil service, despite the interposition of ENA, and the establishment of a uniform code for civil servants, there is still a great amount of bureau-particularism in France. The corps remain strong and their tradition, common schooling, and organizational identification enable them to capture and maintain substantial control of the *direction* or *directions* whose work is closely related to them.[4] These instances of capturing, discontinuity, and variation at the level of the *directions* are not haphazardly distributed. They happen to fit rather neatly

Table 1. RECRUITMENT OF TOP ADMINISTRATORS: CORPS PERSONNEL ACCORDING TO TYPE OF MINISTRY SERVED IN

	Corps				
Category of Ministry	*Grands Corps*	*Corps de Control Administratif*	*Corps d'Administration Centrale*	*Corps Techniques*	*Corps de Services Extérieurs*
Finances	37%	39%	39%	25%	0%
Regaliens	58	9	13	5	70
Techniques	2	19	22	66	1
Sociaux & Ed.	1	31	21	3	28
Primier ministre	3	3	4	1	1
N =	106	70	411	252	128

into the *arenas of power* pattern, thereby giving us an opportunity to analyze the relationship between policy and politics.

Tables 1 and 2 may present the best possible overview of the pattern of bureaucratic politics in France. Although the corps may be the single most important influence on administrative organization and behavior in France, *this influence is segmented along policy lines*. Note first on Table 1 that the *grands corps* played almost no role at all in three of the five types of ministries. Note also that the predominant use of the grands corps, at least in recent years, has been in the so-called Ministères Régaliens, which include the Conseil d'Etat, the Cours des Comptes, most of the Ministry of Justice, most of the foreign affairs and the civil functions of the armies, and the important Ministry of the Interior. This implies that the grands corps do not quite constitute a senior civil service, in the sense of topping all major agencies, but are instead a rather specialized administrative elite. The term *régalien* pertains to those agencies and functions closest to ancient sovereignty or the regalia of the court, implying quite appropriately that the primary use of the grands corps, and perhaps the secret of their influence, is their *maintenance of the realm*. This will be confirmed and reinforced doubly when we turn to the constituent arena and the policy analysis below.

The other corps are also unevenly distributed, in ways that suggest they have a rather specialized usage throughout the government. This is even true of the two most important sources of middle management, the *corps de controle administratif* and the *corps d'administration centrale.*

These segmented lines of influence begin to show up all the more clearly within the arenas-of-power framework. Whether the inspection of Table 2 is done by row or by column, the unevenness of the

Table 2. RECRUITMENT OF TOP ADMINISTRATORS: CORPS PERSONNEL DISTRIBUTED BY THE ARENA OF THE *DIRECTION* IN WHICH THEY ARE EMPLOYED

	Constituent		*Distributive*		*Regulative*		*Redistributive*		*Total Row %*
Grands corps	16%		1%		1%		32%		
(N = 86)		(53%)		(1%)		(1%)		(44%)	99%
Corps de controle administratif	8		5		12		13		
(N = 54)		(43%)		(11%)		(17%)		(30%)	101%
Corps d'administration centrale	41		39		46		49		
(N = 259)		(47%)		(17%)		(14%)		(22%)	102%
Corps techniques	19		54		21		6		
(N = 141)		(40%)		(43%)		(11%)		(5%)	99%
Corps de services extérieurs	16		–		21		–		
(N = 63)		(75%)		–		(25%)		–	100%
Total column %	100%		99%		101%		100%		
N =	294		112		78		119		

The numbers in parenthesis are the row percentages.

distributions is clear and meaningful; the segmentations are in almost every respect along lines consistent with and understandable within the established policy categories.

Note first on Table 2 the great contrast in personnel recruitment (and therefore in each corps' probable influence, between constituent and distributive agencies. The missions of the former are, by definition, *overhead* functions; this means that the primary constituency of each is actually other government agencies, rather than people or interests in the private sphere. This is closely related to the fact that constituent agencies draw most heavily from the grands corps and from the corps d'administration centrale.[5] Agencies in the constituent category draw far less upon the operatives in the *corps techniques.* In contrast, distributive agencies draw from those very operative corps. Among constituent agencies, some management functions are carried out at the periphery by operatives of the *corps des services extérieurs* (because this includes the prefectorial corps). Yet such is distinctly not the case for distributive agencies, whose local activities constantly affect and are affected by the *préfets;* nevertheless, their key personnel are from the corps techniques, with management functions apparently being performed by the same corps or by the corps d'administration centrale. To say the least, these are management personnel of far lower status than those drawn from the grands corps, who constitute 1% of total management personnel.

The situation of the other two types is even more distinctive; the particular pattern of employing the corps in these agencies is solidly consistent with general propositions about policy and politics formulated long before these data were analyzed. Over 80% of the personnel in redistributive agencies were drawn from corps which perform overhead functions. Unlike distributive agencies, here we find a very large proportion of the *highest* status management functionaries: those from the grands corps (32%; or, to put it the other way, 44% of all grands corps personnel were serving in redistributive agencies). Only 6% of the top management personnel in redistributive agencies were operatives (compared to 54% and 21%, respectively, for distributive and regulative agencies).

Regulatory agencies also recruit heavily from overhead or management corps. Yet note the difference. Only 1% of the regulatory personnel were drawn from the grands corps (versus 32% for redistributive agencies). Management seems to fall to the lesser corps d'administration centrale (46%) and to the corps des services extérieurs—meaning primarily the prefectoral corps—from which 21% of regulatory personnel were drawn (as compared to 0% for redistributive and distributive agencies). Regulatory agencies also use more operatives—experts and specialists from the corps techniques—than do redistributive agencies (21% versus 6%).

A pattern is beginning to emerge that is increasingly consistent with the general policy-politics scheme. To link it to the other data, look once again at the case for redistribution, where a fairly clear case for the policy-politics relationship emerges even from the small amount of data in Table 3. Redistributive agencies in France seem to be the most classically bureaucratized. (This will also hold true of the United States.) Their processes are the most internalized. Stress here is almost completely upon management. Few operatives are used, despite the fact that redistributive agencies are "line agencies," dealing entirely with people "in the private sphere." No corps exists primarily for recruitment into and training in these agencies; they are cut off from localities by having little or no field services. These features tend to confirm the central conception of redistributive policy and its attendant politics. The work of redistributive agencies derives from fairly strictly drawn discriminations among classes in the society. Such policies reduce the discretion of administrators, and devices usually emerge to keep check upon that reduced discretion.

Stress is inevitably put upon routine, supervision, and upper and middle management—in a word, overhead functions. Even constituent agencies—whose missions are by definition overhead—draw more upon operative corps than do redistributive agencies (35% versus 6%). To repeat: it is the mission—the policy responsibility of each agency—that has contributed to the distinctiveness of administrative organization. Let us now turn to other data to explore the extent to which these tendencies are sustained.

U.S. AND FRANCE—A CLOSER LOOK

1. *Professionalism.* The French corps is an organizational phenomenon, but it is also an aspect of personnel recruitment policy. The character of training and experience of top management personnel is a matter of intense and continuing concern to any government; nowhere will this kind of concern be more intensely expressed than in France and the United States. However, the actual patterns and practices are not general throughout all agencies; on the other hand, although each agency is likely to have very definite attitudes toward recruitment of top management, actual recruitment practices are not peculiar to each agency. That is to say, there are indeed variations in recruitment practices at the top, but observable variations in recruitment practices distribute themselves along the lines of the policy categories. In the United States and in France there is a very clear difference in the extent to which technologists or "subject matter specialists" are recruited into top management positions. Table 3 leaves little doubt that distributive agencies draw most upon technologists for their top management jobs.[6]

In the United States this is consistently true for the three important technological areas on which the aggregate data could be compiled. For another reading of this phenomenon, part b of Table 3 utilizes interview data which have been scaled in order to rank the importance of outside training, the actual backgrounds of the top personnel, and the attitudes of the respondents toward the utilization of technologists in top positions. Note that "outside professional training" ranks 2 on a 6-point scale among respondents in distributive agencies, while it ranked 6 on the 6-point scale among respondents in regulatory and redistributive agencies.[7]

The datum most closely comparable to the above for France appears in part c of Table 3, proportion of top administrators drawn

Table 3. PROFESSIONALISM: USE OF TECHNOLOGISTS IN TOP MANAGEMENT, U.S. AND FRANCE

	Distributive	*Regulative*	*Redistributive*	*Constituent**
United States				
a. Use of "substantive specialists" (% of agencies in which at least 4% of *top* management are technologists):				
Biological sciences	36%	11%	7%	
Engineers	50	17	14	
Physical sciences	–	–	–	
b. Executive respondents rank value of outside professional training, 1 (high) to 6 (low)	2	6	6	
France				
c. Recruitment of top administrators from the *corps techniques*	54	21	6	19%

*The U.S. data were developed before the fourth category had been worked out. This will be added eventually, but in the meantime the three cuts into the data ought to be sufficient to permit exploration of the policy-politics nexus.

from the corps techniques among each of the types of agencies. Here again, the distributive agencies are by far the most prominent. A striking 54% of all the top administrators among the distributive agencies in France are drawn from the technical corps, as contrasted with 21%, 19%, and 6%, respectively, of the top personnel in the other types of agencies.

These data will acquire greater strength when we look at them again in light of variations in other characteristics; however, it is already possible to suggest a line of argument of considerable importance on the basis of these data alone. The key to the organizational and authority structures of distributive agencies is what Thompson and other students of administration would call "dual authority." Lines of control and communication run from the general managers to subordinates, but also from subject-matter specialists at the center to their counterparts in the field. Since distributive agencies, operating under distributive policies, must operate largely *in the absence of rules* (according to the original definitions of policies), they must make greatest use of substantive knowledge and the authority that accrues from credentials of professionalization[8] as indicated by the Ph.D. or equivalent outside training. This not only makes top managers credible when they issue a command, it increases the probability of coordination through common values rather than through common rules or close supervision.

2. *Organizational Mechanisms for Control and Coordination.* If distributive agencies tend to recruit subject-matter specialists as a means of control and coordination, by what devices do other agencies attempt to do the same? Table 4 is a summary of data on four well-known approaches to control and coordination. Each is associated with a different type of bureaucracy. For example, in the United States and in France, redistributive agencies employ *overhead* mechanisms of coordination. In fact, this relationship is strikingly clear in both countries, inasmuch as that can be expressed by the figures in Table 4, item a. Constituent agencies in France also make moderately strong use of overhead mechanisms, as is partly true in the United States. But the distributive and regulatory agencies do not rely upon this mechanism. And, in addition to overhead, redistributive agencies are also most likely to employ close supervision of lower administrators as a means of control and coordination. Note, in item b of Table 4, that supervision ranks very high among top-level respondents in Corson and Paul's survey of activities in a typical work week. In contrast, supervision rates very low among the weekly activites of top administrators in distributive and regulatory agencies.[9]

The datum relating to close supervision in the French survey is also reported in item b of Table 4 in responses to how many superior officers the higher administrators in French bureaucracies were required to report to. Here again the results parallel the American ones inasmuch as 24% of the higher French administrators testified that they were required to report to three or more superior officers. The fact that this was also true of higher administrators in regulatory agencies brings us closer to the pattern of control in those agencies.

In addition to a moderate reliance upon supervision, regulatory agencies, at least in the United States, tend to rely most heavily upon bureaucratization and hierarchy for coordination and control. This can be seen in items c and d of Table 4 which, when taken together, suggest a fairly strict and repetitive distribution of controls from top to bottom in regulatory agencies. For example, the scaling of interview questions, on matters such as careful promotion within rank and orderliness of lines of command, reveals that respondents from regulatory agencies consistently rate these matters extremely high. Item d, drawn from the aggregate data, shows a tremendously high

Table 4. MECHANISMS OF ADMINISTRATIVE CONTROL: AGENCIES RELY UPON DIFFERENT MEANS OF COORDINATING AGENCY CONDUCT

United States			France*		
a. *Use of Overhead Mechanisms*					
Proportion of *agencies* in which over 10% of the top personnel are in budgeting and accounting	*Distributive*	7%	Percent of top personnel drawn from the two major overhead *corps*	*Distributive*	6%
	Regulative	17%		*Regulative*	13%
	Redistributive	43%		*Redistributive*	45%
				Constituent	24%
b. *Use of close supervision*					
Executives rank supervision activities as important (1) or unimportant (6) in a typical week's work	*Distributive*	6th	Top personnel required to report to three or more superiors	*Distributive*	15%
	Regulative	5th		*Regulative*	24%
	Redistributive	2nd		*Redistributive*	24%
				Constituent	19%
c. *Control through bureaucratism*					
(1) Rank on bureaucratism scale (promotion within rank, etc.)	*Distributive*	4th	(1) Top personnel drawn from *corps des services extérieurs*	*Distributive*	0%
	Regulative	2nd		*Regulative*	21%
	Redistributive	1st		*Redistributive*	0%
				Constituent	16%
(2) Rank on procedure scale (typical week involved staffing, negotiating or representing	*Distributive*	1st	(2) Top personnel who spent *no time* in field (services extérieurs)	*Distributive*	61%
	Regulative	1st		*Regulative*	58%
	Redistributive	3rd		*Redistributive*	71%
				Constituent	63%
d. *Control through hierarchy*					
(1) Proportion of *agencies* in which at least 15% of HQ personnel are GS15 and above	*Distributive*	32%	(1) Number of separate units or divisions within each *direction*	*Distributive*	1-9
	Regulative	72%		*Regulative*	10-21
	Redistributive	50%		*Redistributive*	21+
				Constituent	1-9
(2) Proportion of *agencies* in which 40% of top personnel are in the field	*Distributive*	11%	(2) Have you ever been able to depart from precedent or introduced an innovation? (% yes)	*Distributive*	55%
	Regulative	39%		*Regulative*	51%
	Redistributive	21%		*Redistributive*	44%
				Constituent	49%

*All French data for Table 4 were drawn from a study directed by Darbel and Schnapper. Their findings were published in Darbel and Schnapper (1969, 1972). However, for this paper the data in Table 4 were drawn directly from computer tapes. I am grateful to Mme. Schnapper and the late M. Darbel for providing me with these tapes and for adding items on the *Directions* that made possible the use of the data on bureaucracy in a policy framework. However, responsibility for the particular form and use of the data in this paper is entirely mine.

reliance upon high-level personnel at headquarters *and* in the field. That is to say, regulatory agencies tend to be "top heavy," with rather large proportions of people at levels where discretion and responsibility are expected.

Regulatory agencies in France tend only moderately to follow this trend. In fact, except for the moderately high use of supervisory controls already reported, the data do not reveal any pronounced reliance upon any particular coordinating device among regulatory agencies. Each device shows up as moderate, but no single one is pronounced. This could be an artifact of the data; that is, the data simply do not identify the one of two coordinating mechanisms that are actually in greatest use among regulatory agencies. Another, more substantive possibility is that regulatory agencies in France employ few strong coordinating devices because of the existence of the prefects, a situation very important in France but not shown in these data. It is well known that the prefects and subprefects are responsible for a tremendous amount of the local "police power," and that prefects are expected to coordinate the local activities of the important national ministries, such as interior, justice, and finance where so much of the regulatory activity in France goes on. One indication of this is the fact that the regulatory agencies are most likely to draw their top management personnel from the corps des services extérieurs. As shown in Table 2, 21% of all of the top personnel in regulatory agencies come from the prefectorial corps; this contrasts with 16% of the top personnel in constituent agencies, and 0% of the top personnel in distributive and redistributive agencies.[10]

A SUMMARY AND SYNTHESIS

1. *Redistributive Agencies and Redistributive Policies.* In both the United States and France, redistributive agencies are mainly headquarters agencies. One could call them centralized, even though this is only one type of centralization, albeit an important one. In both countries, overhead is an important coordinating device, and common technological training is very unimportant, despite the technical nature of many welfare-state programs. In neither country do personnel in redistributive agencies spend much time in field offices before moving into positions of top management at headquarters. In both countries redistributive agencies are highly internalized—tied to the center by procedure, by careful bureaucratic promotion, by little

outside professionalism, by dependency upon organization values, and by minimal departure from precedent. They are also coordinated by internal overhead control and close supervision.

Much of this could have been anticipated by logical extension of what was already known about redistributive policies. Redistributive policies embody rules that are relatively clearly defined in organic law. Thus, less discretion is delegated to the agency and the clearer rules of law operate as criteria against which to judge agency action all along the line. Since redistributive rules involve classification, and therefore do not have to await individual action before being applied (as contrasted to regulatory rules), the administrator can routinize his work more in redistributive agencies. This is exactly what we were able to observe. Thus policy characteristics and administrative structure are bound together either in common logic or common causation, or both.

2. *Regulatory Agencies and Regulatory Policies.* Regulatory agencies are also unified, but their unification is based on an entirely different set of principles from those observed among redistributive agencies. In the United States it is quite clear that regulatory agencies are run primarily through "chain of command," which extends from high-ranking personnel at headquarters to high-ranking personnel in the field. In fact, the headquarters of regulatory agencies is quite top heavy, not only because regulatory agencies utilize the largest proportion of "support personnel" there.[11] The fact that the field units have many high-ranking personnel suggests that discretion is delegated farther down the line in regulatory agencies than in redistributive ones. At the same time, they rely heavily upon procedural orientations and routines to keep this discretion within limits.[12]

In France, the situation is fairly comparable. In neither country is overhead a coordinating device in regulatory agencies (as already reported); in both countries top personnel tend to come from management rather than from technologists and other operatives. Both are internalized in the sense that top personnel at the center tend to come through promotion from those who served first at lower levels and in the field operations of the same agencies. They are also comparable in the degree to which discretion seems to be delegated to lower levels. This is indicated by the fact that in the U.S. high proportions of top personnel are in the field. In France the regulatory agencies are the only ones in which large proportions of field personnel move directly to top management at headquarters. Another indication of delegation to lower levels among French regulatory agencies can be found in the following distribution of attitudes: French regulatory administrators were (a) most likely to say they could depart from precedents and were least likely to complain of intervention by higher-ups within their agency or from finance. Yet, (b) they were most likely to complain of inadequate support and excessive centralization.[13]

Once again, many of these administrative patterns might have been anticipated by a prior knowledge of the nature of regulatory policies. Regulatory policies are rich in rules. Rules tend to limit discretion; yet, since regulations must apply to individual behavior, discretion is also necessary and inevitable. Therefore, arrangements have to be made to balance inconsistent demands upon the agency between the operation of rules of general application and the need to apply these rules to individual cases. These policy patterns are highly related to the political patterns observed in the data.

3. *Distributive Agencies and Distributive Policies.* The most outstanding feature of distributive agencies in both countries is the extent to which they rely upon technologists and substantive specialists in positions of top management. This is not simply a distinctive feature of the personnel; it is also an organizational characteristic, inasmuch as distributive agencies in both countries make little use of formal control mechanisms, such as overhead or supervision. Reliance is upon the "internal gyroscope" of each of these highly qualified persons, to conduct themselves individually according to an internalized organizational norm. The French have, of course, formalized this by drawing heavily upon the corps techniques for top management, basing them in turn upon the *grandes écoles,* the high-powered trade schools from which most technically trained personnel in France graduate.

Here again, the relationship between administrative structure and distributive policies is logically compelling as well as empirically quite clear. Distributive agencies are operating in a policy context that is virtually free of substantive rules. There is, therefore, very little if any a priori structure within which management can be guided or can guide itself. Top management can, of course, formulate its own rules; no doubt the top management in every distributive agency contrives substantive as well as procedural rules. Nevertheless, as suggested already, the absence of rules embodied in organic statutes seems to call for heavy reliance upon the substantive knowledge that each responsible administrator can bring to the task.

THE FUNCTIONS OF THE STATE AND THE NATURE OF POLITICS: SOME OPENING THOUGHTS

No claim will be made here that the fourfold scheme of policy analysis has been confirmed. However, two positive claims can be made. First, we have established a presumption in favor of the fourfold scheme. It reveals many interesting and unexpected variations in an area of political science not well developed, with data from a variety of sources gathered by people innocent of the scheme itself. Moreover, the argument is sustained consistently between the policy scheme and the empirical findings.

We have established a second and even stronger presumption of the policy-to-politics approach to analysis; in the long run this is more important than my particular resolution of it. A long-needed step has been taken toward a fusion of public law, public administration, and political behavior—separated artificially for more than a generation. The very idea that jurisprudence can contribute to political behavior theory, and that political behavior can generate conclusions of direct relevance to the analysis of the state, is indeed a desirable trend in political science. The policy approach returns the horse to the front of the cart. The state and its coercive powers must come first in any political analysis in the 20th century. In the context of the modern state, microscopic units of political behavior, however many in number, seem marginal, as iron filings responding to a magnet. The modern state is the magnetic field; it is time to observe the magnet.

The policy approach has particular advantages for those who would engage in comparative analysis. First, policy categorization greatly facilitates comparative politics within one country. Second, this approach could improve the study of comparative politics across two or more countries because policy (especially when defined formally) establishes consistent and easily accessible terms of discourse. One of the most problematic aspects of present comparative politics is "hyperabstractionism," masquerading as "comparative theory." As soon as a politics or political behavior approach to comparison turns from single-country description to cross-country analysis and explanation, the differences between the two or more countries are so great, the terms of discourse are so different, or the indices for the phenomena to be compared are so noncomparable that the analyst must take a very remote perspective to include all the factors. Comparison should begin with an actual inventory of formal government actions in the countries concerned and should move carefully and in small steps outward from that toward the limited aspects of structure and behavior that seem most relevant to the observer. Such a policy inventory would guide the individual researcher and would simultaneously provide a logical basis for putting together the findings of a variety of researchers.

Increasing numbers of political scientists are turning to policy and policy evaluation, simultaneously abandoning their concern for the political process to evaluate the impact of the policy on the society itself. But why would anyone want to take advice or criticism from a political scientist on the impact of, say, ecology policies on the environment? Biologists would do that kind of analysis much better. Why indeed would anyone wish to pay for advice and criticism from political scientists on the costs and benefits of a new bridge or a new mine-safety measure? An engineer would be infinitely better qualified. Are there any kinds of policy impacts on which political scientists have some special claim to expert knowledge? Indeed yes. Political scientists are quite capable of analyzing and assessing the *impact of policies on the political system itself.* The applied political scientist ought to ask: Even if the policies fail to have an impact on the society, what effect do they have on the political system? And if the various policy approaches to a given social problem are all likely to fail, which approach will have the most or least desirable effect on the political system in the interim? Through these questions, political scientists can become good policy analysts and remain political scientists rather than becoming bad engineers, bad economists, or bad biologists.

Thus, somewhere there is an "arenas of power" approach that will make political science the rigorous and relevant social science it wishes to become. This approach will be better than the one in this essay, but I suspect it will consist of a better jurisprudence, a clearer and more operationalized set of policy categories, and a stronger data base. Nevertheless, the elements are likely to be the same.

NOTES

1. Space does not permit elaboration of the rationale. However, this can be found in several earlier publications, beginning in 1964. Perhaps the two most useful sources are Lowi (1970) and Lowi (1972).

2. The U.S. and French agency classifications are the result of a very long process of research, analysis, and discussion among several of my colleagues. In particular I am grateful to Vincent Blocker, Richard Joslyn, Richard Bensel, Judith Hurtmann, James L. Grant, and to Professor Benjamin Ginsberg of the Cornell Department of Government for valuable contributions to the research and the decisions on how to classify each agency. Information on French agencies was drawn from *Journal officiel de la Republique Française* (laws,

statutes, etc., published annually); *Bottin administratif* (1966); and *La revue administrative, revue bimestrielle de l'administration moderne* (1948-). Lists of agencies classified by "arena" are available on request.

3. There are discrepancies in the definitions of *grands corps*. These need not detain us, but a comment might save knowledgeable readers from some confusion. Suleiman (1974), for example, defines grands corps to include the major technical corps (*mines* ponts et chaussées, eaux et forêts) and the prefectorial corps. In contrast, Darbel and Schnapper (1969, 1972) limit their definition of the grands corps to the three examples given in the text above. Without making any judgments on the merits of the two definitions, I will follow the Darbel-Schnapper definition because I am relying heavily on their data. Both works are indispensable for understanding or studying French bureaucracy.

4. For a good discussion and cases of bureau politics of this sort, see Suleiman (1974: Chapter VI). There are few equivalent instances of capturing in the United States. For one, see Kaufman (1960); see also Maass (1951). More cases will be found in the American military and among the bureaucracies in large urban centers. But these are exceptions in the United States that tend to confirm the rule in France.

5. This includes such corps as *administrateurs civils,* PIT, and *agents superiéurs.*

6. Table 4 and the rest of the empirical data on the United States are based upon two sources of data. The first is aggregate data on total personnel, their levels (G.S. ratings) and their function, or "occupational family," as officially defined. These were drawn directly from the records of the U.S. Civil Service Commission. The second source was the data developed by Corson and Paul (1966). The authors were kind enough to turn over all their raw data to me after they had completed their own work on it. Two dissertations, developed under my guidance at the University of Chicago, based their conclusions upon the aggregate and Corson-Paul data. The actual figures used here come mainly from these two theses, and I am most highly indebted to their authors, Grant (1971) and Hartmann (1973).

7. In our scoring, 1 is the highest rating; professionalism scores an actual tie for highest ranking with "procedural orientation" but got second ranking before the rounding off of averages.

8. For a good discussion of "dual authority," see Thompson (1969). For the best case studies of dual authority and subject-matter specialization as a means of coordination through value premises, see Kaufman (1960).

9. Corson and Paul asked respondents to describe a typical week in terms of time spent in supervising, coordinating, evaluating, negotiating, staffing, performing, etc. Their frequencies and weightings were scaled in our reanalysis of the data.

10. Since I have already made some observations about the patterns among constituent agencies in France, and since there are as yet no data for constituent agencies in the United States, I will say nothing further about coordination and control patterns among these agencies at this point.

11. Support personnel are the lower third of the G.S. ratings, GS-9 and below.

12. For example, respondents in regulatory agencies rank procedural matters as the most important types of activities during their typical week, while respondents in redistributive agencies ranked these third. In contrast, supervisory activities were ranked fifth in a typical week, as compared to second for redistributive agencies.

13. These comments are based directly upon statistics drawn from the Darbel-Schnapper survey (1969, 1972) as reclassified in our fourfold policy categorization.

REFERENCES

Bottin administratif (1966). Paris: Sociéte Dido–Bottin.

CORSON, J., and PAUL, R. S. (1966). Men near the top: Filling key positions in the federal service. Baltimore: Johns Hopkins University Press.

DARBEL, A., and SCHNAPPER, D. (1969, 1972). Les Agents du système politique and Le système administratif. Paris: Mouton and Ecole Pratique des Hautes Etudes.

GRANT, J. L. (1971). "The administration of politics: A political theory of public administration." Unpublished doctoral dissertation, University of Chicago.

HARTMANN, J. (1973). "Bureaucracy, democracy and the administrative official." Unpublished doctoral dissertation, University of Chicago.

Journal officiel de la republique française, published annually.

KAUFMAN, H. (1960). The forest ranger. Baltimore: Johns Hopkins University Press.

LOWI, T. J. (1970). "Decision making vs policy making: Toward an antidote for technocracy." Public Administration Review, 30(May/June):314-325.

——— (1972). "Four systems of policy, politics and choice." Public Administration Review, 32(July/August):298-310.

MAASS, A. (1951). Muddy waters: The army engineers and the nation's rivers. Cambridge, Mass.: Harvard University Press.

La Revue administrative, revue bimestrielle de l'administration moderne (1948). Paris.

SULEIMAN, E. (1974). Politics, power, and bureaucracy in France. Princeton, N.J.: Princeton University Press.

THOMPSON, V. (1969). Modern organization. New York: Knopf.

10

POLITICAL CONFLICT, URBAN STRUCTURE, AND THE FISCAL CRISIS

ROGER FRIEDLAND

University of California at Santa Barbara

FRANCES FOX PIVEN

Boston University

ROBERT R. ALFORD

University of California at Santa Cruz

During the last few years, many of the older cities in the United States have experienced in intense form a series of stresses that are sometimes treated as and called "the urban fiscal crisis."[1] Current dramatics notwithstanding, the so-called fiscal crisis is a familiar feature of urban life. Its classic symptoms are widening disparities between revenues and expenditures on the one hand, and rising demands for municipal services on the other. These symptoms are not only a recurrent fact of American urban history, but also, if often in less intense form, a feature of many other cities in advanced capitalist nations. Juxtaposed to the scope of these symptoms, the explanations that have dominated discussion of the so-called crisis in the United States have been remarkably trivial, emphasizing as they do such idiosyncratic aspects of contemporary American cities as the quality of municipal leadership, or the particular functional responsibilities of particular municipal governments, or the irrationalities in revenue collection and service delivery resulting from fragmented local government jurisdictions. Even the somewhat more plausible explanations that have recently come to the fore, emphasizing changing intrametropolitan and interregional patterns of capital investment with the resulting erosion of the municipal tax base (e.g., Sternlieb and Hughes, 1976; Perry and Watkins, 1977; Starr, 1976; Baer, 1976), fail to consider these developments in appropriate historical and comparative perspective. American cities have experienced fiscal strains at earlier historical junctures, at periods when capital was concentrating in the cities, not deserting them. And not all cities, either in the United States or in Western Europe, that are suffering fiscal strains are the victims of territorial shifts in capital investment. In short, while some empirical verification can be found for all of these assertions, they do not propose an explanation of urban fiscal strains commensurate with their perennial and widespread occurrence.

A potentially more illuminating perspective from which to view these urban troubles is suggested by a growing body of work by neo-Marxists on the theory of the state. Perhaps the best known exemplar of this new tradition is James O'Connor. Stated simply, O'Connor (1973) and others postulate that the capitalist state must provide the infrastructure and subsidies which will ensure the profits of monopoly capital; it must subsidize and protect the accumulation process, while continuing to permit the private appropriation of profits. At the same time, the state must absorb popular discontent generated by the social costs of the accumulation process. The theory of the state argued that the fiscal crisis is the result of the increasing demands on government arising from these dualistic functions.[2] This is a provocative perspective, but also has certain flaws. The theory asserts a structural and inherent tendency to crisis, although the visible manifestations of the crisis are in fact variable. Also, the theory of the state remains very general and does not deal with variations in symptoms of fiscal stress from one historical period to another, from one city and nation to another, and even from one function or level of the state to another.

In this paper, we begin our argument with the premise that urban areas are critically important sites at which both economic growth and political integration are organized. Government structures in urban areas must therefore perform key functions both to support urban economic processes and to promote the political integration of the urban population. On the one hand, urban governments must be responsive to the infrastructural and service requirements of capital accumulation, and to changes in these requirements generated by economic growth. On the other hand, they must also manage political participation among the masses of the urban population who do not control capital accumulation and may not benefit from it either. Whether or not these dual functions of urban government are, as the theory of the state argues, inherently and consistently contradictory,[3] they are clearly contradictory at certain junctures in the process of capitalist economic development—for example, during extreme downturns in the business cycle when large numbers of people become unemployed and real wages fall, or during periods of rapid economic concentration and modernization that displace workers and uproot or undermine communities.[4]

Considered apart from specific structural arrangements, such periods might be expected to generate extraordinary convulsions in municipal politics. The electoral-representative arrangements which underpin municipal governments make them vulnerable to popular discontent, and also limit their ability to employ extraordinary strategies of collective mobilization or repression to cope with discontent. At the same time, municipal authorities are helpless to intervene in the economic developments which may have triggered discontent and, indeed, find it difficult to resist even new demands arising from the private sector on which they are fiscally dependent. During such periods, the responses required of city government to successfully accomplish political integration and support economic growth might be expected to intensify, and to become antagonistic or contradictory.

However, such convulsions are not frequent. The reason, we will argue, is that specific structural arrangements are developed on the municipal level that mediate these potentially antagonistic functions posited by the theory of the state, and allow urban governments to cope with both the requirements of economic growth and the requirements of political integration, even during periods of potentially intense conflict. Among the structural arrangements that we think are important in mediating economic and popular pressures are (1) the degree of decentralization or centralization of government functions and (2) the degree of segregation of economic and political functions within urban governments.

All Western nations provide for some degree of decentralization in the governance of cities, but the degree of decentralization varies from nation to nation and from city to city, as does the specific forms of governmental authority which are decentralized or centralized. Similarly, all Western nations provide for some degree of structural segregation between those governmental activities that further economic growth and those that facilitate the political integration of the urban population. And there is also a widespread but varying tendency for these functions to be fragmented among different agencies and programs. These variations in the scope and substance of decentralization of government authority, and in the segregation and fragmentation of government activities, may help to account for differences among nations and cities in the capacity to cope with periodic eruptions of political conflict.

But while these structural arrangements help to diffuse and manage conflict, they also lead to the proliferation of government activities and costs and the contraction of government revenues. The tensions which might otherwise take form in direct struggles between business, industry, and finance on the one hand, and workers and consumers on the other hand, take form instead in escalating demands on municipal agencies—for jobs, services, contracts, tax concessions—with the result that municipal activities and budgets expand, while municipal revenues are reduced. As a consequence, periods of potential social and class conflict become instead periods of fiscal strains.

Finally, the fiscal problems of municipal governments tend to be cumulative as a result of the institutionalization of past concessions. Municipal agencies and activities become a repository of historical demands, and this accumulation of commitments obviously aggravates fiscal strains. Moreover, these existing patterns may inhibit responses to new and emerging requirements of economic growth and political integration. Hence periodic reform efforts to solve the fiscal crisis often concentrate on restructuring of local government in order to purge it of obsolete concessions. These efforts may succeed, at least for a time, in managing the recurrent urban fiscal strains.

Before we go on to elaborate these points, we want to frankly acknowledge that our speculations are based primarily on our knowledge of urban processes and structures in the United States. We have tried to distill from this experience the propositions which might form the basis for more intensive comparative examination of the nature of urban fiscal strains and the institutional arrangements which we think help to explain them. And, although we refer to empirical studies to illustrate our argument, our main object is to suggest a theoretical perspective which at this stage remains largely untested.

ECONOMIC GROWTH VERSUS POLITICAL PARTICIPATION ON THE URBAN LEVEL

Cities are obviously the location of key production and distribution activities in Western economics, although, of course, the economic role of cities varies. Cities contain enormous fixed capital investments reflecting their diverse economic functions, in the form of networks of headquarters offices or manufacturing units, and the agglomeration of what David Harvey (1975) has called the "built environment" necessary for these activities. Government at the urban level supports this economic structure in several ways. Government provides public services that help maintain the labor force through subsidized housing, public education, and health care, for example. Government agencies build and operate the public infrastructure necessary for the profitability of urban enterprises, in the form of transportation networks, water and power systems, and pollution control plants. Government agencies provide the authority to make and enforce decisions affecting the spatial efficiency of the urban economy, in the form of zoning plans, the development of industrial parks, urban renewal projects and, increasingly, metropolitan planning activities. Finally, local government agencies implement macroeconomic policies set at the national level, such as public employment programs or countercyclical public capital investments.

The concentration of economic activities in urban areas results in the concentration of population in urban areas, and the concentration also of popular political participation. At the same time, therefore, as local governments perform key functions for urban economic enterprises, they also become a primary focus for the political activity and organization of large proportions of the population. While the bare fact of concentrated population might of itself tend to give local governments a large role in maintaining popular political allegiance, certain other features of the urban situation tend to enlarge that role and, from time to time, by heightening the potential for group and class strife, to make it problematic as well.

First, local governments are often important loci for popular political participation because they are structurally accessible, the point of daily contact between citizen and state. The relative visibility of local government policies and the relative accessibility of local government agencies make them a more susceptible target of political opposition than other levels of the state. Oppositional political parties thus frequently develop national political strategies around initial urban political mobilization and electoral victories (e.g., the successes of the Socialists on the local level in the early 20th century in the United States, the post-World War II local successes of the Communists in Italy, and the recent successes of the French Communists at the municipal level).

Second, local governments are important providers of social services. The quality and quantity of these social services on the one hand, and their tax cost on the other hand, are increasingly significant components of real family income.[5] In cities with a large unionized working class, such public services become an alternative to improvement in real wages through collective bargaining at the work place, and forms of political participation oriented toward public services become an alternative to trade unionism and political parties oriented toward work-place issues. In cities with large concentrations of nonunionized working class and of marginal groups unable to find productive employment at all, local public service issues can become the main focus of political organization. Thus the social services provided by urban governments attract the political energies and activism of both organized and unorganized segments of the working class, as well as the politically concerned elements of the middle class.

Rapid economic growth or decline not only tends to increase the demands both of capital and of the working population, but creates a large potential for conflict between these demands.[6] Because urban areas are the location of economic growth, they are also the location where changes in group and class structure, and in political alignments emerging out of group and class structure, find their first political expression.[7] Thus during the late 19th century, the expansion of American industry was facilitated by municipal investments in infrastructure as well as municipal contracts, franchises, and even the private appropriation of municipal capital. At the same time, industrial expansion created a new industrial working class, composed of American artisans and tradesmen and of large numbers of immigrants as well. That this working class was rebellious was evident in frequent and bloody strikes. But rarely did working-class mobilizations take the form of challenging business control of municipal government, even when city police were used to break strikes. The processes by which city government defused this potential conflict produced the recurrent fiscal crisis of the late 19th century.

Similarly, during the post-World War II period, all Western nations experienced rapid and sustained growth accompanied by continuous urban concentration. An increasing proportion of production was concentrated in urban areas and the most productive, technically advanced, and economically powerful enterprises were centralized in a handful of dominant metropolitan centers. Urban economic growth generated large demands for public facilities to complement private investment. Structural economic changes also led to demands for new and expensive urban policies to adapt the city's form and services to expanding coordinative and service functions. Rapid economic growth and concentration also generated a continuous flow of population from less developed parts of the country, or from less developed countries, to many major metropolitan centers. Thus millions of Southern Italian workers migrated to the Northern industrial belt of Italy to find employment, and over a million Italian, Spanish, Portuguese, and Arab workers streamed into the metropolitan centers of France, attracted by the jobs in rapidly developing French industry. Millions of blacks and Latins came to the cities of the United States. These rapid influxes of population created a potential for intense political intraclass and interclass conflict.

But political conflict was muted, we will argue, by structural arrangements on the local level which diverted group and class antagonisms into fiscal claims on local government. Urban governments became the shock absorbers of the upheavals produced by the national political economy. The so-called fiscal crisis is one result.

To summarize, over time urban governments come to be structured in ways which allow them both to support economic growth on the one hand, and to regulate and manage political participation on the other. Urban governments are organized in ways which allow them to absorb political discontent through political participation which is limited to agencies and issues which do not impinge upon economic growth.

URBAN GOVERNMENT STRUCTURES AS MECHANISMS FOR COPING WITH CONTRADICTORY FUNCTIONS

Structural arrangements which we think are important in accounting for the capacity of urban governments to cope with antagonistic pressures are institutional separation of the state and the economy, and the structural segregation and fragmentation of accumulation and political integration functions within the state. Some degree of decentralization and structural segregation is common to the urban government structures of advanced capitalist states, but there are variations. We would predict that more advanced forms of institutional separation and more advanced forms of structural segregation permit more successful management of the class and group conflicts generated by economic growth and change. However, we would also predict that the structural arrangements which help to mute and channel conflict tend to produce fiscal strains, so that the political convulsions one might otherwise expect come to be realized as intense fiscal stresses. Political conflict may be an alternative to fiscal strain and may be a strategic alternative under certain historical conditions.

CENTRALIZATION AND DECENTRALIZATION

Before we can consider the variable arrangements for centralization and decentralization, the fundamental institutional separation of state and economy in capitalist societies must be summarized. In general, the state, including urban governments, has been excluded from profitable activity. Embedded in constitutional arrangements, this exclusion is normally an accepted context rather than a legitimate issue for political participation.[8] Where the state is engaged in productive activity, where the state provides some input into private accumulation, it generally does so where the private market *fails* to supply this input (Offe, 1975:129-130). Thus state production is usually relegated to unprofitable forms of social service delivery and material production which are nonetheless necessary for accumulation to proceed.

Governments in capitalist societies consequently are dependent on taxes which are ultimately drawn from incomes or profits generated in the private sector. As long as state financing is dependent upon taxation (or public debt to private financial intermediaries), its autonomy is limited by the necessity to avoid policies that might impinge upon capital accumulation.[9] And to the extent that capital accumulation and public fiscal capacity both depend on continued private control of investment, production, and location decisions, political issues which question that control are extraordinarily difficult to raise.

The degree of dependence of urban governments on the private sector varies, however, because urban governments occupy different positions in the overall structure of state authority. The level of decentralization of this state structure in terms of financing, policy-making, and implementation responsibilities of urban governments will accentuate the vulnerability of urban governments to capitalist demands for expensive tax and policy subsidies. Conversely, decentralization forces urban governments to resist popular demands for expanded social services or progressive taxes which might impinge upon capitalist interests. Where urban revenues are centrally raised, urban policies nationally formulated, and local implementation constrained by national government, local tax and expenditure policies will not be as susceptible to the exigencies of local profitability. Under these circumstances, the central governments will act as an intermediary, reflecting in its policies the overall fiscal dependency of the state, but buffering municipal governments from the immediate and direct necessity of avoiding any policies which impinge upon capital accumulation (Sbragia, 1976).[10]

By contrast, in political systems where urban government revenues are locally raised, expenditure patterns locally determined, and policies locally implemented, the vulnerability of municipal officials to the vicissitudes of local economic activity is acute. The fracturing of governmental jurisdictions in metropolitan areas adds to the vulnerability of particular municipal governments, for then investors can bargain among central city and suburban jurisdictions even when they are tied to the metropolitan area by economic considerations. Increasingly, however, the growth of national and international corporations, and improvements in transportation and communications which made this growth possible, have freed capital from dependence on particular locations. Under these conditions, investors can adjust and readjust—or threaten to adjust and readjust—their production and location decisions, bargaining among metropolitan areas and particular governments in metropolitan areas as in a marketplace, so as to secure the most favorable mix of taxes, infrastructure and business-oriented public services.[11] Moreover, just as the exclusion of the national government from profitable activity is taken for granted, and not easily subject to political challenge, so is the restriction of local governments from intervention in the decisions of investors taken for granted, and not easily made a matter of local political contention. Indeed, the ideological supports for this segregation may be stronger on the local level where the conviction that "freedom" consists in the protection of the "free" market from government intervention is joined to the conviction that fiscal decentralization is the foundation of local self-government. Thus voters in local elections, threatened by the loss of jobs that capital flight entails, often support business subsidies or tax favors and spurn proposals to increase business taxes or business costs. Several state referenda increasing the utility charges of large enterprises but reducing the charges paid by individual households were voted down in the 1976 election in the United States.[12]

Such arrangements, ensuring the vulnerability of local government to the requirements of accumulation and preventing political challenge to these requirements, tend, however, to exacerbate fiscal strains. The capacity of private investors to choose among localities leaves local governments not only helpless to regulate the volume and content of private investments within their boundaries, but often helpless even to control public taxation and service decisions. Thus the city government of New York, and state agencies as well, respond to the threatened flight of capital investment from the city by promising to reduce business taxes, relax pollution controls, and enlarge the public infrastructure and subsidies that attract investors.

These structural arrangements make municipal agencies more easily the prey of particular economic interests who secure public expenditure benefits that may increase private profits without necessarily increasing tax revenues. Many of the central city urban redevelopment projects in the United States were promoted on the grounds that they would stimulate private investments that would not otherwise have taken place, thus enlarging the city's tax base. Redevelopment projects certainly increased the tax yield on the development sites. On the other hand, they not only destroyed manufacturing and small retail employment by demolishing older establishments and replacing them with high-rise offices and luxury residential units (Hartman, 1974; Epstein, 1976), but they did not have any net effects on the aggregate level of high-rise residential construction or net industrial investment (Friedland, 1977). Thus it can be argued that in the end they cost municipalities far more in public investment and public services than was regained in increased tax yields.

Similarly, spurred by developer interests, southern U.S. cities have expanded their boundaries and extended public infrastructure to support suburban residential and industrial developments. The lopsided relationship between developers and political officials, which yields these public concessions does not necessarily yield tax revenues to finance them.[13] A similar relationship between real estate interests and public officials in declining urban areas results in the use of public funds and authority to acquire properties whose real value is rapidly declining for "urban renewal" which never occurs.

Nor can urban government easily sift through particular economic pressures to reach fiscally wise decisions. Not only are criteria of productivity vague and ambiguous in the public sector, but it is extremely difficult for municipalities to predict the revenue effects of public expenditures when they lack any control of private economic decisions.[14] Moreover, political decision makers are structurally bound to short range perspectives by the electoral system itself; profits in politics are earned at the next election, while profits in enterprise are earned over the longer haul.

The movement of financing, policymaking and implementation responsibilities in and out of the public sector is a highly political process which reflects the power of different interest groups, classes, and political parties at different locations in the overall structure of the state (Andersen, Friedland, and Wright, 1976).[15] For example, in late 19th century America, business interests were continually mobilized in the state capitals to use state legislative authority to undercut popular municipal political bosses or to reorganize agencies which failed to adequately serve capitalist interests at the municipal level. At other junctures, the political mobilization of working- or lower-class groups at the municipal level forces precipitous shifts in the structural location of particular programs. For example, the rise of urban protest and the danger of municipal bankruptcy in 1933 forced the nationalization of responsibility for public welfare, a function which had historically been beyond the purview of the federal government. With a measure of economic recovery and the subsiding of protests by the unemployed by 1935, welfare responsibilities were again devolved to the states and municipalities. In Italy, the rise of the Communist party as a dominant force in most large urban centers contributed to the 1973 financing reform that shifted responsibility for the collection and distribution of tax revenues from the cities to the Christian-Democratic controlled central government.

THE STRUCTURAL SEGREGATION OF ACCUMULATION AND LEGITIMATION FUNCTIONS

While vulnerable and responsive to economic interests, urban governments resting on electoral support must also provide opportunities and incentives for popular political participation, particularly during periods of mounting discontent, but it must do this in such a way as to insulate the role of municipal government in the accumulation process from political challenge. Another major mechanism to promote participation while deflecting that participation from policies important for economic enterprises is the structural segregation of these potentially contradictory government functions. While such segregation is in no sense strict or complete,[16] it appears to be a common feature of the cities of advanced capitalist nations. The devices by which it is accomplished include locating potentially contradictory functions in different agencies; structuring these agencies so that access to economically important decisions is difficult while access to integrative ones is relatively easy; and locating these different functions at different levels of government. Each of these devices varies *between* cities and nations and changes *within* them historically, partly as a result of the shifting political strategies to deal with the popular discontent which results in moving potential targets "up" or "down" in the political system.

First, authority over policies that impinge upon the profitability of economic processes are often located in one agency, while authority over policies that are designed to absorb political discontents generated by economic processes are located in other agencies. For example, slum clearance for the profitable construction of luxury apartment complexes and office buildings is delegated to an urban renewal agency, while the construction of low-income housing is located in a public housing agency. This arrangement, found in France and the United States, tends to act as a barrier against the effective mobilization of displaced residents to demand adequate replacement housing. When political mobilization against clearance and displacements does occur, it cannot so easily be fused with mobilization for the provision of alternative low-cost housing, whether on the urban renewal site or elsewhere in the city (Castells, 1972; Friedland, 1977). Another obvious example is the universal separation of agencies responsible for economic development, such as planning or zoning agencies or industrial redevelopment authorities, from the agencies which are responsible for dealing with those made unemployed by economic development, such as welfare or unemployment or manpower training agencies. By such a separation, agencies which have some authority to determine the structure of employment opportunities are insulated from those agencies that deal with people who cannot find work because of lack of employment opportunities. Not accidentally, when unemployment becomes severe and the unemployed are roused to protest, they direct their discontents against the agencies that manage the unemployed, and not against the agencies that might have some leverage in altering the pattern of economic development and labor market demand.

Second, agencies that control the conditions of economic growth are structured in ways which render them relatively autonomous from popularly elected officials and relatively invisible to the urban population at large.[17] By contrast, agencies that deal with policies related to political legitimation are relatively vulnerable to elected officials, and relatively accessible to the general public.[18] Thus transportation and industrial development policies are often delegated to agencies such as port authorities in the United States whose officials are not elected, whose legislative mandates are not subject to short-term renewal, and whose funding is also protected from legislative review, often because the agency is granted the authority to float its own bonds. Freed in this way from partisan and popular political constraints, these agencies develop external constituencies among those economic interest groups that have a keen interest in public policies that influence the parameters of economic growth. The success of these agencies comes to be dependent upon such clientele relations, a dependency made more intense by the insulation of the agency from electoral or popular pressures. The ideology of technical planning and professionalism with which these agencies cloak themselves not only legitimates their insulation, but it also discourages any attempts at popular intervention, for it argues that what is being done is not political but technical, and so neither relevant nor comprehensible to the wider urban population.

By contrast, agencies which attract the political participation of groups who are excluded from the benefits of economic growth or who may even be its victims, are far less autonomous, their policies are far more visible, and their budgets are allocated from general revenues. The mandate for such agencies is continuously under legislative scrutiny and budgetary review, generating constant concern with the politics of bureaucratic survival. The agencies need constantly to mobilize allies from a diverse urban constituency to ensure renewal of their legislative mandate and funding. To cope with the problem of building political support, these agencies must always deal with conflicting demands for representation on their boards and for patronage through public employment and public services. During periods of economic dislocation, they are likely to be deluged with demands for substantive responses to a host of discontents arising out of larger economic processes. But these agencies do not have the authority or the resources to deal with discontents arising from economic processes. Moreover, such efforts would bring the agencies into conflict with other government agencies, and with the far more powerful economic interests served by these other agencies. Consequently, local agencies charged with maintaining popular political allegiances strive always to convert demands generated by broader economic and social change, which are unmanageable, into demands for symbolic representation and public patronage, which are relatively more manageable (see Edelman, 1964).

The observable tendency to respond to popular demands by establishing new programs and new agencies is consistent with this pattern. The new program or agency is a visible, if mainly symbolic, response, and its establishment diverts discontent away from agencies which might make more substantive responses. New programs and agencies also mean the proliferation and fragmentation of symbolic representation and public patronage. Diversified patronage not only fragments broader class alignments, but tends to create the potential for further divisions among the relatively few who are the chief recipients of patronage, and the many who are not. The funding of these agencies through general revenues is also divisive, for the very programs that absorb popular demands are also subject to challenge by the middle- and working-class taxpayers who pay for them.[19]

The third mechanism to structurally segregate accumulation and legitimation functions is to locate them at different levels of government. Policies which affect the rate and direction of urban economic growth are more likely to be decided at a metropolitan, regional, or national level, while policies designed to encourage participation and absorb protest are decided locally. Revenues for such programs are, at least in part, likely to be raised locally. In the United States in the 1960s, for example, the anti-poverty program was designed to allow local policy formation and to encourage participation by the central city poor. Meanwhile, policies providing agricultural subsidies, housing funds, and military contracts (all of which had a large effect on urban poverty) were set nationally, without similar provisions for local discretion of "participation of residents of the areas to be served." Similarly, the financing of programs which benefit dominant economic interests and the middle class—such as highway construction or homeowner subsidies—tends to be arranged so that these programs are funded by less visible national tax revenues (or invisible tax exemptions). By contrast, programs which are oriented toward lower-class groups, such as medicaid and welfare, are both susceptible to local political decisions and funded in part by acutely visible local taxes.

In Britain, nationally organized commercial and industrial interests have been resistant to any granting of regulatory powers over economic activity to local governments. Scarrow (1971) has shown how such capitalist groups have used their institutionalized access at the national level, through national departments, for example, to prevent local bills granting such regulatory powers from passing in Parliament. Thus local government efforts to regulate economic growth are likely to be consistently thwarted in the national political arena.

The tendency to create supramunicipal jurisdictions to handle the financing and production of public capital investments critical to regional economic growth has occurred in many Western capitalist nations. In the United States, regional special districts with their own taxing and spending powers have rapidly emerged to handle public investments such as water, sewers, mass transit, and airports. Their tax and bond financing have been effectively segregated from the regional revenue requirements for schools, parks, and social services of all kinds. The emergence of structures to regionally rationalize the allocation of public investment critical to capital accumulation has also been evident in Italy and France, although the scope and success of regional reform is likely to be dependent on patterns of partisan and bureaucratic linkage between existent local governments and the national administration (Tarrow, 1974).

The increasingly regional nature of capitalist economic and political organization is one stimulus for this development. However, the distinction between levels of government, as if these levels reflected some enduring reality, can be quite misleading, serving to conceal strategies of political domination by making them appear to have legal and technical content rather than political content. "Much so-called imposition by the state is actually policy developed by local groups and interests and implemented through the machinery of state government. Frequently local officials join with other local groups to seek legislation of this kind" (Jones, 1972:4). What this indicates is that decisions to shift either or both policies and agencies from one level to another are themselves a strategy to gain relative political advantage. When dominant economic interests are challenged at lower levels of government, they move to other levels, or create new levels and new agencies beyond the reach of popular opposition.

In short, the formal structure of the state is not socially or politically neutral. To assure that urban governments are responsive to the requirements of accumulation, agencies charged with its management are institutionalized beyond popular or political control. As social needs, arising from economic processes, are translated into political demands, urban governments attempt to absorb and limit the scope and impact of political participation by channeling it to agencies of limited power and high politicization. This organization of political authority organizes some issues out of the political arena and makes other fundamental policies relatively invulnerable to popular political challenge. The political relations between social groups and classes are partially mediated through the formal organization of political authority. Thus the structure of urban government is not determined by the technical requirements of public policy optimal to the solution of urban problems. On the contrary, the organization of urban political authority reflects the power relationships among different social groups and their relative ability to institutionalize those programs and agencies upon which their interests are most dependent.

STRUCTURAL DETERMINANTS OF THE PATTERN OF POLITICAL REPRESENTATION

The character of political structures in urban political systems, like others, shapes political life, determining in large measure the articulation and alignment of groups within those structures, and the issues on which those groups focus.[20] Patterns of class alignment that one might otherwise expect to emerge in cities within capitalist societies are substantially fractured, and conflict diverted, by the political structures of the city. On the one hand, these structures tend to encourage the multiplication and fragmentation of groups focused on relatively minor forms of group recognition, patronage, and service delivery. On the other hand, urban political structures tend to encourage the emergence and coherence of producer groups with larger stakes in the economic benefits yielded by city government activities. Under conditions of relative stability, municipal costs edge slowly upward as a consequence. Under conditions of change and conflict, costs escalate much more rapidly as the demands of producer interests rise, and popular political discontents are channeled into demands for increased recognition, patronage, and services. The structures which normally work to mute conflicts thus become subject to intense fiscal strains.

Even without the mediation of urban political structures, it is probably at the local level that nonclass forms of political identification such as territory and ethnicity are most acutely felt. These multiple forms of identification tend of themselves to strain class alignments. But municipal political structures work to heighten nonclass bases of identification by organizing formal representation, patronage and public services on territorial and ethnic bases.[21] The result is that interest groups based on territory and ethnicity predominate in municipal politics, fragmenting broader class interests and encouraging intraclass competition and animosities.

This multiplication of group interests and the promotion of group competition has the consequence of splintering the middle, working, and lower classes, and thus diverting them from demands that would threaten the role of municipal government in the accumulation process, even during periods when economic change stimulates popular discontents. Moreover, the very proliferation of groups and group antagonisms and the complementary proliferation of municipal agencies and programs, helps to create an ideological image of the state as a neutral broker between multiple interests of politics as merely a marketplace in which many buyers and sellers meet to their mutual advantage—in other words, the image of a pluralist democracy.

In Western Europe, the fragmented and competitive character of municipal politics is partially offset by the existence of strong national political parties and strong unions with a class orientation. In the United States, by contrast, the fragmentation and competition of municipal politics is virtually unfettered, dominating the American political culture. The result is that the role of urban government in the accumulation process is rarely challenged by coherent popular opposition. But this is not accomplished without adding to municipal costs. Over time, as group demands multiply, so do the minor programs and public positions which encourage a fragmentation and competition between neighborhoods and ethnic groups. As a consequence, municipal activities proliferate in overlapping and inconsistent networks and municipal budgets are slowly driven upward. During periods of rapid economic change and dislocation, this pattern accelerates, as discontents that might otherwise take form in popular mobilization against dominant economic interests instead take form in intense demands on municipal agencies for the symbols of ethnic and neighborhood recognition, and for patronage and services.

At the same time as much of the urban population is inducted into a municipal politics of group strife over symbols of recognition and the minutiae of service delivery and consumption, municipal government structures stimulate the political organization of producer groups. But the pattern of producer group organization and alignment is extremely complex, for producer groups are located in both the public agencies and in private sector activities that depend on public sector expenditures, and in both those agencies oriented toward economic growth and those oriented toward political legitimation. In contrast to the broader urban population, all of these producer groups have large economic stakes in the delivery of municipal services or the construction of municipal projects or the use of municipal services to maintain effective demand. Capitalist producer groups are of course more powerful, partly because the pattern of internal structural segregation gives them greater leverage by making it extremely difficult for other groups to intervene and resist their ability to wrest concessions from urban governments. Working- and middle-class producer groups located in the agencies or activities that promote economic growth also acquire greater leverage as a result of structural segregation and the association of those agencies with profitable activity. Moreover, during periods of political unrest, producer groups in agencies oriented toward political integration are able to use the pressures generated by popular discontent to increase their leverage as well. One result is the crazy-quilt pattern of political alignments and conflicts that cross-cut broader class identifications that is often noted in municipal politics.

Another result is the capturing of municipal activities and budgets by particular producer interests. While the political articulation of producer groups located in accumulation agencies ensures the responsiveness of municipal government to the requirements of economic growth, it also tends to introduce large distortions or irrationalities into the urban economy, distortions that have become increasingly important in accounting for fiscal strains. Producer interests are able to use the political leverage ensured them by structural arrangements to drain the municipal treasury for private profit.[22]

For instance, in their analysis of the possibility of controlling medical inflation in the United States, Marmor et al. (1975) suggest that effective governmental strategies to curb inflation are likely to incur the intense political opposition of health care producer interests. Because consumers have diffuse interests and producers have concentrated interests, political elites are more likely to be overwhelmed by pressures from the latter. Marmor et al. (1975:81) conclude: "The political process is unlikely to right the distributive wrongs of the economic market place when a similar set of actors dominate both."

Among the most notorious examples of producer group domination and of the structural arrangements which made such domination possible in the United States are the New York Port Authority and the Triborough Bridge and Tunnel Authority. These agencies were legally structured to minimize the possibility of popular political influence on their internal structure or their operations, and to maximize their vulnerability to key financial interests, whose decisions to buy bonds and provide loans were critical to the operation of the authorities (Caro, 1974). At the same time, the operations of the authorities also made them a natural focus of political activity by construction industry interests. Together, these producer groups exercised virtually unchallenged domination of agency activities. But while the potential for political conflict was thus reduced, public expenditures escalated.

In general, producer interests operating within insulated agencies are free to remove vast tracts of land from the tax rolls, and at the same time to increase the public debt to private creditors as they continue to produce public works such as roads, bridges, and tunnels in deference to the producer interests to whom they are linked. Despite nominal use of competitive bidding, state contracted production is characterized by cost overruns, byzantine layers of lucrative subcontracting, payoffs and kickbacks, and unproductive expenses of all kinds.

In a similar fashion, producer interests develop around government programs which maximize effective demand,[23] leading to the subsidization of consumption of housing, transportation, and medical services in ways that are responsive to the producer pressure rather than to the overall requirements of either economic growth or popular demand. The use of government by producer groups in this way subverts any popular or consumer control of prices or products. For the urban economy, the results are often the uncontrolled inflation of costs and the anarchic production of services and goods. For urban government, the results are fiscal stress.

STRUCTURAL AND INCREMENTAL EXPANSION

Studies of Western capitalist nations have shown the incremental way in which city, state or provincial, and national expenditures grow (Fried, 1975; Wildavsky, 1964; Meltsner, 1971). Levels of previous expenditure for a given agency, program, or governmental unit have been found to be the strongest predictor of current expenditures, even controlling for economic and political characteristics. Such incremental budgetary processes are often argued to be due to the nonprogrammatic decision-making rules used by governmental officials in a politically and fiscally complicated world. Alternatively, they have been analyzed as deriving from the ability of dominant interests to insulate critical agencies from legislative control (see Alford and Friedland, 1975).

The significance of budgetary incrementalism for the purpose of our analysis of the structural arrangements which produce fiscal crisis is somewhat different. Budget allocations reflect responses to demands arising from the functions of accumulation and legitimation. Once entrenched in agencies and programs, these demands come to be self-perpetuating, protected in part by the development of bureaucratic stakes in the continuation of a particular agency or program.[24] As a consequence, municipal fiscal and legal resources cannot be reallocated to respond to new demands arising from economic processes or from popular political participation. Existing interest groups, often entrenched within the agencies, protect older budgetary commitments. Instead of killing off old programs which may be politically and economically obsolete, new public programs are added to the existing ones, particularly when external demands escalate. These additions contribute to the tendency toward fiscal crisis.

Structural arrangements aggravate this tendency. Because urban governments, as we have argued, are often bureaucratically fragmented into a maze of agencies and jurisdictions, many of which are highly autonomous from political control, bureaucratic aggrandizement is difficult to control. Once established, public agencies use the web of conflictual political demands and bureaucratic clients to assure their continuation and expansion, and even demonstrate a capacity to activate demands to justify their expansion. As a consequence, city budgets show a continuous tendency for incremental expansion, even in the absence of intense external demands.

The classic studies of budgeting procedures show in great detail how multiple agencies at multiple levels convert the politics of the budgetary process into a series of incremental bargains and negotiations over small increases, with seldom any challenge to the existence of any component budgeting unit, nor to the existence of an ongoing program. (See Wildavsky, 1964, and the various studies of the "Oakland Project.") The consequences are consistent and continuous pressures to increase agency budgets, always protecting historic commitments.

During periods of intense stress and rising demands, these bureaucratic tendencies do not vanish. Instead, the emergence of external pressures becomes the basis on which large new expenditures are added to old ones. Political conflicts do not challenge the fundamental patterns by which public resources are allocated, but rather take the form of demands for additional allocations and additional programs. As a result, public expenditures are rarely restructured, they are only increased, sometimes slowly and sometimes rapidly. As they increase, so do fiscal strains.

To summarize the argument, the segregation of accumulation and legitimation functions in different kinds of agencies or different levels of government insulates the state's role in accumulation from political challenge and absorbs popular participation in accessible locations without substantial power. Yet this structural segregation means that the political authority that orchestrates the causes of social problems is insulated from that which manages their political consequences, and is thus without power to deliver a substantive response. Instead, agencies and programs tend to multiply and budgets expand to cover the flood of demands legitimated by each agency's legislative mandate. The bureaucratization of accumulation functions removes political controls on the growth of these agencies and programs and allows their profitable manipulation by those producer interest groups which have most at stake in their continued operation. Conversely, the channeling of participation of those who do not benefit from accumulation to politicized agencies renders such agencies vulnerable to patronage demands, wasteful stop-go patterns of program expansion, and costly maneuvering for political and bureaucratic allies in a highly unstable environment. Finally, incremental financing and budgeting prevents any fundamental restructuring of tax bases or expenditure priorities. Such patterns of expenditure and revenue growth are encouraged by the structural segregation of accumulation and legitimation functions and the related selective representation of group and class interests. Under conditions of rapid economic and political change, new programs are added rather than old ones replaced, adding to fiscal strains. The general result is that municipal activities at any given historical moment constitute an aggregation of functions, agencies and expenditures which may no longer be functional to the requirements of either accumulation or legitimation.

FISCAL CRISIS AS AN OCCASION AND STRATEGY FOR COPING WITH FISCAL STRAINS

The post-World War II experience of major metropolitan centers in the West seems to us to reveal the effects of these structural arrangements. The postwar period saw the concentration and expansion of economic activity in many major cities, with accompanying investments in infrastructure and business-oriented services by municipalities. At the same time, the displacement of many people from agriculture, and the need for labor generated by expansion in the cities, led to the concentration in the cities of large new populations, usually distinguished by race or ethnicity from the older populations. The conflicts that erupted during this period of dislocation, however, were mainly conflicts between working- and lower-class groups fractured by neighborhood, race, and ethnicity, and focused on competition over the provision of public services and, in some places, the traditional patronage of public employment. To cope with rising conflicts and rising demands, municipal services and patronage expanded.

In response to these different pressures, public expenditure for urban capital projects, social services, and public employment grew by leaps and bounds. By the late 1960s, municipal and regional governments began to suffer budget deficits, rising debt, and increasing dependence on state (or provincial) and national government fiscal aid. "In all of the Western democracies the costs of social programs have grown considerably in the post-war period. In the United States and western Europe, government spending tended to rise faster than gross domestic product of the economies between 1961 and 1972, with social transfer payments rising even faster than general government spending" (Heidenheimer et al., 1975:275).

Economic decline only exacerbated these fiscal strains, and the political tensions underlying them. In the late 1960s and 1970s, serious recessions in many countries exacerbated the discrepancy between urban revenues and expenditures. Revenues shrank, but popular political demands did not, and in fact were heightened by unemployment, reduced real wages, and inflation. As urban expenditure, taxation, and debt increased together, many cities were thrown into a politically intractable fiscal crisis. Municipal workers were increasingly organized and resisted cutbacks with paralyzing strikes. City residents tried to hold onto existing services, or even to press for improved services, confronting urban bureaucracies with rent strikes, fare reduction campaigns, and housing occupations.[25] Major corporations resisted any threatened service reduction or tax increase that would cut into their profitability with threats of relocation to other cities, and even to other countries.

The dilemma of cities in capitalist societies is how to maintain a structure of expenditure and taxation that can stimulate stable economic growth, while at the same time maintaining the popular legitimacy of governmental institutions, even when the potential for political conflict becomes intense. The series of structural arrangements described above tend to convert political conflict between groups and classes into demands on the state which force state expansion. But this process also tends to create fiscal strains. Public expenditures increase faster than the state's ability to finance them from its own revenues. Thus fiscal strains are a recurrent feature of capitalist cities.

These fiscal strains result in increased pressures for higher taxes on business and industry, indirectly push up wage costs, and potentially constrain the expansion of public services and infrastructure upon which corporate profitability is dependent. Under these conditions, fiscal strains provide capitalist groups with an occasion and a strategy to increase their control over the city's budget.

The process by which capitalist groups politically manage fiscal strains seems to follow a natural historical sequence, if New York City may be taken as a prototype, although perhaps an extreme one. First, financial and other capitalist interests declare an emergency, publicly redefining fiscal strains as a "fiscal crisis." Second, the fiscal crisis is attributed to natural economic laws beyond the control of political parties, governmental units, corporations, and banks themselves. Capitalist arguments that urban governments must balance their budgets, that there simply is not enough money, are elaborated by explanations of the inevitable erosion of the economic base of the cities as a mobile capital responds to the "natural laws" of profit maximization.

Third, capitalist interests assert control. Bankers refuse to finance the urban debt. Industrialists and developers make their investments conditional upon expanded subsidies and services, and reduced taxes. Business-backed reform groups push for policy changes to increase public sector productivity and reduce waste and duplication.

Depending on the level of indebtedness, the locational dependency of investors, and the political power of the reform groups, the parameters of urban policy are reorganized. On the one hand, structural changes may be introduced which remove even formal policy and budgetary authority from electoral control, as when an Emergency Finance Control Board was created in 1975 in New York City with the authority to supersede the budgetary decisions of city officials. On the other hand, expenditures and revenues are selectively reorganized to favor business through reduced taxes, enlarged subsidies and a relaxation of public regulation in matters such as environmental pollution. Public employment and neighborhood services which are less necessary to private profitability are cut back. In New York City, for example, half of the Hispanics and two-fifths of the blacks on municipal employment have been fired (Piven and Cloward, 1977:13), most of whom were located in public agencies created to absorb the political protest of the 1960s. Finally, policy proposals for more progressive revenues are suppressed. For example, in the Banker's Agreement of 1932, loans were extended to the city of New York on condition that proposals for taxes on stocks, savings banks, and life insurance companies would be dropped (Darnton, 1977:226).

In conclusion, we believe that municipal expenditures tend to expand, fueled by the dynamism of group and class conflict. Given the structural arrangements we have described, when popular discontent intensifies, expenditures escalate more rapidly than revenues, producing the various symptoms we have called fiscal strains. At these junctures, capital mobilizes within the framework of these urban structures to declare a fiscal crisis and subdue popular demands. Whether this strategy is viable in the long run seems doubtful, but this conclusion rests on a faith in the possibility of an emergence of political challenges which, at least in the United States, are not yet visible.

NOTES

1. For further information on growing local government expenditure demands in the limited fiscal capacity in the United States, see U.S. Senate, Subcommittee on Housing and

Urban Affairs, *The Central City Problem and Urban Renewal Policy,* 93rd Congress, 1st Session, U.S. Government Printing Office, 1973, Washington, D.C. We use the terms "stress" and "strain" interchangeably, and distinguish these tendencies from the strategies for managing them, which include defining them as a "crisis."

2. O'Connor uses a somewhat different language. He locates the fiscal crisis of the capitalist state in the ways in which public authority must increasingly absorb both the social and the private costs of capital accumulation. On the one hand, monopoly capitalism requires the state to increasingly socialize the costs of constant and variable capital. On the other hand, the tendency toward surplus capacity under monopoly capitalism produces enormous social costs which must also be absorbed by the state. The state's absorption of the social and private costs of accumulation, combined with the continued private appropriation of the social surplus, produces an inherent tendency toward fiscal crisis (O'Connor, 1973). It is of course this last condition, the private appropriation of the social surplus, which distinguishes the capitalist state from the state in other industrial and industrializing societies. These governments may also, as Daniel Bell asserts, face the twin problems of maintaining accumulation and legitimation, but they have greater authority to direct economic development, and are also able to appropriate the surpluses resulting from development, to cope with the problems of legitimacy (Bell, 1974:37-38).

3. Much of the time, perhaps most of the time, a stable and prosperous economy is also a precondition of the legitimacy of the state, for the breakdown of the accumulation process leads to the loss of jobs, declining real income, and the series of dislocations which give rise to political discontent. We are not prepared, therefore, to argue the inherent and continuous contradiction between accumulation and legitimation functions, but argue only that these functions become antagonistic at specific historical junctures.

4. In the past, periods of intense labor-management conflict which have politicized larger urban populations have also made city governments in the focus of conflictual demands. This tends not to occur in the contemporary United States, perhaps because of the enlarged role of unions in mediating such conflicts, but it is still important in other Western nations, Italy being one example.

5. "Tax revenues, including the payroll taxes that help finance social security, have been rising everywhere as a percentage of Gross National Product. . . . Average annual tax revenue per capita for the period 1965-1971 amounted to $1394 in Sweden, $1177 in the United States, $911 in France, $846 in Germany, $795 in the Netherlands and $708 in Britain" (Heidenheimer et al., 1975:227-228).

6. For an examination of the role of economic dislocations in the emergence of working and lower-class protests in the United States, see Piven and Cloward, 1977b.

7. Samuel Huntington, commenting on O'Connor's thesis, argues that the fiscal crisis is not due to "capitalist economics" but "is in fact a product of democratic politics" which reflected the egalitarian reform movements of the 1960s. It should be clear from our discussion that we think Huntington is partly right; "democratic politics" were an important component of the urban fiscal crisis in the United States. We disagree, however, with Huntington's effort to sever the political demands of the egalitarian movements of the 1960s from the "capitalist economics" which gave rise to them.

8. Claus Offe (1975:125-126) has defined the capitalist state by this exclusion from profitable activity. We think that the extent of control over the capitalist economy and its ability to participate in the production and distribution of a society's surplus should be treated as a historically variable characteristic of capitalist states. States vary, for example, in their ability to produce surplus directly through nationalization of industries or utilities, to capture private surpluses generated by public investment through betterment taxes, or to appropriate them directly through progressive taxation. The determination of this variation and its political and economic correlates remains largely unexplored.

9. There are of course other conditions which ordinarily ensure the subordination of the state to capital as well, not least its susceptibility to economic interest group pressure

and its overall dependence on relatively stable economic conditions as a precondition of political stability.

10. It is important to note that even in those systems where urban expenditures are financed from central public banking systems, subnational governments nonetheless remain responsible for the discretionary implementation of public capital construction. In the United Kingdom in 1967, local governments accounted for 80% of total public capital investment; in France, 66% (Sbragia, 1976:5).

11. In the United States, intercity competition for private investments allows corporations access to public subsidies for investments that would have been made in any case. A recent study of municipal issuance of industrial aid bonds in the U.S. found that although corporations used alternative location to secure access to publicly subsidized debt financing, the majority of industrial projects, and seven-tenths of the dollar value, would have occurred in the same location without public subsidy (Apilado, 1971).

12. Max Weber pointed out this dilemma of the decentralized municipality: "Within compulsory associations, particularly political communities, all property utilization that is largely dependent on real estate is stationary, in contrast to personal property which is either monetary or easily exchangeable. If propertied families leave a community, those staying behind must pay more taxes; in a community dependent on a market economy, and particularly a labor market, the have-nots may find their economic opportunities so much reduced that they will abandon any reckless attempt at taxing the haves or will even deliberately favor them (Weber, 1968:352).

13. We are indebted to Al Watkins for this point.

14. Offe argues that the capitalist state is not only restricted to unprofitable production, but that it lacks "decision rules" by which to organize the content, method, output, and distribution of production. As a result, state activity is inefficient and ineffective, characterized by continuous political conflict, and continuous efforts at organizational reform (Offe, 1975).

15. The level of urban decentralization is not technically determined by the most appropriate unit to achieve economies of scale, for example, nor by some inexorable logic of centralization.

16. We readily acknowledge the difficulties of empirically assessing the consequences of specific urban government activities on the urban economy or on the political integration of urban populations. The difficulty is compounded because some activities clearly bear both on the urban economy and on urban politics and, indeed, specific activities may have diverse and contradictory consequences. Some municipal activities, however, clearly bear directly on economic processes, while others clearly bear directly on the problems of managing political participation and integration. We present this model of structural segregation as a potentially illuminating way of explaining the allocation of municipal functions, and await the help of our colleagues in dealing with the difficulties of empirically specifying the consequences of diverse municipal government activities.

17. In Oakland, California, city officials "avoid the public in order to bring revenue into the system." By various tactics "indirect taxes and nominal charges are introduced into the tax structure which reduce the tax consciousness of the payer and result in low-yielding taxes and small, attentive tax publics. Public participation is also made difficult, so as to keep these tax publics small, fragmented, and quiet." (Meltsner, 1971:8). This is an example of how key public decisions critically affecting accumulation (the tax burden on large property owners) are bureaucratized, rather than politicized, through conscious political decision.

18. Peter Marcuse suggests that our argument that political integration functions are relatively open and visible, while accumulation functions are insulated from popular intervention, has an analogue in the familiar dichotomy between legislative and administrative activities, the one being relatively visible and subject to intervention, while the other is relatively removed from public purview or interference.

19. This point was made by Allan Schnaiberg in response to an earlier draft of this paper. See also Alford, 1975a, and Alford, 1975b.

20. Our conception of the structural segregation of state agencies and programs, and the consequences of segregation for the political fragmentation of class alignments, has a strong analogue in recent work by leftist economists on the structural arrangements underlying the segmentation and balkanization of the labor force. See for example Reich et al., 1973, and Edwards et al., 1975. We are indebted for this point to Ann Markusen.

21. Katznelson (forthcoming) refers to the distinctive "serialization" of class in the United States: "What has been 'exceptional' about the American experience of class is that the split between work and community has been reproduced ideologically and institutionally in ways that have fragmented patterns of class in a qualitatively distinct way. Elsewhere in the West, the tendency to parcelization has been partially countered by competing 'global' institutions and meaning systems of class."

22. See McConnell, 1966, for an analysis of how private producer interests have "captured" different segments of the state at the national level.

23. Two structural tendencies have necessitated increasing state involvement and particularly urban state intervention in the organization of consumption. On the one hand, the monopolization of capitalist enterprise, combined with enormous increases in industrial and organizational productivity have rendered the scope of domestic effective demand increasingly problematic for all Western capitalist nations. On the other hand, the increasing spatial and functional complexity involved in the reproduction of labor power through diverse social services and material goods also renders the content and distribution of consumption problematic (Castells, 1976).

24. John Mollenkopf makes the important point that the specific organizational arrangements of particular agencies promotes this effect. For his elaboration of this argument, and his exposition of the functions of specific organizational arrangements for muting conflict, see Mollenkopf, 1977.

25. For general essays on the "politics of turmoil" in the 1960s in the U.S., see Cloward and Piven, 1974; Castells et al., 1974. For France, see Castells et al., 1974.

REFERENCES

ALCALY, R. E., and MERMELSTEIN, D. (eds., 1977). The fiscal crisis of American cities. New York: Vintage.

ALFORD, R. R. (1975a). Health care politics. Chicago: University of Chicago Press.

--- (1975b). "Ideological filters and bureaucratic responses in interpreting research: Community planning and poverty." In N. J. Demerath III, O. Larsen, and K. F. Schuessler (eds.), Social policy and sociology. New York: Academic Press.

ALFORD, R. R., and FRIEDLAND, R. (1975). "Political participation and public policy." Annual Review of Sociology, 1:429-479.

ANDERSEN, G., FRIEDLAND, R., and WRIGHT, E. O. (1976). "Modes of class struggle and the capitalist state." Kapitalistate, 4-5(summer):186-220.

APILADO, V. (1971). "Corporate-government interplay: The era of industrial aid finance." Urban Affairs Quarterly, (December):219-241.

BAER, W. C. (1976). "On the death of cities." Public Interest, 45(fall):3-19.

BELL, D. (1974). "The public household." Public Interest, 37(fall):29-68.

CARO, R. A. (1974). The power broker. New York: Vintage.

CASTELLS, M. (1972). "Urban renewal and social conflict in Paris." Social Science Information, 2(2):93-124.

--- (1976). "Urban sociology and urban politics: From a critique to new trends of research." In J. Walton and L. H. Masotti (eds.), The city in comparative perspective. Beverly Hills: Sage.

CASTELLS, M., CHERKI, E., GODARD, F., and MEHL, D. (1974). Sociologie des Mouvements Sociaux Urbains, Enquete sur la Region Parisienne (vols. 1 and 2). Paris: Ecole Des Hautes Etudes en Sciences Sociales, Centre d'Etude des Mouvements Sociaux.

CLOWARD, R. A., and PIVEN, F. F. (1974). The politics of turmoil: Essays on poverty, race and the urban crisis. New York: Vintage.

Congressional Budget Office, United States Congress (1975). "New York City's fiscal problem: Its origin, potential repercussions, and some alternative policy responses." Washington, D.C.: U.S. Government Printing Office.

DARNTON, J. (1977). "Banks rescued the city in a similar plight in '33." In R. Alcaly and D. Mermelstein (eds.), The fiscal crisis of American cities. New York: Vintage.

EDELMAN, M. (1964). The symbolic uses of politics. Urbana: University of Illinois Press.

EDWARDS, R., REICH, M., and GORDON, D. (1975). Labor market segmentation. Lexington, Mass.: D. C. Heath.

EPSTEIN, J. (1976). "The last days of New York." New York Review of Books (February 16).

EYESTONE, R. (1971). The threads of public policy: A study in policy leadership. Indianapolis, Ind.: Bobbs-Merrill.

FRIED, R. C. (1975). "Comparative urban performance." In F. I. Greenstein and N. W. Polsby (eds.), Handbook of political science (vol. 6). Reading, Mass.: Addison-Wesley.

FRIEDLAND, R. (1977). Class power and the central city: The contradictions of urban growth. Unpublished Ph.D. dissertation, University of Wisconsin–Madison.

FRIEDMAN, L. (1968). Government and slum housing. Chicago: Rand McNally.

HARTMAN, C. (1974). Yerba Buena: Land grab and community resistance in San Francisco. San Francisco: Glide Publications.

HARVEY, D. (1975). "The political economy of urbanization in advanced capitalist societies: The case of the United States." Pp. 119-163 in G. Gappert and H. M. Rose (eds.), The social economy of cities. Beverly Hills: Sage.

HEIDENHEIMER A. J., HECLO, H., and ADAMS, C. T. (1975). Comparative public policy: The politics of social choice in Europe and America. New York: St. Martin's Press

HUNTINGTON, S. P. (1975). "The democratic distemper." Public Interest, 41(fall):9-38.

JONES, V. (1972). "Bay Area regionalism." Quoted in F. W. Wirt, Power in the city: Decision making in San Francisco. Berkeley: University of California Press.

KATZNELSON, I. (forthcoming). City trenches. New York: Pantheon.

LUPSHA, P. (1975). "New federalism: Centralization and local control." Paper delivered at the Annual Meeting of the American Political Science Association, San Francisco.

MARMOR, T. R., WITTMAN, D. A., and HEAGY, T. C. (1975). "The politics of medical inflation." Journal of Health Politics, Policy and Law, 1:69-84.

McCONNELL, G. (1966). Private power and American democracy. New York: Knopf.

MELTSNER, A. J. (1971). The politics of city revenue. Berkeley: University of California Press.

MOLLENKOPF, J. (1977). "Untangling the logics of urban service bureaucracies: The strange case of the San Francisco Municipal Railway." Paper presented at the Conference on Urban Political Economy, American Sociological Association and International Sociological Association, Santa Cruz, California.

O'CONNOR, J. (1973). The fiscal crisis of the state. New York: St. Martin's Press.

OFFE, C. (1975). Stress and contradiction in modern capitalism: Public policy and the theory of the state (associate editor with Colin Crouch and Robert Alford. Principal Editor, Leon N. Lindberg). Lexington, Mass.: Lexington Books.

PERRY, D., and WATKINS, A. (1977). "Contract federalism and the socioeconomic realignment of yankee and cowboy cities: Two stages of urban decay." Paper presented at the Conference on Urban Political Economy, American Sociological Association and International Sociological Association, Santa Cruz, California.

PIVEN, F. F., and CLOWARD, R. (1977a). "The urban crisis as an arena for class mobilization." Radical America, 11(January-February):9-17.

--- (1977b). Poor people's movements: Why they succeed, how they fail. New York: Pantheon.

PRESSMAN, J. L., and WILDAVSKY, A. B. (1973). Implementation. Berkeley: University of California Press.

REICH, M., GORDON, D., and EDWARDS, R. (1973). "The theory of labor market segmentation." American Economic Review, (May):359-365.

SBRAGIA, A. (1976). "Public housing and private profit: Some inferences for comparative policy studies from an Italian case." Paper delivered at the Annual Meeting of the American Political Science Association, Chicago.

SCARROW, H. A. (1971). "Policy pressures by British local government." Comparative Politics, 4(October):1-28.

STARR, R. (1976). "Making New York smaller." New York Times Magazine (November 14).

STERNLIEB, G., and HUGHES, J. W. (1976). "New York: Future without a future?" Society, 13(May/June):1-23.

TARROW, S. (1974). "Local constraints on regional reform: A comparison of Italy and France." Comparative Politics, 7(October):1-36.

U.S. Senate, Subcommittee on Housing and Urban Affairs (1973). The central city problem and urban renewal policy. 93rd Congress, 1st Session. Washington, D.C.: U.S. Government Printing Office.

WEBER, M. (1968). Economy and society: An outline of interpretive sociology (vol. 1, edited by G. Roth and C. Wittich). New York: Bedminster Press.

WILDAVSKY, A. (1964). The politics of the budgetary process. Boston: Little, Brown.

ABOUT THE CONTRIBUTORS

ROBERT R. ALFORD is Professor of Sociology at the University of California at Santa Cruz, where he is director of a new interdisciplinary Ph.D. program. He is also author of *Party and Society* (1963), *Bureaucracy and Participation* (1969), and *Health Care Politics* (1975). His coauthored article is part of a larger comparative research project which will extend the analysis from one largely based on the United States to several European countries as well.

CHARLES W. ANDERSON is Professor of Political Science at the University of Wisconsin–Madison. He has long been a student of comparative public policy both in advanced industrial societies and in the developing nations. His current research focus, reflected in his contribution to this volume, is on basic normative problems of policy evaluation. His publications include: *The Political Economy of Mexico, Politics and Economic Change in Latin America, Issues of Political Development, The Political Economy of Modern Spain* and *Statecraft.*

DOUGLAS E. ASHFORD is Director of the Western Societies Program in the Center for International Studies and a professor in the Department of Government, Cornell University. Over the past three years he has conducted a seminar on the policy process in the industrial democracies with Professors T. J. Pempel and Peter Katzenstein. He has published a number of articles on local government and public policy in Great Britain and is currently completing a book on the strategy for local reorganization in Britain and France. His recent monograph, *The Limits of Consensus* (Western Societies Occasional Paper No. 6, 1976), is a preliminary comparison of the two systems.

AMY BRIDGES is a member of the editorial board of *Politics and Society*. Her work has appeared in the *American Journal of Sociol-*

ogy, Review of Radical Political Economics, Politics and Society, and *Science and Society.* She is currently a Ph.D. candidate in the political science department of the University of Chicago.

ROGER FRIEDLAND is Assistant Professor of Sociology at the University of California at Santa Barbara. He completed his Ph.D. at the University of Wisconsin in 1977, with a study of "Corporate Power and the Central City." He has also coauthored a review of the literature on "Political Participation and Public Policy," with Robert R. Alford, which appeared in the first *Annual Review of Sociology* (1975). His coauthored article in this volume is part of a larger comparative research project with Robert R. Alford and Frances Fox Piven.

MARTIN O. HEISLER is an Associate Professor of Government and Politics at the University of Maryland. He received his Ph.D. at the University of California at Los Angeles in 1969. He is editor and coauthor of *Politics in Europe: Structures and Processes in Some Postindustrial Democracies* (1974) and of the September 1977 issue of *The ANNALS* of the American Academy of Political and Social Science, devoted to the subject of "Ethnic Conflict in the World Today." He is also series editor of "Comparative Studies of Political Life" and author or coauthor of papers on comparative public policy, European politics, and ethnic relations. His current research is devoted to the policy aspects of ethnic and regional autonomy movements in advanced industrial societies.

WAYNE L. HOFFMAN received his Ph.D. in Political Science from the University of Chicago in 1976. He has taught at American University and has written in both the urban politics and public policy fields.

E. W. KELLEY is Associate Professor of Political Science at Cornell. He has published books and articles in methodology, philosophy of science, comparative politics and coalition behavior, and American and comparative public policy.

THEODORE J. LOWI is the John L. Senior Professor of American Institutions at Cornell University. Before coming to Cornell in 1972 he was Professor of Political Science at the University of Chicago. He spent 1967-1968 on a Guggenheim in Paris and another year in Paris in 1973-1974. During 1977-1978 he was a Fellow at the Center for Advanced Study in the Behavioral Sciences. His major publications include *At the Pleasure of the Mayor* (1962), *The End of Liberalism* (1969), *The Politics of Disorder* (1971), and *American Government: Incomplete Conquest* (1976). He is coauthor of *Poliscide* (1976), a study of science policy. *Arenas of Power,* a book in preparation for 1977-1978, is a study of public policy of which the contribution in this volume will be a part.

THEODORE R. MARMOR teaches and does research in public policy at the University of Chicago. He is currently director of a project funded by the Robert Wood Johnson Foundation on the implementation of prospective national health insurance plans. Professor Marmor received his Ph.D. from Harvard University in 1966, continuing to teach there and at the Universities of Minnesota and Wisconsin. The author of *The Politics of Medicare,* Marmor has published work on the politics of different social politics in a variety of scholarly and general journals.

STUART S. NAGEL is Professor of Political Science at the University of Illinois and a member of the Illinois bar. He is the coordinator of the *Policy Studies Journal* and the secretary-treasurer of the Policy Studies Organization and has been Series Editor of the Sage Yearbooks in Politics and Public Policy since its inception. He is the author or editor of *Policy Studies and the Social Sciences, Policy Studies in America and Elsewhere, Improving the Legal Process, Effects of Alternatives, Environmental Politics, The Rights of the Accused: In Law and Action,* and *The Legal Process from a Behavioral Perspective.* He has been an attorney to the Office of Economic Opportunity, Lawyers Constitutional Defense Committee in Mississippi, National Labor Relations Board, and the U.S. Senate Subcommittee on Administrative Practice and Procedure.

PAUL PERETZ is currently an assistant professor at the University of Texas at Dallas. His primary interest is in the field of macroeconomic policymaking and he has done work in prices and incomes policy in the United Kingdom and the processes leading to inflationary economic policies in the United States.

B. GUY PETERS is an Associate Professor of Political Science at the University of Delaware. Since receiving his doctorate in 1970, he has contributed many articles to leading journals in the United States and Europe and has coauthored books dealing with European as well as American politics. Professor Peters is the author of *The Politics of Bureaucracy: A Comparative Perspective* (1977) and is coauthor of a forthcoming cross-national study of central economic policies and conditions in advanced industrial societies. He recently completed a major research project on the "Quality of Life" in urban settings in Western societies, which was funded by the Ford Foundation.

FRANCES FOX PIVEN is Professor of Political Science at Boston University and the author (with Richard Cloward) of *Regulating the Poor* (1971) and *Poor People's Movements* (1977). An urban planner by professional training, she formerly taught at Columbia University and the City University of New York. Her coauthored article in this volume is part of a larger comparative research project which will extend the analysis from one largely based on the United States to several European countries as well.

ROBERT F. RICH is Assistant Professor of Politics and Public Affairs at Princeton University. He has conducted utilization studies on the application of survey data in seven federal bureaucracies, the effectiveness of U.S. Foreign Service Reporting, and the practices of the National Science Foundation/RANN division program managers. Most recently, he has served as Principal Investigator on a Commission on Federal Paperwork study on administrative practices in the area of unemployment compensation.

HENRY TEUNE received his Ph.D. from Indiana University in 1961. Since then he has been teaching political science at the University of Pennsylvania. He has coauthored *The Integration of Political Communities*, *The Logic of Comparative Social Inquiry*, and *Values in the Active Community*. He is involved in cross-national comparative research on social change. His forthcoming book will be on the dynamics of development change.

INDEX OF NAMES

INDEX OF NAMES

A

B

H

I

J

K

INDEX OF SUBJECTS

INDEX OF SUBJECTS

H

I

P

Q

R